The Musical Novel

What is a "musical novel"? This book defines the genre as musical not primarily in terms of its content, but in its form. The musical novel crosses medial boundaries, aspiring to techniques, structures, and impressions similar to those of music. It takes music as a model for its own construction, borrowing techniques and forms that range from immediately perceptible, essential aspects of music (rhythm, timbre, the simultaneity of multiple voices) to microstructural (jazz riffs, call and response, leitmotifs) and macrostructural elements (themes and variations, symphonies, albums). The musical novel also evokes the performance context by imitating elements of spontaneity that characterize improvised jazz or audience interaction.

The Musical Novel builds upon theories of intermediality and semiotics to analyze the musical structures, forms, and techniques in two groups of musical novels, which serve as case studies. The first group imitates an entire musical genre and consists of jazz novels by Toni Morrison, Albert Murray, Xam Wilson Cartiér, Stanley Crouch, Jack Fuller, Michael Ondaatje, and Christian Gailly. The second group of novels, by Richard Powers, Gabriel Josipovici, Rachel Cusk, Nancy Huston, and Thomas Bernhard, imitates a single piece of music, J. S. Bach's *Goldberg Variations*.

European Studies in North American Literature and Culture

The Musical Novel

Imitation of Musical Structure, Performance, and Reception in Contemporary Fiction

Emily Petermann

Rochester, New York

Copyright © 2014 Emily Petermann

All Rights Reserved. Except as permitted under current legislation, no part of this work may be photocopied, stored in a retrieval system, published, performed in public, adapted, broadcast, transmitted, recorded, or reproduced in any form or by any means, without the prior permission of the copyright owner.

First published 2014 by Camden House
Reprinted in paperback 2018

Camden House is an imprint of Boydell & Brewer Inc.
668 Mt. Hope Avenue, Rochester, NY 14620, USA
www.camden-house.com
and of Boydell & Brewer Limited
PO Box 9, Woodbridge, Suffolk IP12 3DF, UK
www.boydellandbrewer.com

Paperback ISBN-13: 978-1-64014-027-1
Paperback ISBN-10: 1-64014-027-1
Hardcover ISBN-13: 978-1-57113-592-6
Hardcover ISBN-10: 1-57113-592-8

Library of Congress Cataloging-in-Publication Data

Petermann, Emily.
 The Musical Novel : Imitation of Musical Structure, Performance, and Reception in Contemporary Fiction
 pages cm.—(European Studies in North American Literature and Culture)
 Includes bibliographical references and index.
 ISBN-13: 978-1-57113-592-6 (hardcover : acid-free paper)
 ISBN-10: 1-57113-592-8 (hardcover : acid-free paper)
 1. Music in literature. 2. Music and literature. I. Title.

PN56.M87P44 2014
809'.933578—dc23

2013051185

Contents

Acknowledgments	vii
Introduction	1
1: Theorizing the Musical Novel	16

I: The Novel Based on a Musical Genre: Jazz Novels

2: Elements of Sound in Jazz Novels	49
3: Structural Patterns in Jazz Novels	70
4: The Performance Situation in Jazz Novels	106

II: The Novel Based on a Particular Piece of Music: J. S. Bach's *Goldberg Variations*

5: Structural Patterns in Novels Based on the *Goldberg Variations*	149
6: Composition, Performance, and Reception in Novels Based on the *Goldberg Variations*	187
Conclusion	211
Appendix: Diagrams of Intermediality in Selected Novels	219
Works Cited	223
Index	235

Acknowledgments

> *you know*
>   *if i could write a nice long blues*
> *you know*
>   *a nice long blues*
> *you know*
>   *it sure would feel good to my writing hand*
> *you know*
>   *you know*
> *you know*
>
> —Jayne Cortez, "You Know," 103

> *Blessed Cecilia, appear in visions*
> *To all musicians, appear and inspire:*
> *Translated Daughter, come down and startle*
> *Composing mortals with immortal fire.*
>
> —W. H. Auden, from "Anthem for St. Cecilia's Day," 174

CECILIA, PATRON SAINT OF MUSICIANS, is often invoked as a muse and source of inspiration. The present study aims to demonstrate that her influence not only acts on musicians, but also extends to authors of literary texts. Inspired in turn by these texts that seek to "write a nice long blues" or use other musical forms, I have written this book out of an ongoing fascination with interarts phenomena.

Just as a musical novel is often a hybrid joint production with inspiration coming from all sides—musical and intertextual—this book reflects a debt of gratitude to a number of helpers. I am grateful to a number of readers for useful critical feedback, especially to Reingard M. Nischik and the members of her research colloquium in Konstanz, Germany. I am also indebted to Lauren Holmes and Carolyn Sinsky for their collaboration on the intermediality section of the first chapter, which grew out of a research seminar with Pericles Lewis at Yale University in the spring of 2008. My *Schreibgruppe*—Simone Paulun, Svenja Menkhaus, and Anja Krüger—read drafts of nearly every section of the book and contributed greatly to its coherence and polish. Michael Basseler, Mario Dunkel, Chiara Frigeni, and Barbara Giehmann also read and commented on individual sections, providing very useful feedback for final revisions. Many thanks to Madita Oeming for providing the excellent photograph for the book's cover. I am also very grateful to Jim Walker and Julia Cook at Camden House for their meticulous efforts in shepherding this project towards publication. Any remaining errors, of course, are entirely my own.

This project was supported financially by a number of sources. I am grateful to the Landesgraduiertenförderung of the state of Baden-Württemberg for a generous fellowship, to the Landesstiftung Baden-Württemberg for financing my exchange year 2007–8 at Yale University, to Wellesley College for the Ruth Ingersoll Goldmark Fellowship that supported me at the beginning of my research in 2006, and to the Office of Equal Opportunity at the University of Konstanz and the German Academic Exchange Service for contributing to the costs of traveling to conferences.

Several portions of the book were presented at conferences that contributed important feedback on my work in progress: the intermediality theory section was presented with Lauren Holmes and Carolyn Sinsky at the Twentieth Century Colloquium of the Yale English Department in May 2008; a section on jazz performance was presented at the International Association of Word and Music Studies (WMA) in Vienna in June 2009 and appeared in *Word and Music Studies: Essays on Performativity and on Surveying the Field*, edited by Walter Bernhart and Michael Halliwell (Amsterdam: Rodopi, 2011), as "Jazz Novels and the Textualization of Musical Performance" (reprinted here with permission from Rodopi); sections of the jazz chapters dealing with Jack Foster's *The Best of Jackson Payne* were presented in a modified form at the British Association for American Studies (BAAS) in Norwich, England in April 2010; sections dealing with Xam Wilson Cartiér's creation of a distinct jazz voice were presented at the WMA conference in Santa Fe, August 2011; and the section on the concept of time implied by the theme-and-variations form was intended for the first conference of the WMA Forum in Dortmund in November 2010 and appeared in a modified form in *Time and Space in Words and Music: Proceedings of the 1st Conference of the Word and Music Association Forum, Dortmund, November 4–6, 2010*, edited by Mario Dunkel, Emily Petermann, and Burkhard Sauerwald (Frankfurt: Peter Lang, 2012), as "The Concept of Time Implied by the Theme-and-Variations Form: Novels Based on Bach's *Goldberg Variations*" (reprinted here with permission from Peter Lang). I am also grateful for the wealth of positive responses I have received in conversations at a variety of conferences, especially from the many emerging scholars that make up the Word and Music Association Forum.

Thanks also go to my parents, family, and friends for their continued patience as I have been wrapped up in this project for what must have seemed like a very long time. And especially to Rudi, who has always believed in my success and given me the support and freedom to sing whatever song is in me.

Introduction

> *To be second is not to be secondary or inferior; likewise,*
> *to be first is not to be originary or authoritative.*
> —Hutcheon, *A Theory of Adaptation*, xiii

THIS QUOTATION CONCISELY FORMULATES one of the main assumptions of this book: the musical novel, a literary subgenre that engages with musical pretexts, is valuable in itself, as well as in its relationship to a musical model that contributes to its overall form. As in any intertextual work, this intermedial involvement with music does not yield a merely derivative product, but instead adds a layer to the "palimpsestuous" (Genette, *Palimpsests*) structure of the musical novel.[1] The ways in which specific musical elements have been adopted and imitated by novels will be the focus of this book.

Literature's changing relationship to music over time has been intimately linked to the critical perception of music and its status in the relative hierarchy among the arts. While music in the eighteenth century was perceived to be accessible solely through the senses and was therefore less valued in an age that cherished intellectual involvement with the arts, the romantics praised music precisely for its inability to express ideas.[2] As Enrico Fubini describes it in *History of Music Aesthetics*:

> Music had no need to express anything that could be expressed in ordinary language. . . . Music could capture the very essence of the world, the Idea, the Spirit, the Infinite. And the farther it was from having any sort of meaning or philosophical content, the higher the degree to which it was endowed with the power to do these things. (262–63)

The romantics saw music's seeming fusion of form and content as an ideal to be emulated by the sister arts of painting and poetry. Walter Pater emphasizes this unity epitomized in music above all other arts:

> It is the art of music which most completely realizes this artistic ideal, this perfect identification of matter and form. In its consummate moments, the end is not distinct from the means, the form from the matter, the subject from the expression; they inhere in and completely saturate each other. . . . In music, then, rather than in poetry, is to be found the true type or measure of perfected art. (158)

Statements such as his famous dictum of 1877 that "all art constantly aspires to the condition of music" (156) thus indicate merely that the other arts should also strive toward this unity of form and content, not that they should give up the specificity of their own medial forms to become like music in any formal sense. Such formal experimentation would have to wait for a stronger focus on the formal aspects of music itself.

Eduard Hanslick is considered the first to make a scientific study of music and his 1854 volume *Vom Musikalisch-Schönen* founded a new formalist school of music theory, albeit one that only much later seeped into discussions in the fields of the other arts. He attacked romantic ideas about musical aesthetics for their amateurism, arguing not only that music's content and form were ideally united, but also that music possessed no content that could be in any way separated from that form. Music's beauty resides in the internal formal relations of a work, and not in any external ideas—whether emotions, the sublime, or programmatic content—that a listener might project on the music. Such formalist conceptions of musical aesthetics continued to characterize the modern period, as in Igor Stravinsky's statement that music is "essentially powerless to *express* anything at all, whether a feeling, an attitude of mind, a psychological mood, a phenomenon of nature, etc. . . . *Expression* has never been an inherent property of music" (cited in Fubini, 368; italics and ellipsis in Fubini). This emphasis on music as a form without content has a strong impact on the way music begins to be perceived in literature of the modern period, as the focus shifts from the musical ideal to much more concrete experimentation with musical form.

Music's strong fascination for literature is by no means restricted to the nineteenth century;[3] on the contrary, the two poles of romantic and formalist conceptions of music can both be found in literature up to the present day. While some texts focus on the romantic conception of the inspired musical genius or use music as a means of creating a particular atmosphere or evoking emotions, others, especially since the modern period, engage in textual adaptations of musical structures and techniques. Those experiments may extend over the entire form of the novel rather than being restricted to shorter episodes (see e.g. the polyphony of the "Sirens" chapter in James Joyce's *Ulysses*, 1922, or the evocation of counterpoint in sections of Aldous Huxley's *Point Counter Point*, 1928). Though novels such as Anthony Burgess's *Napoleon Symphony* (1974), Albert Murray's *Train Whistle Guitar* (1975), Anne Michaels's *Fugitive Pieces* (1996), Richard Powers's *The Gold Bug Variations* (1991), and Arthur Phillips's *The Song Is You* (2009) have yet to be joined together as a group by literary criticism, these experiments have become frequent and significant enough to merit treatment as a subgenre of their own: the musical novel.

A musical novel, as I define it, is musical not primarily in terms of its content, but in its very form. Like other subgenres of the novel such as the graphic novel or the artist novel, the musical novel crosses medial boundaries. Unlike the artist novel, the musical novel contains a musical presence not primarily on the level of content, but rather on that of form. And in contrast to the graphic novel, which consists of both words and images, the typical signs of the foreign medium of music are not materially present, but are only imitated by the text.[4] Though some musical novels include musical notation as epigraphs or other paratextual devices, often quoting from particular pieces, this physical inclusion of musical notation is at most a minor phenomenon.[5] Novels of this type take a genre or individual work of music as a model for their own construction, borrowing techniques and forms that they use to structure the narrative. These borrowed elements range from immediately perceptible, essential aspects of music (rhythm, timbre, and the simultaneity of multiple voices or instruments) to microstructural (jazz riffs, call-and-response patterns, or leitmotifs) and macrostructural elements (larger forms such as a theme and variations, a symphony, or a jazz or pop album). Additionally, novels may evoke the context of musical performance and reception by imitating elements of spontaneity that characterize improvised jazz or the varied responses of a number of audience members. Though music often plays a role in the content and themes of the novel, this genre definition of the musical novel relies on a significant or overarching presence of some variety of music on a formal, structural level; any explicit thematization of it is strictly optional.

Though these texts attempt to adapt musical forms to a literary context, they clearly do not become music—nor, I would argue, do they seek to. It is precisely by evoking musical form within the context of what remains a literary text that these novels are able to incite a metareferential reflection on the limits and strengths of the novel as such. The generic term "musical novel" clearly refers to a kind of novel, one that is musical in a structural manner, and not to a kind of music. Because of the different types of signs employed by the two media, much imitation of techniques foreign to the literary text must remain partial, analogical, or suggestive. This does not prevent the text from producing impressions in the reader that may be similar to those produced by the music so imitated. Intermedial imitation of this kind is thus an evocation of a foreign medium, not a transformation into that medium or a complete translation from that medium into another.

The extent to which music pervades the text of a musical novel may vary. In some texts music is a consistent presence on more than a merely content-based level, and yet a critic would be hard pressed to identify a specific musical form for the novel as a whole (see e.g. Robert Schneider's *Schlafes Bruder*, 1992;[6] Anne Michaels's *Fugitive Pieces*, 1996;[7] and Richard Powers's *The Time of Our Singing*, 2003[8]). Other musical imitations are much more specific, whether aimed at reconstructing musical practices—Arthur Phillips's *The Song Is You* (2009) is preoccupied with the way digital technologies and new modes of listening such as the iPod shuffle shape our experiences of popular music—or at particular pieces of music such as Beethoven's *Eroica* Symphony (the model for Anthony Burgess's *Napoleon Symphony*) or his *Chorfantasie* op. 80 (the starting point for Gert Jonke's *Chorphantasie*, 2003[9]).

For the purposes of this study, I have restricted my text selection to novels that can unambiguously be said to imitate either the musical genre of jazz or the particular theme and variations by J. S. Bach known as the *Goldberg Variations*. In these cases, the preoccupation with a musical model, whether a genre of music or a specific piece, permeates the text as a whole and is primarily formal. Though they do not all focus on the same aspects, the novels based on jazz imitate specific techniques such as the riff, call-and-response, or the chorus structure, as well as seek to evoke the performance situation with its qualities of spontaneity and the creation in performance of jazz improvisation. Many other novels use jazz as a shorthand for a particular social and ethnic group, to create atmosphere, or as a symbol of artistic creation, but I reserve the label "jazz novel" for those that also imitate (elements of) its structure.

Similarly, Bach's *Goldberg Variations* may figure as a representative of classical music and high culture, of a baroque ideal of order, or many other concepts, but I have chosen to analyze only those novels that pick up multiple elements of its structure—theme and variations, its numerical patterns, even microstructural elements such as time markings or the use of a minor key for certain variations. It is clearly not the case that every element of musical form can be detected in the texts based on these musical models. First of all, the different sign systems employed (verbal vs. musical signifiers) each have their own strengths and limitations and not everything that music can do *can* be accomplished by a text. On the other hand, the novel risks failing as a work of literature if it approaches too closely the form of music, as Alan Shockley said of such "failed novel[s]" as Burgess's *Napoleon Symphony* (116). Shockley praised Burgess's work as an "astounding achievement on many levels" (114), but acknowledged that its relative lack of a narrative led to its poor critical reception, such that it can be considered a success as a musical composition but not as a work of literature. Scholars of word and music studies should thus resist the temptation to pedantically search for exact parallels to all musical techniques or to criticize the text for not going further in approaching music, as a partial approximation or evocation of such techniques may be more successful than a thorough musicalization of the text.

As with all formal experimentation, the musical novel places relatively high demands on the reader. Confronted with a text that breaks with expectations of traditional narrative structure, he or she must seek to make sense of the form of these unusual novels. In some cases, that involves struggling with disparate plot strands, temporal shifts, a seeming disjunction between chapters that can be seen as variations on a theme that may or may not have been stated directly, shifting points of view or narrative voices, or a different use of repetition, rhythm, or other patterns than is frequently found in prose texts. Accepting such postmodern narrative surprises is one thing, understanding their purpose is yet another. Readers of a musical novel may not require knowledge of the musical model and its structures to make sense of the text, but such awareness is certainly an aid in perceiving the many layers that go into such a text and in interpreting the form in relation to the text's content and broader cultural context. The ideal reader of a musical novel can thus be assumed to be part of an in-group that will recognize references to a particular musical piece, genre, or form and make assessments of the novel's structure in relation to that model, partaking of shared knowledge between the reader, the text, and the author.

Though the musical novel has yet to be defined as a genre by scholarship, the field of word and music studies has been rapidly gaining in attention over the last several decades. An early pioneer in the field was Calvin S. Brown, whose influential monograph *Music and Literature* was published in 1948 and was followed by numerous articles on individual works of literature that occupy themselves with musical forms, including theme and variations ("Josef Weinheber's Hölderlin Variations" and "Theme and Variations as a Literary Form"). His work was taken up by scholars such as Steven P. Scher, a scholar of German literature who proposed influential categories for describing different kinds of interaction between words and music: word music, formal and structural analogies, and verbal music (see e.g. *Verbal Music in German Literature* and "Notes Towards a Theory of Verbal Music"). Though these categories have the disadvantage of lacking sharp delineations, they provide a useful starting point for examining the relations between the two media and distinguishing the direction of influence of one medium on the other.[10]

Werner Wolf's 1999 study *The Musicalization of Fiction* is probably still the most systematic and thorough approach to what could be called a genre of musical fiction, and will be examined for its theoretical foundations in intermediality studies in chapter 1. His analyses in that volume focus primarily on Anglo-American fiction of the modern and postmodern periods (concluding with an analysis of Gabriel Josipovici's 1987 short story "Fuga"), but in other articles he has also extended this research focus to more recent texts such as Huston's *Les Variations Goldberg* and Josipovici's *Goldberg: Variations*. Other scholars have examined music in literature primarily since the modern period, as in Alex Aronson's 1980 study of music in works by high modernist authors, Daniel Melnick's 1994 work on dissonance in modern fiction, Brad Bucknell's 2001 book on musical aesthetics in the work of moderns such as Joyce and Stein,

Erik Alder's and Dietmar Hauck's 2005 study of music in the work of E. M. Forster and Anthony Burgess, and Alan Shockley's impressive 2009 study of music in selected works of Joyce and Burgess, along with more recent experiments in polyphonic writing.

Furthermore, the International Association for Word and Music Studies, which aims "to promote transdisciplinary scholarly inquiry devoted to the relations among literature, verbal texts, language and music,"[11] has since 1997 provided a forum for numerous additional research projects operating at the intersections of the two media.[12] The broad scope of the organization, however—encompassing not only the study of musical fiction but also studies in opera and other vocal music, shared capacities of the two media such as description, musical aesthetics, sound poetry, and many other topics—means that terminological precision and a continuing focus on the general theoretical framework of the field remain desiderata in word and music studies.

The focus of work on musical fiction has long been overwhelmingly restricted to the role of European classical music in literary texts. An increasing interest in the influence of other musical genres such as jazz, world music, and pop on literary texts can be seen in a few isolated studies published over the past few years,[13] but there is still a large gap between the amount of work on textual imitations of classical music by Bach and Beethoven and on imitations of music from other traditions. This book takes a first step toward filling this gap by extending systematic analysis of musico-literary intermediality to novels that imitate jazz (chapters 2–4). Combining analyses of jazz novels with analyses of texts that imitate Bach's *Goldberg Variations* (chapters 5 and 6), this study aims to compare the treatment of two different musical traditions and demonstrate that very similar literary techniques may be employed in imitating music, regardless of its musical genre.

This book is organized in such a way as to unite the analyses of several novels in one chapter rather than have separate chapters on individual texts. Because the primary goal is to demonstrate some of the many ways that literature can imitate music, the book does not consist of a series of discrete text analyses that would aim to provide a complete discussion of each individual text. Instead, it is structured according to the elements of music that are imitated in a number of different texts, which allows for a more efficient comparison of the textual strategies used in such imitation and the isolation of individual musical forms and techniques that occur in a relatively large group of musical novels. The discussions of each text are thus restricted to the most salient musical elements present and do not attempt a complete analysis of any individual novel. The consideration of plot elements, ideology, symbolism, or numerous other aspects of the texts must thus be relegated to the margins in the interest of a coherent focus on the imitation of music. Also, this focus on musical elements means that some novels are treated in several sections of different chapters. For example, Albert Murray's *Train Whistle Guitar* (1975) is used to demonstrate musical rhythms in chapter 2; the riff, jazz choruses, and call-and-response patterns in chapter 3; as well as improvisation and ensemble performances in chapter 4. On the other hand, other novels may only figure in the discussion of one particular musical strategy. Thomas Bernhard's *Der Untergeher* (1983) is such an example. It differs so dramatically in structure from the other novels based on Bach's *Goldberg Variations* that it does not figure in the analyses of the theme-and-variations structure in chapter 5, but it is an excellent case for considering the role of the performer in chapter 6.[14]

The theoretical foundation of this study can be found in theories of intermediality and of semiotics, which together make up chapter 1, "Theorizing the Musical Novel." As a genre based fundamentally on the integration of strategies borrowed from another medium, the musical novel is intermedial by definition. As defined above, such novels are not merely *about* music—though this is very often also the case—but, crucially, attempt to translate selected musical forms or techniques into text. Theories of intermediality such as Werner Wolf's, as expounded in *The Musicalization of Fiction* (1999), provide useful terminology for distinguishing between intermedial thematization and imitation. The first part of chapter 1 discusses Wolf's model of intermediality and compares it with other models such as that of Irina Rajewsky (*Intermedialität*, 2002) before outlining a new model based not on categories or types of intermediality but on features that may be present or absent in any given case. This new model, which includes tree diagrams as graphic representations of intermedial features (see examples in the appendices), provides a tool for examining cases such as the musical novels analyzed in the later chapters.

Semiotics, the study of signs, forms an integral part of this theory of intermediality. Because the two media involved in a musical novel—text and music—comprise two separate sign systems, the scope available for transfer from one medium to the other is restricted and conditioned by the types of signs used in each medium. The second part of chapter 1 begins with an overview of theories of semiotics such as those independently proposed by the "founding fathers" of the field, Ferdinand de Saussure and Charles S. Peirce, as well as more recent structuralist approaches by Roman Jakobson, Umberto Eco, and others. Because such theories all begin with language as the primary sign system, I then go on to explore musical semiotics in particular, focusing most closely on work by Jean-Jacques Nattiez. Together, these semiotic approaches allow a more differentiated discussion of the ways in which language is capable of imitating music and of the primary differences and similarities between the two media that play a role in novels constructed on a musical model.

I have chosen as a text corpus two distinct groups of musical novels, groups that are intended to exemplify two fundamental types of textual imitation of music: the imitation of a musical genre and the imitation of a single musical work. Part 1, "The Novel Based on a Musical Genre," is thus devoted to jazz novels, which do not focus on a single jazz piece or performance, but on an entire genre of music. Within this genre, of course, there are considerable historical and stylistic differences, whether between the early New Orleans jazz played by Buddy Bolden around 1900 and the large swing bands of the 1930s or between the hard bop of Charlie Parker and the cool jazz of Miles Davis—or even between Davis's own bop, cool, and fusion phases. It is significant, however, that the elements of jazz picked up by musical novels are for the most part not distinctive of a particular period or style, but are perceived as characterizing jazz as a whole.[15] These widely disparate musical phenomena can thus be treated within a single framework. The three chapters on jazz novels focus on elements of sound, structure, and performance in the jazz novel, taking as examples eleven novels by Albert Murray (*Train Whistle Guitar*, 1975; *The Spyglass Tree*, 1991; *The Seven-League Boots*, 1995; and *The Magic Keys*, 2005), Michael Ondaatje (*Coming Through Slaughter*, 1976), Xam Wilson Cartiér (*Be-Bop, Re-Bop*, 1987; *Muse-Echo Blues*, 1991), Toni Morrison (*Jazz*, 1992), Christian Gailly (*Be-bop*, 1995), Stanley Crouch (*Don't the Moon Look Lonesome*, 2000), and Jack Fuller (*The Best of Jackson Payne*, 2000).

In contrast to novels that imitate jazz as a genre, the novels discussed in part 2, "The Novel Based on a Particular Piece of Music," are all based on a single piece of classical music: Johann Sebastian Bach's *Goldberg Variations*. Though this piece plays a role in numerous other works on a smaller scale, I focus on five contemporary novels, most of which make their interest in the *Goldbergs* visible in their titles: Nancy Huston, *The Goldberg Variations*, 1996 (first published as *Les Variations Goldberg* in 1981 and translated into English by Huston herself); Thomas Bernhard, *Der Untergeher*, 1983 (translated as *The Loser*, 1991); Richard Powers, *The Gold Bug Variations*, 1991; Gabriel Josipovici, *Goldberg: Variations*, 2002; and most recently, Rachel Cusk, *The Bradshaw Variations*, 2009. Because these five novels all deal with the same piece, they provide a unique opportunity to compare the different ways texts may approach a given piece of music. Though four of the five novels have been studied with relation to their musical model—those by Huston, Bernhard, Powers, and Josipovici—they have yet to be analyzed as a group or compared with one another.[16] While the jazz novels examined in chapters 2–4 present a case of an entire musical genre being imitated in text, the "Goldberg" novels take a more specific structural model, that of a single piece of music.[17] At the same time, the two groups of texts allow for comparison of jazz and classical musical models, though the analyses will show that many of the techniques used to imitate these forms are in fact shared.

The text analyses in chapters 2–4 are grouped according to the elements of jazz that are imitated in the novels. The model of intermediality proposed in chapter 1 distinguishes between the imitation of fundamental, immediately perceptible elements of music such as sound, that is, of rhythm and timbre; structural elements such as riffs, call and response, and chorus patterns; and elements of context such as improvisation and the live performance situation. These different levels provide the basis for the three chapters on jazz novels.

Chapter 2, "Elements of Sound in Jazz Novels," focuses on the imitation of the sound of jazz, specifically on rhythm and timbre. The analyses demonstrate that poetic techniques such as meter and the coinage of poetic, idiomatic neologisms serve as a bridge between the media of prose fiction and music, sharing features with both. Another such bridge can be found in reference to railroad trains, which have a long tradition of association with blues music and which are exploited in some of the novels as a source of rhythmic patterns.

Chapter 3, "Structural Patterns in Jazz Novels," turns to the elements of jazz structure that are imitated in the novels, starting with the repetition of highly recognizable phrases that evoke jazz riffs. Other features considered here include the structure of a jazz piece as a series of distinct units called choruses, the structure of a greatest-hits album, and call-and-response patterns. Call and response, in particular, may occur on different diegetic levels, whether between characters within the novel, such as in the sermons embedded in texts such as Stanley Crouch's *Don't the Moon Look Lonesome* and Jack Fuller's *The Best of Jackson Payne*, between different narrative voices, or between the narrator and the reader, both of which can be seen in Toni Morrison's *Jazz*.

Chapter 4, "The Performance Situation in Jazz Novels," concludes the examination of jazz novels with a focus on contextual aspects of jazz music. Because jazz of all types is so intimately associated with the live performance and especially with improvisation, this is a particularly salient aspect for treatment in the novel. Here again, the differences in signs pose a challenge for the textual imitation of these aspects, but the texts resort to a variety of strategies to translate musical improvisation and audience interaction into text. One such strategy, as exemplified by Toni Morrison's *Jazz*, is the adoption of techniques from oral storytelling and gossip as a means of evoking a linguistic situation that is rooted in spontaneous performance. Another such strategy is the creation of a distinct narrative voice that corresponds to the performer and that pushes the author or composer into the background. There may also be multiple narrators, which can be seen as imitating ensemble performances and collective improvisation. Such narrators suggest that they are engaged in composing the text themselves, often by making use of the present tense or by switching between tenses, as in Xam Wilson Cartiér's novels *Be-Bop,*

Re-Bop and *Muse-Echo Blues*. The audience is included in the construction of textual meaning in the manner of a live jazz performance through second-person address, but also by reacting to narrators that revise their text as they go. This may be done frequently throughout the novel or may be restricted to "breaks," during which the narrator "solos" on a motif that has been presented previously. Examples of different types of solo improvisation are discussed with regard to three very different novels: Albert Murray's *Train Whistle Guitar*, Toni Morrison's *Jazz*, and Christian Gailly's *Be-bop*.

As in the section on jazz novels, the analyses of novels based on Bach's *Goldberg Variations* are grouped according to the musical elements imitated. The elements of sound—rhythm and timbre—are much less distinctive in novels based on the *Goldberg Variations* than in those based on jazz, so that a comparable chapter on sound is not needed in this second analysis block.[18] Chapter 5, "Structural Patterns in Novels Based on the *Goldberg Variations*," forms a parallel to chapter 3 on jazz structural elements. The examination of musical structure is here divided into macrostructural elements—the imitation of the larger form and symmetry of the *Goldberg Variations*—and microstructural elements, or details of structure that are restricted to individual variations. In the first section, the focus is primarily on the imitation of the theme-and-variations form, including an identification of the themes that form the basis of variation in each novel, as well as the principle of variation employed in each case. The mathematical structure of the *Goldbergs* with its focus on multiples of two and three also provides a basis for imitation, as when the "pattern of three"—by which every third variation is a canon beginning at progressive intervals—yields a tripartite plot structure in Powers's *The Gold Bug Variations*. The chapter considers time notation and the use of major and minor keys as microstructural elements, while a concluding section explores the concept of time implied by the theme-and-variations form. Rather than conceiving of time—or the plot of the novel—as something linear and progressive, novels based on a theme and variations are inclined to present it as cyclical. This can be seen in recursive structures, in a return to the beginning at the end of the story, and in frequent reference to the calendar as a marker of temporal cycles.

Chapter 6, "Composition, Performance, and Reception in Novels Based on the *Goldberg Variations*," is occupied with the three main roles in the communicative triangle, building on the semiotic models of linguistic and musical communication that I present in chapter 1. In the case of the musical performance, those roles are filled by the composer, as the sender of the message; the performer, as the messenger; and the listener or audience, as the recipient of the message. The musical performance or work then corresponds to that message, which is analyzed in its immanent structure in chapter 5. Here, the three remaining roles are considered independently, insofar as the novels permit such a separation. First, I consider the legend of the *Goldberg Variations*' composition, according to which the piece was commissioned as accompaniment for an insomniac in his sleepless nights. Gabriel Josipovici's *Goldberg: Variations* seizes on this legend as the foundation of its narrative structure, in which a writer takes the role of the performer in attempting to fulfill a similar commission. Interestingly, this constellation ends up equating the composer and the performer, as the writer Goldberg not only reads, but must also write the pieces he reads to his employer. The analysis of Nancy Huston's *The Goldberg Variations* also demonstrates that the performer and composer roles are intimately connected and that any performance is per se a creative act.

The performer role can be further specified as either professional or amateur, a distinction that divides my two analyses of performer figures in these novels. While Thomas Bradshaw in Rachel Cusk's *The Bradshaw Variations* diligently struggles with his piano lessons, Glenn Gould in Thomas Bernhard's *Der Untergeher* is portrayed as a romantic artistic genius. Both novels provide interesting insights on the role of the performer in any performance and his or her relationship toward the piece and toward the audience.

Finally, the audience makes up the third component of the communicative triangle. Nancy Huston's *The Goldberg Variations* presents the reactions of thirty listeners to a performance of Bach's piece, exemplifying the varied levels of interest in and experience with baroque music. Though the thirty monologues are eventually revealed to be the imaginative creations of the performer and primary narrator Liliane, they nevertheless demonstrate how the recipient—whether listener or reader—is necessarily an active participant in the construction of musical or textual meaning. A very different listening experience is portrayed in Richard Powers's *The Gold Bug Variations*, in which the performance in question is captured on a record. This record and its materiality provide the opportunity for fruitful reflection on the status of the "original" work in an age in which performances are no longer fleeting and momentary but can be captured on disc for repeated listenings. At the same time, the importance of the listener continues to mean that each instance of listening is singular and changes from person to person and with the passage of time. All these novels join in destabilizing the authority not only of the composer/author in postmodern fashion, but also that of the performer and of the original work.[19] Not only is each performance fundamentally unique; the same can be said, these novels implicitly argue, of each reading of a novel as well.

This comparison that is provoked between the musical performance and the novel is typical of intermediality wherever it appears. The juxtaposition of elements from two different media and the breaches in reader expectations caused by unfamiliar techniques cause the reader to reflect on what the text is capable of and where its limits lie. This reflection on the borders between text and music is profoundly metareferential and is one of the primary functions of intermedial imitation. By transposing elements of music from jazz, from Bach's *Goldberg Variations*, or from any of a number of other genres and pieces, novels can explore new forms and devices and show the reader not only their own limitations—what music can do that the texts would like to be able to do—but also their strengths. The fact that these novels successfully integrate musical forms and create impressions akin to those evoked by a musical performance is a demonstration of the power, creativity, and flexibility of the contemporary novel.

Notes

[1] As Sarah Dillon elucidates in her study of the palimpsest, the usual adjectival form is *palimpsestic*. Gérard Genette's coinage of the term *palimpsestuous* allows for a distinction between the "process of layering that produces a palimpsest" (*palimpsestic*) and "the structure that one is presented with as a result of that process" (*palimpsestuous*) (Dillon, 4).

[2] The present discussion of musical aesthetics from the eighteenth up to the twentieth century is based on a more in-depth treatment in Enrico Fubini, *The History of Music Aesthetics*.

[3] A case can be made for experimentations with musical form going back much further; William Freedman, for example, sees the "*Origins of the Musical Novel*" in Laurence Sterne's *Tristram Shandy* (1759–1967). Considering the number of other ways in which this novel anticipates modernism and postmodernism, however, it seems appropriate that this kind of formal experimentation with musical models should also play a role in its structure.

[4] A somewhat closer parallel to the musical novel is the photographic novel or the iconotext (see Wagner, 15–16), which in addition to reproducing actual photographs may also evoke photographic techniques in its construction in a manner similar to the imitation of music in the musical novel. See, for example, Krüger.

[5] For example, Xam Wilson Cartiér's *Muse-Echo Blues* (1991) includes a piano transcription of an improvised Charles Mingus solo entitled "Piano improvisation *Myself When I Am Real* (*Adagio Ma Non Troppo*)" as the second of two epigraphs to the novel. Similarly placed, but with rather different implications, Gabriel Josipovici's *Goldberg: Variations* employs a stylized musical stave, although without musical notes, to mark the beginning of each chapter in the novel. By using musical signs rather than textual means, these examples illustrate the phenomenon of multimediality, in which the typical signifiers of more than one medium are physically present. In intermediality, on the other hand, only one medium is physically present and gestures toward, thematizes, or imitates the signs of a foreign medium, which it does not actually possess. For a detailed discussion of intermediality, including the distinction between intermediality and multimediality, see chapter 1.

⁶ The title of Robert Schneider's novel *Schlafes Bruder* (*Brother of Sleep*) is taken from the chorale "Komm, O Tod, du Schlafes Bruder" in Bach's cantata *Ich will den Kreuzstab gerne tragen* (I will gladly carry the cross-staff; BWV 56), on which the novel's protagonist, a romantic musical genius, improvises on the organ. Though music permeates the atmosphere of this text and the other two novels in Schneider's Rheintal trilogy, there do not seem to be recognizable imitations of structural elements from that music imitated in the text and Schneider in an interview has explicitly rejected the possibility of (his) fiction imitating larger musical forms such as that of a fugue, and confirmed that he sought to evoke individual musical techniques such as the crescendo (Kruse, 98–99).

⁷ Anne Michaels's *Fugitive Pieces* is inspired in part by a Brahms's Intermezzo no. 2, op. 117, evoking the piece's atmosphere but not re-creating its formal structure in any consistent way. The novel also refers to Beethoven's *Moonlight Sonata* as an example of the subjectivity of assigning meaning or images to instrumental music, as well as making more general references to lullabies and other music. In all these cases, music is overwhelmingly linked in the novel to conceptions of time and memory.

⁸ Richard Powers's *The Time of Our Singing* revolves around a family that demonstrates hybridity not only racially but also musically, making reference to a wide variety of musical styles from classical vocal repertoire by Schubert and Bach to Renaissance madrigals, popular standards, gospel, jazz, and rap. Music in this novel is combined with an interest in physics that also connects it to the musical-scientific structure of Powers's earlier novel *The Gold Bug Variations*, while the attempt to make sense of temporality through various models including music is something it shares with Michaels's *Fugitive Pieces*.

⁹ Gert Jonke's *Chorphantasie*, which bears the subtitle *Konzert für Solo-Dirigent auf der Suche nach dem Orchester* (concert for solo conductor in search of the orchestra), is a play inspired by the premiere of Beethoven's *Chorfantasie* (*Fantasie für Klavier, Chor und Orchester in c-Moll*, op. 80) on December 22, 1808, in which the orchestra is reputed to have played so badly that Beethoven felt compelled to interrupt the performance and begin again. Jonke's conductor faces even more dramatic challenges, since the orchestra is missing altogether, so he begins by conducting the audience instead. The play is structured into three acts, labeled as movements ("Satz") and bearing the musical markings "Allegro ma non troppo," "Andante con variazioni," and "Allegro appassionato mit Schlusschor," respectively. These markings do not correspond to those in the Beethoven piece, however, though there are some recognizable structural parallels, such as the use of variations in a middle section and the concluding choral section.

¹⁰ See e.g. Werner Wolf's discussion of the terminological imprecision of Scher's category "verbal music" in *The Musicalization of Fiction* (59–60; diagram 3, 70).

¹¹ Quoted from the association's home page: http://wordmusicstudies.org.

¹² The recent establishment of a forum for emerging scholars (the Word and Music Association Forum, founded in 2009 by Mario Dunkel, Emily Petermann, and Beate Schirrmacher) demonstrates the high level of interest that continues to be brought to the field by graduate students and postdocs, a trend that

suggests that work in this area is just beginning and much more can be expected in the future.

[13] An important exception is Claus-Ulrich Viol's 2006 study of pop music in British fiction, *Jukebooks*. Michael Meyer's 2002 edited collection *Literature and Music* also includes essays on texts dealing with jazz, folksongs, and spirituals, as well as classical musical genres, though it does not propose an overarching theory of musical fiction, but instead collects essays on individual authors and texts. A more recent example that considers popular music among a variety of other musical models is Gerry Smyth's 2008 book *Music in Contemporary British Fiction*. He includes a chapter on "Musical Genre in the Novel," which examines examples of novels inspired by music of various traditions such as folk, jazz, rock, hip hop, and world music, albeit fairly briefly. See also Hoene (2012) on Indian classical music in postcolonial South Asian diasporic literature, as well as Jean-Louis Pautrot's (2006) and Eric Prieto's (2003) work on jazz in French literature, among others. Though there has been widespread attention to the phenomenon of jazz in (especially African American) literature, as mentioned above and discussed in the section on jazz novels, it has rarely been dealt with within the context of word and music studies, and such analyses belong to a different discursive tradition.

[14] For a good analysis of the musical structures in *Der Untergeher*, see Hens (1999).

[15] It is important to emphasize that my focus in this work is not on jazz or classical music as they really are, but rather on what the novels *say* they are. This is a study not of music but of musical novels, such that the music itself figures only peripherally, as an introduction to the role of music in the texts. I will thus begin each analysis chapter with only a brief look at the musical elements involved before turning to their adaptation in text.

[16] A 2010 article by Theodore Ziolkowski does analyse four of these five texts as a group (he does not include Cusk's *The Bradshaw Variations*). His paper lacks the space to go into a detailed comparison of the structure of these four novels, however, which will be the task of chapters 5 and 6.

[17] That several novels have chosen to adapt the structure of this same piece of music in their own construction appears to be a unique case. Indeed, there have been very few other imitations of specific pieces of music like this, most prominently Burgess's *Napoleon Symphony*, but also his "K. 550 (1788)" in *On Mozart: A Paean for Wolfgang* (1991), as well as Gert Jonke's theater play *Chorphantasie* (2003) and his novel *Schule der Geläufigkeit* (1977; published in English translation as *Homage to Czerny: Studies in Virtuoso Technique*, 2008). Tolstoy's *Kreutzer Sonata* is sometimes mentioned in this context, but although the novella places a particular Beethoven composition at its climax and positions it prominently as the story's title, there seems to be little structural imitation of the piece. As I will argue in the sections on the Goldberg novels, however, though this group is something of an anomaly when seen within the larger context of musical novels, the kinds of imitation of musical structure they exhibit can also be found in a variety of other texts, even if they are less pervasive or unified.

[18] This somewhat surprising shift in emphasis may be related to the relative emphasis on individuality in tone and performance style in jazz music in contrast

to the desire for homogeneity in classical instrumentation. Similarly, with a classical piece of music the "work" is perceived as being embodied in the written score and less in any individual performance, which attempts to a much greater extent to reproduce a single idealized "original." Together, these different ideologies associated with jazz versus classical music may account for a stronger focus on formal elements in the imitation of classical music and less on the context of the performance. As the analyses in chapter 6 will show, however, postmodern texts simultaneously break with this expectation by questioning the roles of composer, performer, and audience, drawing their representations of music surprisingly close to those in jazz novels.

[19] This is of course reminiscent of Walter Benjamin's theory of the mechanically reproducible artwork and the way this process destroys the aura and authority of the original work, as I will discuss in chapter 6.

1: Theorizing the Musical Novel

Though artists and critics alike have often explored the relationships between the arts, a shared critical vocabulary has yet to be developed. Scholars in diverse fields have approached the subject from various disciplinary positions, such as media and communication studies, comparative literature, individual philologies, musicology, and art history, offering many perspectives on the issue, but leading to widespread terminological ambiguity and the lack of a common discourse. In response, I propose a model of intermediality that aims at a more precise terminology and methodology for analysis. In the first part of the chapter, I offer definitions of key terms and a differentiation between intermediality and the related phenomena of transmediality, multimediality, and intramediality or intertextuality, before briefly discussing prior models. The section concludes with a detailed presentation of my own model. A diagram can be found in the appendix. Graphically represented, this model provides a tool with potential cross-disciplinary applications for the analysis of different media products ranging from musical novels to multimedial dance productions, from instances of intermediality in painting to those in mono- or multimedial musical works. Sample diagrams of three of the musical novels analyzed in this study are also included in the appendix.

In addition to intermediality, semiotics forms an important basis for the analyses of textual imitation of music in the novels selected. An attempt to be "like music" involves the transposition of a different kind of sign and signification into literature. The analyses will thus draw on theories of verbal and musical signs in order to examine the specific processes of signification that are common to both media as well as those aspects of musical signification that remain foreign to the text.

Intermediality[1]

Terminology and Definitions

When Samuel Taylor Coleridge first used the term "intermedia" in 1812, it represented a conceptual fusion of different media and had programmatic-aesthetic implications for intermedial art works. Coleridge used the word "to define works which fall conceptually *between media* that are already known" (Higgins, 23). Yet his application of the term to allegory, which he called an "intermedium" between person and personification, makes it clear that his definition is still quite a ways away from today's usage (Paech, 17).

Intermediality, as I define it, is any crossing of medial borders *within* a given work or media product. Throughout, I will be using the term "media product" rather than "text," as the former can encompass examples from any medium, whether themselves monomedial or multimedial: a film, a piece of music, a statue, a graphic novel, a poem, a jazz performance, etc. The term "work" is being used as a synonym for media product; while this term could be seen as privileging the work of art over nonartistic products, this theory of intermediality can be equally applied to media products as diverse as reviews of musical or dance performances, illustrated magazines or newspapers, and photojournalism. Intermediality as conceived here refers to the relationships between media that are visible within a single media product rather than the processes of adaptation or transfer involved in the creation of that product. The media product is by this definition not itself intermedial, but may exhibit intermediality in its relations to another medium or other media. The media product itself is firmly located within one medium, whereas it is the *relationship* to the foreign medium that is intermedial, as this relation is what actually extends across media borders. For example, a novel remains a work of literature, even if it makes use of filmic techniques or descriptions of musical works. Those techniques and descriptions are intermedial phenomena, while the novel as a whole exists within the medium "literature." These intermedial relations can be seen within the media product itself, whether through reference to (thematization) or imitation of that other medium.[2]

This definition of intermediality differs in several important respects from current usage. The term "intermediality" has often been defined so broadly that it can apply to *any* phenomenon that can in some sense be located between media.[3] This includes processes of media-combination that may lead to the formation of new media,[4] the transfer of content from one medium to another,[5] and reference to or imitation of foreign media within another media product. The present model proposes a conceptual separation of these first two aspects—what I will call multimediality and transmediality, respectively—from the third, intermediality proper.

Intermediality is a separate phenomenon from multimediality, though in practice multimedial works almost always contain intermedial relationships as well. I restrict the term "multimediality" such that it refers only to the material presence of two or more media in the same work or phenomenal space (as in a gallery installation of paintings and music), which need not relate to each other in any manner other than their juxtaposition. Because intermediality refers not to a media product as a whole but to relations within a media product, it can be found not only in a work in which only a single medium is materially present with its own signifiers but also in a work that is itself multimedial, such as a film, a graphic novel, vocal music, or a dance performance. In such a case one medium may refer to, imitate, mirror, or otherwise relate to the other medium in the multimedial product, just as it may relate to a medium that is not materially present. The presence of two or more media in a single product, which I label "multimediality," thus frequently leads to intermedial relations between the media involved, although they need not relate to one another. Multimediality is thus a distinct phenomenon from intermediality—a context in which intermediality may occur, but is not itself intermediality.

Multimediality has generated its own field of study, and in fact, research on media studies generally focuses on multimedial phenomena, even when the term "intermediality" is used.[6] Multimedia studies are often focused on the *process*[7] of interactions between media and the effects created by their juxtaposition, as well as on the historical development of new complex media out of multimedial contexts.[8] In this model of intermediality, however, I focus primarily on the media *product* as a concrete realization of a semiotic system and on its interactions with other semiotic systems, in an approach that is primarily synchronic rather than diachronic. A diachronic focus on intermediality as a process leads to thorny questions about the intentions of author or composer, intentions that cannot be proven or disproven. I therefore advocate a synchronic examination of intermedial relations in a work-immanent context, though that work is of course itself the result of processes that have gone before. In other words, I work under the assumption that the process by which a given work is created—to the extent that the process is relevant for the signification of that product—leaves its traces in the product.

Intermediality must also be distinguished from what Rajewsky and others have called transmediality. Transmediality refers to media-nonspecific phenomena that can appear in various media without being marked by the specific techniques and structures of those media (Rajewsky, *Intermedialität*, 13).[9] In this context, it is sufficient to emphasize the lack of medium-specificity involved in such phenomena. For example, if a painting and a play both make use of the Greek myth of Oedipus, they need not be regarded as referring to a particular textual version of that myth, but instead to content that belongs to the collective memory of Western society and is independent of a particular medium. Likewise, the aesthetic ideals of a given period may manifest themselves in painting, music, and literature, without there necessarily being a direct influence between any two of those media. If, however, the medium-specificity of one of those media is also represented in another medium, it becomes a case of intermediality.

The term "transmediality" may also be applied to adaptations of a media product from one medial context into another, as when a novel is made into a film or play. Such "adaptations" may of course involve a direct reference to the source medium, a reference that would be intermedial. Research on adaptation as a process, however, has focused on the continuity of content between the source work and its adaptation, as well as on the need for medium-specific modification of that material in its new media context (see e.g. Nischik, Leubner). Linda Hutcheon in *A Theory of Adaptation* lists a number of elements that can be considered "adaptable content": the "story," "themes," "characters," and "the separate units of the story," which are changed in terms of "plot ordering," "pacing," "focalization or point of view" (10–11). In the majority of cases, those works considered adaptations interact with the content or story of their sources, giving a new form to existing content.[10] Intermedial imitation, on the other hand, is an adoption of formal aspects of a source and their re-creation or approximation in a new medial context, while content need not be directly involved. For this reason, the present study with its focus on musical form does not make use of work on adaptation, which can instead be largely subsumed under the category of transmediality.

Finally, another branch of inquiry needs to be distinguished from intermediality—that of intramediality. This term refers to phenomena that occur within the boundaries of a single medium. In the case of literature, this is more familiar as intertextuality, a field closely related to that of intermediality, as it also deals with references to another semiotic system (the foreign text or genre). In fact, work on intertextuality has sparked much of the current interest in intermediality.

The critical ambiguity surrounding the term "intermediality" arose in large part because of the radical openness of the concepts of "text" and "textuality" that emerged with the rise of structuralism and poststructuralism in the 1960s. Ferdinand de Saussure's description of language as a system of signs in *Cours de linguistique générale* (1916) paved the way for Julia Kristeva's concept of culture and everything within it as a *texte general* ("Le Texte clos," 103). The idea that "everything is a text," or at least able to be understood and analyzed as a text, led to descriptions and analyses not only of any kind of written object, literary or otherwise, but also of music, dance, the visual arts, bodies, social structures, and cultural formations as "texts"—or, more precisely, as *like* texts: highly structured semiotic systems. While the broad application of semiotics had many rich effects in terms of the expansion of cultural criticism into areas beyond literature and the arts,[11] the ease with which the term "text" is still interchanged with "semiotic system" or "system of signs" has led to confusion, not least in distinguishing intertextuality and intermediality within the field of literary studies.

Kristeva's definition of intertextuality is broad enough to include the concept of intermediality used here as well: "le terme d'*inter-textualité* désigne cette transposition d'un (ou de plusieurs) système(s) de signes en un autre" (the term *intertextuality* designates this transposition from one (or more) system(s) of signs into another; Kristeva, *La revolution du langage poétique*, 59). For Kristeva, then, intertextuality primarily concerns *systemic* relationships and processes, rather than diachronic, author-oriented processes of composition, and furthermore need not be limited to linguistic signs or literary structures.

Indeed, many studies of intermediality as defined here refer to it as intertextuality (see e.g. Daly and other essays in Hoesterey and Weisstein, 1993). Given the current broad definitions of text, the confusion of terms is understandable. In addition, one might look at the expansion of the concepts of "translation," "quotation," and other previously text-based terms into other media as sources of ambiguity surrounding intermediality. As one critic, disturbed by the widespread confusion between the terms, concludes:

> The broad concept of both texts and intertextuality introduced to the volume [Hoesterey and Weisstein, *Intertextuality*] makes it difficult to delimit intertextuality from intermediality. But then, any reader curious about intermediality would probably expect an analysis of MTV and perhaps computer-generated virtual reality rather than one of *Laokoon* and the more traditional union of the arts reflected in the current volume. (Moeller, 71)

The present use of the term "media," significantly wider than the "new media" or "mass media" so often associated with the term, attempts to resolve the biases and limitations associated with the term "intermediality" on the one hand, and the problematically vague conception of "intertextuality" on the other.

My use of the term "medium" depends to a large extent on Werner Wolf's definition of it as "a conventionally distinct means of communication or expression characterized not only by particular channels (or one channel) for the sending and receiving of messages but also by the use of one or more semiotic systems" (*Musicalization of Fiction*, 40). I thus do not see the term "medium" as restricted to a narrow concept of a technological channel of communication, as for example in the Lasswell formula: "If who says what, through what channels (media of communication), to whom, what will be the results? And how can we measure what is said and its result?" (Harold D. Lasswell, cited in Schanze, 25). Nor do I use the term to cover "any extension of ourselves" as in Marshall McLuhan's famously broad take on medium (23). A medium supplies the outer form of a given message, corresponding to the signifier in Saussure's concept of the sign (Eicher, 16). Wolf's definition includes both aspects of communication and expression and also emphasizes the various semiotic systems involved.[12]

Existing Models of Intermediality

Views of the arts as essentially similar date back at least as far as the ancient Greeks. Simonides of Keos famously pronounced poetry to be "speaking painting" and painting to be "silent poetry,"[13] similar to Horace's dictum "ut pictura poesis."[14] On the other hand, in *Laokoon* (1766), Gotthold Ephraim Lessing advocated a separation of literature and the visual arts, based on the different types of signs used in each. In the nineteenth century, discussions of the relationships between the arts were primarily based on philosophical models, as exemplified by Richard Wagner and his idea of the *Gesamtkunstwerk* (total work of art) and Walter Pater's assertion that "all art constantly aspires to the condition of music" (Pater, 86). Such approaches remained prevalent among modernist artists, writers, choreographers, and composers as they worked to transcend the boundaries and capacities of individual media.

Among contemporary theorists, this type of approach is best represented by the work of Daniel Albright, especially his *Untwisting the Serpent: Modernism in Music, Literature, and Other Arts*,[15] which describes the ways in which many of the most innovative modernist artworks were in fact collaborations among the arts. He focuses on the intensified effects produced when various art forms merge, whether the media are in dissonance with each other (asserting their difference), or in consonance (dissolving their differences into an essential unity).

In the practical analysis of a particular work, however, I advocate a more specific and systematic approach. This need not exclude, nor should it, more philosophical and artistic reflections on the meaning and effects of intermediality. However, an analysis that begins with specifics is likely to be stronger, and I see my system as a tool for analysis rather than a philosophical interpretation of intermediality per se. In developing this model, the two systems I have drawn on most extensively are those of Werner Wolf and Irina Rajewsky.

Werner Wolf, in *The Musicalization of Fiction*, was the first theorist to systematically articulate the various types of intermediality that may occur in fiction with relation to music.[16] Although he focuses exclusively on text and music, in many respects his system can be extended to other intermedial phenomena. I have drawn on Wolf's work in some detail, adapting many of his terms. My primary divergence from Wolf's model is in my definition of intermediality. As discussed above, I see it as a fundamentally different phenomenon from multimediality (though potentially occurring in the same work), whereas Wolf uses a broader conception that includes any combination of media, and thus includes multimedia as well. This difference leads to Wolf's development of the terms "overt" and "covert intermediality," which relate to the number of media materially present—terms that are not applicable to the definition of intermediality used here.

What I call intermediality corresponds to his category of covert intermediality, while his overt category refers to what I have called multimediality.

Wolf's division of intermedial phenomena into what he calls "thematization"—"explicit 'telling'" in which the "other medium [is] indirectly present in a work merely as a signified or as a referent" (*Musicalization of Fiction*, 44)—and "imitation"—"in which some kind of iconic similarity between (parts of) a work characterized by one medium and another medium suggests the presence of this second medium within the (dominant) first one" (57)—is a useful distinction that is preserved here. The term "imitation" evokes the concept of mimesis, as an attempt to make something absent present, in this case not "reality" itself, but another medium. It should not be understood with the negative connotations of copying as opposed to originality (i.e., "*only* imitation"). As Linda Hutcheon has observed: "to be second is not to be secondary or inferior; likewise, to be first is not to be originary or authoritative" (*A Theory of Adaptation*, xiii). Though the term "imitation" has provoked some debate,[17] it has become quite established in the field of word and music studies and will thus be retained here in the sense of "borrowing techniques from" or otherwise "making present."

In *Intermedialität*, Irina Rajewsky builds on Wolf's work by presenting a system that strives to include all combinations of media. One of the main strengths of Rajewsky's systematic approach is her discussion of intermediality in relation to such categories as intramediality and transmediality, as discussed above. Rajewsky's typology is also distinguished by its applicability to a wide variety of media constellations, rather than being characterized by bias toward one medium or media group. Within her category of intermediality, which she defines as phenomena that cross media boundaries, involving what are conventionally seen as at least two distinct media, she distinguishes three main categories: media combination (multimedia), media transposition (similar to adaptation), and intermedial references.[18]

Rajewsky's category "intermedial references" is what I consider intermediality proper. These are forms of constituting meaning in a given media product through relation to a specific product or the semiotic system of another conventionally distinct medium. Rajewsky differentiates a number of subcategories within intermedial references. Unfortunately, the categories overlap awkwardly and despite her extensive glossary the distinguishing features between them are often unclear.[19] If this abundance of categories is replaced by features, the following factors emerge as significant in her model: the degree of the phenomenon—whether or not it extends throughout the whole work (a distinction not included in the present model); the production of altermedial illusion (i.e., the defining characteristic of what is here called imitation, and which is distinct from thematization); the presence or absence of explicit marking (this, too, is related to the thematization/imitation distinction); and the use of shared aspects (media-nonspecific) versus imitation/translation of foreign aspects (medium-specific). An important point on which I agree with Rajewsky is her claim that the *relationship* to another media product or medium is intermedial, rather than the media product as a whole ("Intermedialität 'light'?," 44). Intermediality thus characterizes particular phenomena, rather than the media product itself.

Although I have maintained Wolf's and Rajewsky's structured approach to intermediality, I have found difficulties in that their terms overlap even within their own systems, and their emphases suggest a categorization of a particular work rather than, as in the present approach, a delineation of the multiple forms of intermediality within that work. Thus, this model focuses on the description of a single instance, rather than intermediality in general. Superficially, my tree diagrams in the appendix would seem to resemble those used by Wolf. An important distinction, however, is that his diagram (see e.g. *Musicalization of Fiction*, 50) depicts all the different types of intermediality and implicitly suggests that any intermedial phenomenon can only fit in one of the categories given. I instead use a separate tree for each work involved, with separate branches for each variety of intermediality present. My tree diagrams represent not categories but *features* of intermedial phenomena, which may be present or absent in any combination. In this way, the phenomena present in any given work can be graphically represented, providing a visual image of possible features. This approach yields a more useful guide to analysis than producing categories that cannot in practice be kept distinct. It can be more easily applied to individual works, yet maintains integrity as a representation of abstractions.

While this model is deeply indebted to previous theoretical work, it streamlines, elaborates, and restructures earlier systems to achieve greater clarity. Above all, it is designed to be a heuristic tool for analysis rather than primarily a theoretical description of intermediality. While Rajewsky, for example, has a single system of charts for all forms of intermediality, in this system each individual work or instance is the basis for its own tree chart, which will then serve as an analytical tool. The following section aims to explain the graphic representation of the model printed in the appendix. The text analyses in chapters 2–6 can be seen as practical examples of its application. The appendix includes sample tree diagrams for the individual musical novels discussed throughout this study.

A New Model of General Intermediality: Relations among Semiotic Systems

As discussed above, intermediality and multimediality are two separate phenomena, though they may be present in the same media product. This first level of the tree diagram allows the critic to represent these phenomena in a given work as distinct branches.[20] Under intermediality, then, there is a branch for each possible intermedial relationship within a given media product, isolating the different types of interactions that may then be further explored. A textual work that contains references to both painting and music, for instance, would have a branch to describe the relationship between text and painting (A → B), and another branch to describe the relationship between text and music (A → C). In a multimedial work, there could be additional branches to demonstrate the reciprocal relationships among the various media (B → A; C → A).[21]

Thematization and Imitation

Following Werner Wolf, I recognize two primary intermedial phenomena: thematization and imitation (*Musicalization of Fiction*, 44 and passim).[22] It is important to bear in mind, however, that the two are not mutually exclusive. They frequently occur together, and in some cases may be difficult to distinguish from one another. For instance, a passage of a novel describing a piece of music is an example of thematization; if this description also mimics the sound or structure of the piece itself, then it is also an example of intermedial imitation. Thematization consists of an explicit reference to a medium that is not materially present in a given media product.[23]

Thematization has been treated in the critical literature on intermediality as banal (Rajewsky, "Intermedialität 'light'?," 47), yet Rajewsky has correctly identified two important functions of thematization. First, it has a marker function, making explicit reference to the foreign medium, which imitation provides only implicitly. Second, thematization, even as a mere mention of the other medium, serves as a guide to reception, causing recipients to view the media product in light of the foreign medium so referenced. The reference thus contributes to meaning constitution in that media product, often provoking a metareferential reflection on the nature of both media (see Rajewsky, "Intermedialität 'light'?," 48–49, 56, 58–59, 62).

Imitation occurs when techniques of the medium that is materially present are used to metaphorically suggest the presence of a foreign medium, as when the structure of a poem is modeled on a fugue or a piece of music evokes a specific painting. Although Wolf differentiates thematization and imitation as "telling" and "showing," I have chosen not to use these terms because of their bias toward text-based media products. Imitation itself is inherently implicit. When imitation is made explicit, for example by a descriptive title, the act of explication is an instance of thematization. As with thematization, the forms of imitation are frequently medium-specific.

This model specifies the imitated aspect for each phenomenon, meaning the real or perceived aspect of the foreign medium that the media product imitates. Just as a single work may include both thematization and imitation, it may also thematize or imitate more than one aspect of the foreign medium. While these aspects may vary widely from medium to medium and from work to work, I have developed a set of common possibilities for both the imitated aspect and its corollary, the thematized aspect. These aspects include:

- Effect (the real or perceived effects a medium has on its audiences).
- Surface (immediately perceptible elements; in the context of visual art this includes color, whereas in the context of music it includes elements of sound such as melody or rhythm).[24]
- Structure (formal elements on the micro or macro levels, such as poetry's rhyming couplets or the musical form of a theme and variations).
- Inherent qualities (basic elements, such as the spatial nature of sculpture or the temporal nature of music).
- Context (aspects of the situation surrounding the artwork, such as the proximity to other paintings in a museum or audience interaction during a jazz performance).
- Content (for example, the plot of a novel or the subject of a representational painting).

Because content is not medium-specific, it may only be thematized.[25] An attempted imitation of content would instead consist of an adaptation, or translation across media. The reproduction of content without an attending imitation of aspects of a foreign medium is not sufficient to suggest the presence of a foreign medium. Imitation presupposes difference, and is therefore not applicable to aspects like content that transcend medial borders. Instead, such a reproduction of content is classified as transmediality.

The five aspects listed here are not meant to encompass every instance of intermedial thematization or imitation, or to act as final labels, but rather to guide the critic to potentially significant areas for examination by suggesting possible questions. They are one of the most flexible elements of the model and should be understood as placeholders on the tree diagram. In the course of an analysis these aspects will either be elaborated on, by identifying more precise elements of each, or be replaced with different, more medium-specific terms. In this volume, for example, the analysis chapters have been organized around the aspects of music imitated, whether surface (rhythm and timbre, chapter 2), structure (riff, chorus structure, and call and response in chapter 3, as well as theme and variations in chapter 5), or context (live performance and improvisation in chapter 4, composition versus performance in chapter 6). Inherent qualities of the medium music and its effect on listeners will be referred to where they are relevant for the textual imitations, as they have an influence on the surface, structure, and contexts involved.

Means and System

Under all aspects on both branches, I have placed features labeled "means" and "system." The term "means" refers to the methods by which the media product thematizes or imitates that aspect of the foreign medium. The term "system" refers to the system that is being thematized or imitated. This may be an individual media product (whether real or fictitious), a genre, or simply the foreign medium as such.[26] Any reference to or imitation of an individual work also entails an implicit reference to or imitation of the genre and medium of that work. This is indicated on the tree by the use of arrows from the individual work to the genre, and again to the medium. It should be noted that the system may also be an abstract or idiosyncratic conception of a foreign medium, just as thematized and imitated aspects of the foreign medium may be perceived rather than objectively demonstrable. For example, this model does not distinguish between imitations of music based on observable physical properties, such as its capacity for polyphony, and imitations based on ideological associations, such as the spiritual qualities often attributed to it. In both cases, an attempt is made to evoke a foreign medium.

The different means available for thematizing another medium or media product will vary depending on the specific media involved. Text-based media would seem to be the most versatile in terms of thematization. In these, explicit references can include mentions or descriptions of another work, genre, or medium, whereas implicit references include allusions. Other media, however, also have means of thematization at their disposal. A painting can thematize another medium through the use of depiction, whereas a piece of music might thematize the medium of dance, for example, by using musical idioms from traditional dance types such as the gavotte or tango.[27] This would be explicit thematization, as ignorance of an idiom on the part of a listener does not negate its material presence. An example of implicit thematization in music would be a piece of vocal music that uses nonsense syllables rather than text, such as jazz scat singing, which draws attention to the medium of language through its marked absence. Just as the distinction between mention and description in a text is primarily one of degree, thematization can also be more or less prominent in other media.[28]

While thematization is always accomplished by using a medium's own means, imitation can involve either shared means or foreign means. A work may either imitate means that are available to the foreign medium, but not literally possible for the medium of the work, or it can use means that are shared by both media. Shared means in the case of poetry and music, for example, include their ability to mark the passage of time using sound, though in the case of poetry the sounds need not be actualized by reading aloud. By foregrounding rhythm and meter in ways characteristic of music, a poem can evoke the qualities of music. On the other hand, while music is able to produce multiple sounds simultaneously, this is not literally possible for a written text. Therefore, its attempts at counterpoint, harmony, and ensemble playing can only be metaphorical imitations of foreign means that the text does not actually share with music.

At this level of the tree diagram, more specificity will be needed for individual analyses, which can be added based on the particular media constellation involved. It should be clear that the specific means available to a text when thematizing or imitating another medium are not the same as those available to a sculpture, a dance performance, or a jazz song. The term "thematization" does reflect a certain bias toward text-based media products, but I hope to have shown that thematization is at least possible in other media as well.

Music in Literature: A Particular Case of Intermediality

One such media constellation is the case of texts imitating and thematizing music, which forms the core of this book. The musical novel exhibits intermediality in the form of explicit references to individual works of music, such as Johann Sebastian Bach's *Goldberg Variations*, which are mentioned not only in the titles of several novels (i.e., Gabriel Josipovici's 2002 *Goldberg: Variations*, Nancy Huston's 1981 *Les Variations Goldberg* [1996 *The Goldberg Variations*], and Richard Powers's 1991 *The Gold Bug Variations*) but also are discussed on the level of the novels' content. These novels thematize the work as a whole, its structure, the sound of a particular performance, whether live or recorded, the performance situation, as well as other aspects. At the same time, these novels also make implicit references to the *Goldberg Variations* in the form of imitation. The theme-and-variations form is an example of musical structure that is imitated by the novels using shared means, as both media are able to repeat a theme and vary it, though the specific theme itself differs in its "translation" from music to text. The imitation thus both makes use of shared means and also employs an analogical imitation of foreign means.

Semiotics

Semiotics: The Science of Signs

In the previous section, I defined intermediality as a phenomenon in which a foreign medium is involved in the signification of a given media product, through thematization or imitation of that medium. The word "signification" is a clue to further questions that must be asked: How can one medium "mean" another? How does a medium signify or produce meaning in general? An answer to these questions first requires consideration of theories of the sign, or semiotics. Semiotics "seeks to identify the conventions and operations by which any signifying practice (such as literature) produces its observable effects of meaning" (Culler, 48). A general examination of such signifying practices is essential for an understanding of the processes involved when a text attempts to adopt or imitate the semiotic means of music.

Though theories of semiotics or the science of signs have a long history,[29] Ferdinand de Saussure is credited with one of the first explicit theories of the sign and its nature, which is intricately connected to the birth of the modern discipline of linguistics. One of Saussure's most fundamental claims about the nature of the sign is, I believe, applicable not only to human language but to other sign systems as well. This is the binary division of the sign into signifier and signified. What is frequently misunderstood is the abstract nature of *both* sides of the sign. The signifier is not material or concrete, does not consist of the actual acoustic properties of a spoken word, for example, but the abstract sound pattern as stored in the mental lexicon (66). Similarly, the signified is not a material referent, but the abstract concept or meaning also as stored in the lexicon (67), though signified and referent seem to be frequently confused with each other. The blurring of these two terms likely stems from Saussure's use of nouns with concrete referents as his examples—that is, "tree"—though more abstract words like "to be," "not," and "the" are also signs with signifieds (concepts like *existence, negation,* and *definiteness*), though more clearly divorced from a concrete referent in the extralinguistic world.

The American philosopher Charles Sanders Peirce spoke not of the signifier and signified as two halves of a sign, but of a sign and its interpretants (Jakobson, "A Few Remarks on Peirce," 251). Introducing the concept of the interpretant—and especially Peirce's use of the plural—emphasizes the nonidentity between the meanings a sign has for the addresser and for the addressee, between different addressees, or even for the same addressee in different contexts, thus contributing a constructivist or phenomenological perspective to the study of the sign. It is unfortunate, however, that he proposes a separation of the conceptual side (Saussure's signified) from that which is used to represent it (signifier), and apparently reduces the sign as a whole to the signifier. Though a definition of the sign as the signifier alone would be more in keeping with common lay usage,[30] this would seem to imply that a sign can exist without a signified, which is surely false. A signifier that is not linked to any signified does not constitute a sign. Peirce himself saw the possibility of signification as essential to the nature of a sign: "The sign demands nothing more than the possibility of being interpreted, even in the absence of an addresser" (Jakobson, "A Glance at the Development of Semiotics," 206). Though Peirce is correct in emphasizing a plurality of interpretants for any given form, some kind of bond between form and content must be inherent in the concept of the sign itself. For this reason, I will continue to use Saussure's terms, while recognizing that there is never an exact one-to-one relationship between signifier and signified.

Though there is a convention among users of a sign as to the range of its meaning, this is not a completely stable or permanent relationship. The signifieds of a given signifier represent a range of meaning that can shift over time and among users. If the relationship were perfectly stable and precise, communication would never fail and there would be no ambiguity. On the other hand, if the relationship between signifier and signified were completely variable, no communication would be possible, so there must be agreement to a certain extent among users on the nature of the bond between the two components of the sign.

Peirce examined the various types of signs in great detail and set up a lengthy taxonomy of sign classes. Of the 59,049 possible classes (reducible to 66) and ten trichotomies (Culler, 23), one trichotomy has entered general usage not only in the field of semiotics but well beyond. This consists of the three types of sign known as *icon*, *index*, and *symbol*. Roman Jakobson has emphasized the role of the axes of similarity (or the paradigmatic axis) and of contiguity (or the syntagmatic axis) in distinguishing these three sign types ("A Glance at the Development of Semiotics," 215). The icon is a sign in which the signifier bears some natural resemblance to its signified, or is similar to it in some way. Typical examples are photographs and realistic paintings, a curved arrow on a traffic sign to indicate the direction of a turn, or the musical imitation of natural sounds. The index, instead, relies on a natural contiguity between the signifier and its signified. The classic examples of an index are pointing gestures and deictic words in language such as "here" and "there," "this" and "that." The relationship between the signifier and signified of a symbol is arbitrary, rather than natural, and depends on a conventionalized association between the two. Linguistic signs are overwhelmingly arbitrary and conventional, as Saussure argued, as are red or green traffic lights, the ringing of bells in certain patterns to indicate either the time of day or the beginning of church services, and gestures like the peace sign or a salute.

It is important to remember, however, that the three types rarely exist in isolation, and that the classification of a sign into one of these types relies not on its purely arbitrary or purely natural relationship between signifier and signified, but on the dominance of one tendency over the other (Jakobson, "Quest for the Essence of Language," 349). Iconic elements have been argued for in language (such as word order or the addition of morphemes to indicate the plural number), whereas paintings rely on conventions that are genre, period, and culture specific. Even graphs and other visual diagrams, which have been argued to be prime examples of icons (Johansen, 381–83), depend on a conventional association, that is, of the horizontal axis with time, which only seems natural because the convention has become so well established in our culture.

In "A Glance at the Development of Semiotics," Jakobson added a fourth type to this trichotomy, based on his distinction of the three previous types according to the binaries of similarity/contiguity and natural/conventionalized. The one combination remaining after the various types of signs have been classified according to natural similarity (icon), natural contiguity (index), and conventional contiguity (symbol) is conventionalized similarity, which he identified as characterizing the work of art or "artifice" (215). This insight is important for its relativization of ideals of mimesis: the work of art aims at being like reality in ways that are artificial rather than natural, that is, established by cultural convention. Those conventions may be those of a particular school of painting, certain plot structures, or musical patterns (i.e., in a recitative) that are accepted as being similar to speech rhythms.[31]

Another of Jakobson's contributions to the study of the sign and processes of signification is the division of communication into six aspects, which are the factors addresser, addressee, context, message, contact, and code ("Linguistics and Poetics").[32] In accordance with this more encompassing view, which avoids looking at a message in isolation, the scholar of musical semiotics Jean-Jacques Nattiez builds his theory on Jean Molino's model of three levels or dimensions of all signification. He divides semiotic communication into the poietic level (processes of creation and production, focused on the addresser or sender of the message), the esthesic level (processes of perception, focused on the addressee or recipient of the message), and the immanent or material level of the message itself.

The definition of sign as I will be using it is thus as follows: a sign consists of the two linked facets of signifier and signified in the Saussurean sense, both distinct from a possible (but not necessary) concrete referent and from the material (acoustic, visual, etc.) embodiment of the sign. It remains an open question as to whether a sign can ever be completely free of a referent. The important point in this context is that a referent need not be extrinsic to the sign system but can be intrinsic, yielding meaning that is self-referential. Some words and morphemes have a purely intralinguistic function, referring not to objects in the outside world but to other parts of a sentence and linking them syntactically. Other sign systems have similar options of extrinsic and intrinsic reference, so it is essential not to restrict a sign's meaning to something in the outside world. Jean-Jacques Nattiez, for example, sees music as the superimposition of two semiological systems, one of external or semantic reference, and one of intramusical or structural reference. This is connected to a fundamental distinction between the poietic and esthesic levels and the immanent level of the work's internal structure: "One of the semiological peculiarities of music is owed to the existence of *two* domains, intrinsic and extramusical referring" (Nattiez, 117; italics original). Likewise, external referents can be abstractions, imagined rather than real entities, such that a referent should not be mistaken for a concrete "thing."

A sign is thus located within the mind, which forces semioticians to recognize and examine the differences in signs as present in the minds of different users. Still, despite these differences, communication *is* possible, which means that some degree of agreement on the connection between signifiers and signifieds must exist within members of an interpretive community. This agreement, incomplete as it may be, incorporates both the poietic or production side and the esthesic or response side of signification. Specifically, these two facets will be considered with reference to the musical novels as results of both processes of poiesis (the creation of the text as a signifying system) and esthesis (the authors' response to the music that inspired these texts).

A Semiotics of Music

This brings us to the question of the musical sign. One of the most striking similarities between music and language[33] is their shared temporal nature. Both consist of sounds presented sequentially, in time. Neither, however, is purely linear, as the individual sounds consist of bundles of features: in language, each phoneme is distinguished by the features of voicing, place, length, and manner of articulation; in music, each note is distinguished by pitch, timbre, length, and instrumentation. Though language also employs several features at once, particularly suprasegmental elements such as tone, intonation, and stress, music's capacity for presenting multiple pieces of information simultaneously extends far beyond that of language. Music exploits the axis of simultaneity almost as thoroughly as that of successivity, with the linear phenomenon of melody being complemented in many musical systems by that of harmony. While utterances by participants in a conversation or different statements in a written text must generally be presented sequentially, one at a time, in music various instruments or voices may perform at once, yielding chords that are integral to the harmonic structure of the work and producing either consonance or dissonance.[34] This greater ability of music to say more than one thing at the same time, so to speak, is something largely lacking in language-based art forms, and is one that is frequently aspired to in experimental literature.

It is a matter of some debate whether music can have a "meaning" outside of itself. Critics such as Adorno claim that whereas music is "similar to language," "it does not form a system of signs (113). Jakobson refers explicitly to music's "auditory signs" (see e.g. "Visual and Auditory Signs"). Again, the different definitions pose problems: Adorno denies music the character of a sign system because "what is said cannot be abstracted from the music" (113). Albert Gier identified a key difference between musical and linguistic signification as the lack of denotation in music (63). According to his model, a musical sign consists of a signifier and a signified, just as in language. The difference is that a linguistic sign also refers to something extralinguistic, a referent in the world outside of the text; music usually does not. When Adorno states that music is not made up of signs, it is the lack of an external referent that he sees as a barrier to definition as a sign.

Gier argues that music does not denote anything outside itself, which is not, however, the same as claiming that music lacks meaning. On the contrary, the musical sign draws its significance from its position within the musical structure and is dependent on its context. As Umberto Eco claimed, music is a semiotic system that is "purely syntactic and [has] no semantic depth" (88). This is similar to the distinction between introversive and extroversive semiosis as proposed by Jakobson. He sees music as a language that signifies itself:

> Instead of aiming at some extrinsic object, music appears to be *un langue qui se signifie soi-même*. Diversely built and ranked parallelisms of structure enable the interpreter of any immediately perceived musical signans to infer and anticipate a further corresponding constituent . . . and the coherent ensemble of these constituents. Precisely this interconnection of parts as well as their integration into a compositional whole acts as the proper musical signatum. (cited in Nattiez, 111)[35]

Music, then, constitutes meaning primarily through reference to itself: through repetition or variation of what has gone before and through the production of expectations of what is to come. Jakobson sees the essence of a musical sign as the reference to what follows, based on the three central operations of "anticipation, retrospection, and integration" ("A Glance at the Development of Semiotics," 215). Likewise, for Adorno, "in music nothing is isolated, and everything only becomes what it is in its physical contact with what is closest and its spiritual contact with what is distant, in remembrance and expectation" (116). The meaning of a musical sign is thus primarily located in its position within the system,[36] much as Saussure argued for linguistic signs, with the important difference that language's power to refer extralinguistically is not paralleled in music, which remains much more introverted. Though music is not alone among the temporal arts in this capacity for self-reference, it is unique in its apparent lack of reference to anything outside itself,[37] to the extent that theories of the relationships between the arts have repeatedly held up the autonomy of music from reality as a model for other art forms, as in Walter Pater's famous dictum that "all arts constantly aspire to the condition of music" (86).[38] Adorno also emphasizes the artistic quality of music,[39] seeing music's similarity to language in its ability to "say" something, but its difference in that *what* it says remains mysterious. "This quality of being a riddle, of saying something that the listener understands and yet does not understand, is something it shares with all art. No art can be pinned down as to what it says, and yet it speaks" (122).

There are those, however, who do ascribe extramusical meaning to music, emphasizing its power to elicit emotion or to express certain feelings or atmospheres, or pointing to musical imitation of extramusical sounds and the leitmotiv as examples of musical signification that go beyond mere self-reference. Generally, for such a connection between a piece of music (or an excerpt of it) and some idea, emotion, or situation in the extramusical world to be shared by multiple listeners requires either an unambiguous context or explicit naming, often relying on another medium such as language. Program music, for example, which is held up as a prime example of music with an extrinsic reference, is highly dependent on the title and naming of its intended program. Without the paratextual labels, most programs would be uninterpretable as such, as the music itself lacks the specificity needed to suggest such an explicit meaning. Phenomena such as the imitation of nonmusical sounds by musical instruments or voices (such as thunder, animal noises, bells, etc.) do involve an extramusical referent, but are a decidedly marginal feature of music. Other devices that evoke a particular meaning for the listener are dependent on knowledge of traditions or conventionalized patterns. Such meanings are not on the level of denotation, but of connotation—associations that can be seen as belonging to a pragmatics of music (Gier, 65). A narratological approach to describing this distinction between music and text sees the text as possessing both a *discours* level and a level of *histoire* (see Todorov). On the other hand, music exists solely on the level of *discours* and does not narrate a *histoire* (Gier, 67).

If we accept that music does not have a denotation or extramusical referent, we are still faced with the problem of connotation or associations and moods that the music evokes in the listener. Few would dispute that music has meaning for its listeners or for composers and musicians, but the bulk of this meaning is nebulous and extremely varied. Just as the meaning of an individual story for someone whose mother read it to them as a child as an index pointing to that childhood experience would not usually be considered part of the meaning of the story itself, the associative meanings of a piece of music or a performance may also be considered extrinsic to the music itself. Similarly, we must question whether a composer's dedication of a piece to a patron—certainly central to the piece's meaning for those two people—is relevant for an understanding or appreciation of the piece itself. Which meanings can actually be considered part of the work? Is every audience interpretation of a performance part of its meaning? Can a work contain meaning that is divorced from a historical and cultural context? To what extent can the work be divorced from an artist's intentions or from the recipient's perceptions of it?

Reception theory or reader response theory[40] emphasizes the role of the recipient in the production of meaning. Culler argues for the reader as the center of a semiotic account, as "the place where the various codes can be located: a virtual site. Semiotics attempts to make explicit the implicit knowledge which enables signs to have meaning, so it needs the reader not as a person but as a function: the repository of the codes which account for the intelligibility of the text" (38). Returning to models of semiotics such as Jakobson's six aspects of communication or Nattiez's tripartition, it becomes clear that a media product such as a text or a piece of music does not exist in isolation, but is the result of creative processes and requires interpretation on the esthesic side. Yet the wide range of possible interpretations and the inaccessibility of readers' or listeners' responses may lead semioticians to despair of ever fully understanding the way a media product achieves meaning for its recipients. I thus agree with Allan R. Keiler that the appropriate approach to musical semiotics—and indeed to literary semiotics as well—is an examination of the immanent level, which can yet reveal information about both the poietic and esthesic processes to either side: "Only some theory about the internal organization of the object, thus making explicit the complexity of that object, will enable one to ask pertinent questions about musical (or linguistic) performance" (Keiler, 142).[41]

In this study, the object of analysis will be the musical novels themselves, which are of course the result of creative acts by their authors. At the same time, they are a record of the perceptive processes of those authors as listeners and interpreters of music. The texts reflect a particular understanding of the music involved, which is necessarily different from "the music itself." In considering the role of jazz or of the *Goldberg Variations* in these novels, I will use the music as seen in recordings and performances as a reference for my analyses when possible, but the music that exists in these texts is an idea, a conception of music that will frequently differ from both my own personal conception and from any consensus reached by musicologists. A consideration of music's meaning *for these texts* is thus inescapable, and examination of the immanent level of the texts themselves thus automatically includes an implicit examination of the processes of music reception and text production involved in their creation.

The plethora of musical meanings that are involved in the signification of these texts can be divided into two groups: those references that are intrinsic to music and those that are extrinsic to the music itself. Intrinsic referring is found in texts that emphasize the internal structure of the music, its use of repetition, parallels, and other patterns. This type is best demonstrated in the novels discussed in chapters 5 and 6, the novels based on Bach's *Goldberg Variations.* Extrinsic reference, on the other hand, comes to the fore when music is invested with extramusical significance, such as the evocation of emotion; with aspects of the performance situation; with associations such as a particular social context, freedom, an aesthetic ideology, or sociopolitical aspects; or with connections between music and a character, place, or situation. Such extrinsic referring is very common among the jazz novels discussed in chapters 2–4, more so than in the *Goldberg* novels, where the music is strongly associated with a mathematical structure and less with sociopolitical aspects. I will return to possible reasons for this disparity in the analyses of these novels and especially in the concluding discussions, but both intrinsic and external referring occur in both types of musical imitation and interact to a great degree. The imitation of a particular structural element often serves to evoke music as a parallel to the literary text, precisely because of the extramusical associations of that form of music. Though my primary focus remains on imitations of structural elements and of contexts of performance and reception in both groups of texts, such that intrinsic reference plays a more prominent role throughout this study, I will consider the functions of the imitation of music and the related question of the extramusical meanings music bears for the texts in question.

Notes

[1] This section on intermediality is based on the paper "Towards a New Typology of Intermediality," cowritten with Lauren Holmes and Carolyn Sinsky and presented at the Graduate Student Conference of the Twentieth-Century Colloquium at Yale University on May 1, 2008. My use of the pronouns "I" and "my" should be seen in the light of my great debt to that collaboration.

[2] For the distinction between thematization and imitation, see the discussion of Werner Wolf's model of intermediality, below.

[3] See Rajewsky's definition of intermediality as any phenomenon that crosses media borders, involving at least two media conventionally seen as distinct: "Mediengrenzen überschreitende Phänomene, die mindestens zwei konventionell als distinkt wahrgenommene Medien involvieren," in *Intermedialität,* 13 and passim. Here and throughout this book, all translations are my own unless indicated otherwise.

[4] See Schröter's category of synthetic intermediality ("synthetische Intermedialität"), 130–35.

[5] See Schröter's category of formal or transmedial intermediality ("formale oder trans-mediale Intermedialität"), 136–43. Confusingly, this type is said to include both transmedial phenomena (the transferal of media-nonspecific elements) and the use of formal elements specific to other media.

[6] See Schröter, Müller. Critics such as Paech and Spielmann, for example, do not consider what I am calling intermediality, labeled "intermedial references" in Rajewsky's system, to fall within the category of intermediality at all, since they reserve that label for multimedial forms such as film. Rajewsky, "Intermedialität 'light'?," 43.

[7] See Paech, 15, on intermediality as a medial transformational process.

[8] See Higgins's concept of intermedia as intricately related to the avant-garde and the innovation of new media.

[9] Another approach to content that proliferates across media without making reference to a source medium is found in "transmedia storytelling," a term coined by Henry Jenkins: "A transmedia story unfolds across multiple media platforms, with each new text making a distinctive and valuable contribution to the whole. In the ideal form of transmedia storytelling, each medium does what it does best—so that a story might be introduced in a film, expanded through television, novels, and comics; its world might be explored through game play or experienced as an amusement park attraction. Each franchise entry needs to be self-contained so you don't need to have seen the film to enjoy the game, and vice versa. Any given product is a point of entry into the franchise as a whole" (Jenkins, *Convergence Culture*, 95–96). The important point of connection to transmediality as defined by Rajewsky is that "there is no one single source or ur-text" (Jenkins, "Transmedia Storytelling 101," n.p.). In contrast, there is a sense in transmedia storytelling that the different contribution of each medium's version is necessary to complete the picture, which is lacking in other accounts of transmediality.

[10] Julie Sanders defines an adaptation as "a more sustained engagement with a single text or source than the more glancing act of allusion or quotation, even citation, allows" (4), but only one of the three categories of adaptation she borrows from Deborah Cartmell, "analogue" (22), can be considered to engage with the *form* of the original work. Sanders's and Hutcheon's work on adaptations are relevant for the present study, however, in that they emphasize the value of works that have often been disparaged as "derivative" or mere "copies" rather than original work. Hutcheon's assertion that "an adaptation is a derivation that is not derivative—a work that is second without being secondary. It is its own palimpsestic thing" (*A Theory of Adaptation*, 9) can be equally applied to intermedial imitations such as the musical novel.

[11] For instance, semiotics, structuralism, deconstruction, ideological criticism, feminist criticism, and psychoanalytic critique all derive their approach, in part, from this notion of the text as an independently functioning entity whose structures, dynamics, and limitations can be fully described without reference to the intent of the author.

[12] I also include media groups, as when a poem imitates the visual arts in general rather than specifically painting or drawing. Likewise, a text can imitate sound that is not strictly speaking music, as speech can also be seen as a medium under this definition. As this example demonstrates, a medium or media group need not be restricted to an art form.

[13] "Poema pictura loquens, pictura poema silens," which literally means: "poetry is a speaking picture, painting a silent [mute] poetry." First recorded by Plutarch, *De gloria Atheniensium*, 3.347a. Cited in *Encyclopedia of Poetry and Poetics*, entry for "Ut pictura poesis."

[14] Literally "as is painting, so is poetry," this line is translated by Leon Golden as "painting resembles poetry" (Horace, line 361).

[15] The title is a reference to the myth and sculpture of Laocoön as representative of the problems and possibilities inherent in any intertwining of the arts.

[16] Wolf built on prior studies by Calvin S. Brown and Steven P. Scher, who promoted the interrelations of music and literature as a field of academic study. See especially Brown, *Music and Literature*, and Scher, *Verbal Music in German Literature*.

[17] "Some recent theorists dismiss i[mitation] because it seems to rely on a rhet[oric] of 'presence' (insisting on 'sameness' by suppressing the 'difference' that haunts all representations); others point out that both in practice and in theory i[mitation] invokes that very 'difference' which it is purported to suppress" (*The New Princeton Handbook of Literary Terms*, 129).

[18] Rajewsky originally introduces these concepts in *Intermedialität* with the German terms "Medienkombination," "Medienwechsel," and "Intermediale Bezüge," respectively. The English terms stem from her article "Intermediality, Intertextuality, and Remediation." In media transposition, the content of one media product is transformed into another medium, so that only the second medium is materially present. This overlaps awkwardly with the larger category of transmediality. The primary difference between the two is that media transpositions involve a clear case of "which came first," whereas the content in transmediality is of a more ambiguous source, part of a culture's collective memory (*Intermedialität*, 13). The distinction between these two categories is production oriented rather than product oriented. In the media product itself, I regard both cases as transmediality, since evidence of the "source" medium is not necessarily present in the finished product. Media transposition only involves the crossing of media boundaries in the *process* of adapting the content of one medium to another—the finished product need not involve more than one medium in its signification. Clearly, an adaptation may also make reference to the source medium as such. This reference, as for example when a film adaptation of a novel uses a framing device in which an actor depicts the author writing the story that then will be acted out, is intermedial, but the adaptation itself is not inherently intermedial.

[19] In a footnote in "Intermedialität 'light'?" Rajewsky relativizes her use of categories somewhat, suggesting that types or poles with room for variation in between would be a more accurate characterization: "Angemessener erschiene es mir heute, nicht von klassifikatorischen, sondern von Typenbegriffen ... auszugehen, oder auch von zwei Polen zu sprechen, zwischen denen sich intermediale Systemreferenzen bewegen können" (45n38; I would now consider it more

appropriate to speak not of categories but of types, or of two poles between which intermedial system references can oscillate).

[20] Though this study deals only with a model of intermediality, similar models could be outlined for multimediality and intramediality. A model of multimediality could include features such as the dominance of one medium over another or the question of authorization—that is, whether or not the different media elements were created or approved by a single author, for example. A parallel tree for intramediality could conceivably use many of the same features as found in this model of intermediality. Both would be united under the heading "intersemiotic relations within media product X."

[21] A demonstration of these multiple branches can be found in the diagram for Richard Powers's *The Gold Bug Variations*, found in the appendix, which includes a branch for the text's references to painting as well as for those to music.

[22] Eicher points out that the dichotomy between realization ("Realisation") and thematization ("Thematisierung") was introduced by Aage Hansen-Löve along the lines of the linguistic categories of "use" and "mention/refer to" (25).

[23] I differ from Wolf in that I see *any* reference to a foreign medium, no matter how slight or seemingly irrelevant, as an instance of thematization. Determining the significance of a reference is subjective, and it is therefore impossible to define thematization in such a way as to exclude a subset of references on the grounds of importance. In this model, instances of thematization differ in degree rather than kind. Under this definition, many media products that do not foreground intermedial relationships contain instances of intermedial thematization that may be considered trivial. It is therefore up to the critic to determine how relevant a given instance is for the analysis at hand.

[24] "Surface" elements should not be misunderstood as superficial in the sense of insignificant or unimportant. This model divides a media product into various layers, regarding as the "surface" those elements that are immediately perceptible, in contrast to elements of "structure" that only become apparent when the work as a whole is considered and analyzed. Though not directly derived from it, this is comparable to the distinction between foreground and fundamental line or Ursatz in Schenkerian musical analysis.

[25] Of course, content is always to some extent shaped by the form in which it is conveyed. Still, if content is presented in another medium without an attending reference to or imitation of that medium-specificity, it falls under the category of transmediality as defined above.

[26] This is a point made in much work on intermediality to date, such as Wolf's distinction between a general reference to the other medium and to specific works or genres (*The Musicalization of Fiction*, diagram I, 47), drawing on work by Broich and Pfister. Andreas Böhn extends the concept of the "Formzitat" (form citation) from intertextual to intermedial system references, emphasizing that in the intermedial form citation the medium becomes the form and both media are the topic of reflection (42). Rajewsky also uses intertextuality and system references as a starting point for her discussion of intermedial relations (*Intermedialität*, 65–69).

[27] I disagree with Wolf that "in music . . . the 'thematization' of extramusical reality is all but impossible" (*The Musicalization of Fiction*, 45), though I agree that

it is a much more peripheral phenomenon than in visual and verbal media. The lesser referential capacity of music makes such references less common, but they are still possible, for example, through the use of onomatopoeia or the quotation of other works of music as a means of referring to their contexts (i e., in an opera or dance), etc.

[28] Titles and other paratexts can of course also refer to another medium through textual means. These markers are often important indications of other intermedial phenomena that might be less explicit. They also point to the fact that many media such as painting and music are in themselves multimedial, as they use the medium of text as part of their signification. Though these paratexts remain at the margins of the work, they serve an important function in explaining the work or guiding its reception. See Wolf on paratextual reference as one of several types of thematization (*The Musicalization of Fiction*, 56).

[29] In "A Glance at the Development of Semiotics" Roman Jakobson outlines the development of semiotics, the origins of which he traces back to antiquity, through John Locke, Johann Heinrich Lambert, Józef Marja Hoene-Wronski, Bernhard Bolzano, and Edmund Husserl to Charles Sanders Peirce and Ferdinand de Saussure.

[30] Saussure made this argument explicit: "In current usage the term *sign* generally refers to the sound pattern alone, e.g. the word form *arbor*. It is forgotten that if *arbor* is called a sign, it is only because it carries with it the concept 'tree,' so that the sensory part of the term implies reference to the whole" (67).

[31] Alternatively, one can take such examples as a demonstration of any supposed icon's reliance on conventions, rather than as an additional type of sign. The classification of an entire artwork as a single sign is itself problematic, so I prefer to talk about iconic, indexical, and symbolic elements within a work.

[32] "The six factors of the speech event" are presented graphically on page 22 and explained on pages 22–25. The six factors correspond to six functions: emotive, conative, referential, poetic, phatic, and metalingual.

[33] I am here referring to natural human languages, which—with the exception of sign languages—are in their primary forms spoken. Written language is thus a second-order sign system, and literature could be seen as forming even a third order. See Clüver on the literary text as sharing a channel of communication with the nonliterary text ("Inter Textus," 40). Rajewsky suggests regarding the text as a medium in order to avoid this confusion ("Intermedialität 'light'?," 35n16).

[34] It is of course possible for two speakers to speak simultaneously or for multiple letters to be printed on top of each other, but these messages are then much less comprehensible. Such experiments fail precisely because the signs of language must unfold sequentially in time to be understood.

[35] The reader should not be led astray by Jakobson's use of the word "langue" (language) in this context. Jakobson is arguing for an essential difference between music and language and if he calls music a kind of language, it is only in the broad sense of a system of signs.

[36] See Jakobson: "In general, though, in music as opposed to language it is the tone system itself that bears meaning" ("Musicology and Linguistics," 457).

[37] Jakobson sees evidence for the inherent lack of an external referent in music in the fact that a lack of material reference in painting and sculpture has an unintentionally distancing effect, though not in music, where an external referent is not expected the way it is in the visual arts ("Visual and Auditory Signs," 334).

[38] Self-reflexivity has been taken as a criterion for the aesthetic function of a work of art, causing music to be perceived as the most aesthetic of the arts. See Gier, 67.

[39] Compare the "poetic" or literary quality of poetic language, which is also defined as its removal from everyday usage. See the discussion of literary alienation [*literarische Verfremdung*] in Link, 100–120.

[40] See e.g. Iser, "The Reading Process" and *The Act of Reading*.

[41] For a contrasting view cf. Blacking, who objects to the division into material and pragmatic aspects, refusing to separate the work from its performance situation.

Part I. The Novel Based on a Musical Genre: Jazz Novels

In the realm of musico-literary studies, very little attention has been paid to the role of jazz in prose. In African American studies, on the other hand, there is a wealth of criticism on a "jazz style" or "jazz aesthetic,"[1] the "blues idiom,"[2] and the significance of black music for black writing. Most studies of jazz in fiction have concentrated on individual authors (especially Ralph Ellison, Langston Hughes, and Toni Morrison) or works, with varying degrees of precision in their application of musical terminology to literary texts. Alan Munton's essay "Misreading Morrison, Mishearing Jazz" is an astute (if somewhat exaggerated) attack on the frequently dilettantish and impressionistic criticism of individual works of jazz fiction. A large body of work on jazz and fiction or poetry has been published in the last fifteen years or so. Examples of this trend include several articles on jazz and literature in *The Jazz Cadence of American Culture*, edited by Robert G. O'Meally (1998); the 2000 collection *Black Orpheus*, edited by Saadi A. Simawe; Wilfried Raussert's *Negotiating Temporal Differences: Blues, Jazz, and Narrativity in African American Culture* (2000); the two issues of the journal *Genre* in 2004 devoted to the topic *Blue Notes: Toward a New Jazz Discourse*, edited by Mark Osteen; Robert Cataliotti's 2007 collection of essays on jazz fiction, *The Songs Became the Stories: The Music in African-American Fiction, 1970–2005*; and most recently, the 2009 collection *Thriving on a Riff: Jazz and Blues Influences in African American Literature and Film*, edited by Graham Lock and David Murray, which collects essays presented at the "Criss Cross Conferences" in Nottingham in 2003 and 2004. Still, the bulk of this work focuses on jazz as a symbol of black culture and remains on the level of the stories' content. There have been very few overarching theories of the phenomenon of jazz prose as such.[3]

Despite LeRoi Jones's (Amiri Baraka's) assertion in *Blues People* that "blues is *not*, nor was it ever meant to be, a strictly social phenomenon, but is primarily a verse form and secondarily a way of making music" (50, italics original), his well-known book on the history of African Americans as seen through their musical traditions places a "tremendous burden of sociology" (Ralph Ellison, "Blues People," 249) on that music. Ellison's criticism of Jones in his review of *Blues People* could equally apply to a wide range of literary critics who have explored the role of the blues and jazz in African American literature:

> It is unfortunate that Jones thought it necessary to ignore the aesthetic nature of the blues in order to make his ideological point, for he might have come much closer had he considered the blues not as politics but as art. . . . For the blues are not primarily concerned with civil rights or obvious political protest; they are an art form and thus a transcendence of those conditions created within the Negro community by the denial of social justice. (257)

The vast majority of studies of the blues and jazz in literature focus exclusively on African American literature, though these musical forms have influenced other groups of writers within the United States as well as on a global scale. What is even more striking in the context of the present study is the overwhelming focus on these musical forms as symbols of African American culture. Houston A. Baker Jr.'s *Blues, Ideology, and Afro-American Literature* is a classic example of this kind of discourse. Echoing LeRoi Jones's book quoted above, Baker sees African Americans as a "blues people," and he conceives of the blues "as a matrix . . . what Jacques Derrida might describe as the 'always already' of Afro-American culture. They are the multiplex, enabling *script* in which Afro-American cultural discourse is inscribed" (3–4, italics original). Yet despite a deep interest in the meaning of the blues for African American culture and specifically literature, Baker seems not to consider the form *as music* at all. The blues are appreciated for their symbolic and ideological value, as the discourse of African American experience, which ignores their specific musical characteristics. This approach also reduces the spectrum of the blues' possible meanings to the experiences of a particular social group, narrowing that group (only *African* Americans, as opposed to all Americans), yet at the same time expanding it (*all* African Americans, rather than just blues musicians).

David Yaffe, in his 2006 study *Fascinating Rhythm*,[4] examines the portraits of jazz and jazz musicians in literary texts and in musicians' autobiographies, comparing jazz writing with jazz history. These analyses are firmly on the side of content rather than form, and yield the conclusion that jazz has taken many guises in American writing: "as orgasm, as preadolescent fetish, as protest, as 'a beam of lyrical sound,' as primitivism, as ethnic crossover, as modernism, as something 'clean, sparkling, elusive,' as conjecture, as an 'angel headed hipster,' as breathlessness, as the Buddha, as pimping, as signifyin'—but seldom as itself" (196). Like Baker, Yaffe is interested not in the form of jazz or the blues, but in what they mean. In comparing the portrayal of jazz with "jazz itself," Yaffe discovers that the two are highly different, and that most jazz writing confirms and heightens myths surrounding the jazz musician and his craft.

In these and numerous other cases, critics consider jazz primarily on the level of the novel's content rather than its form. At most, they conceive of parallels between modes of expression that can be likened to the blues, orality, or improvisation, but rarely consider concrete musical elements in the texts themselves. Examples of this type of study include Gayl Jones's analyses of orality in African American literature in *Liberating Voices*, Gates's exploration of "signifyin'" in *The Signifying Monkey*, and Albert Murray's concept of the blues hero explored not only in his novels but also in works of nonfiction such as *The Hero and the Blues*.

Yet these writers do not deny the possibility of texts imitating jazz techniques, although they focus on different aspects. Thomas Huke, on the other hand, actively objects to the idea that such structural elements inform the narrative composition of jazz novels. In his 1990 book *Jazz und Blues im afro-amerikanischen Roman von der Jahrhundertwende bis zur Gegenwart*, Huke discusses the role of the black musician as an exemplary figure in African American fiction and relates the music to a specific life experience and ideology (3). Though he includes Albert Murray and Xam Wilson Cartiér in his analyses, he denies that African American authors make any noticeable attempt to apply jazz techniques to their writing, in contrast to beat writers of the same period such as Jack Kerouac (232). In addition, he vehemently opposes the very possibility of imitating a performance aesthetic in "jazz novels" (a term he would certainly object to), on the grounds that

> Ein Roman bleibt mit seinem Text für jeden Leser gleich. Er ist überarbeitet, fixiert und vom Autor bewußt so gestaltet. Ein Blues oder ein Jazzstück leben in der Aufführung, der *performance*. Vor allem im *folk blues* wird diese *performance* immer den äußeren Umständen, der Stimmung des Aufführenden und dem zuhörigen Publikum angepaßt. Das ist beim Roman nicht der Fall, denn sein Text bleibt für jeden, der ihn liest, gleich. Was man aus ihm "herausliest", das kann sich ändern; das ist aber mehr ein Problem des Lesers, nicht des Romans. Der Unterschied zwischen *oral culture* und Schriftkultur ist die Begründung dafür. (231)

> [A novel's text remains the same for each reader. It has been reworked, fixed, and intentionally shaped in this way by the author. A blues or a jazz piece lives in the performance. In folk blues especially this performance is always adapted to the external circumstances, to the mood of the performer and the audience. This is not the case for a novel, because its text remains the same for each person who reads it. What one "reads out of it" may change, but that is more a problem of the reader, not of the novel. The reason for this is the difference between oral culture and written culture.]

While I certainly do not object to a distinction between oral and written culture such as Huke emphasizes here, the following analyses will argue that jazz novels do in fact attempt to approach orality through their use of poetic techniques and furthermore encourage the reader to actively participate in constructing the text. In this way, the novels are by no means "the same for each reader."

Michael Jarrett, on the other hand, is very much interested in how a text can write jazz. His 1999 work *Drifting on a Read: Jazz as a Model for Writing* examines specific features of jazz music and their translation into "*jazzography*: what people say jazz is" (2; italics original). His four main jazz tropes, which he calls "*satura*, obbligato, rapsody, and *charivari*" (ix; italics original), stand for mixing or hybridity, improvisation, real/fake distinctions, and noise, respectively. While these tropes find their way into the features of jazz I isolate and analyze in this chapter, Jarrett's unusual approach is hardly a conventional description or scholarly analysis. Instead of focusing on how these jazz tropes inform literary texts, *Drifting on a Read* is more of a handbook for *how to write* with them. His own prose style is playful and poetic, demonstrating each of his tropes in turn, as if in a creative writing workshop focusing on a jazzy style. The task of systematically examining the various ways in which features of jazz have been imitated in text thus remains incomplete and will be the aim of the next three chapters.

In general, studies of jazz and the blues in literature demonstrate that African American art forms are frequently taken as exemplifying a particular history and experience of a cultural group rather than examined as aesthetic objects in and of themselves. In jazz novels, too, their jazz content is often seen and analyzed solely against the background of African American culture rather than as an imitation of music. Evidence of this can be seen in the relative lack of attention from scholars of word and music studies given to the subgenre of the jazz novel thus far. As Huke observes with regard to writers, rather than critics, they are not generally interested in the objective situation, that is, in an authentic representation of jazz music, but instead focus on the "feeling" associated with the music (231). The following chapters aim to demonstrate that several of the authors involved go beyond a vague jazz-like feeling to apply forms and techniques to their writing that are borrowed from jazz music. The analyses will demonstrate that these elements can be analyzed every bit as systematically as those taken from classical music.

Jazz, Blues, and Other Forms of "Black Music"

A word of explanation is perhaps necessary to justify my treatment of texts based on jazz and blues under the single heading of "jazz novels." Jazz music is a highly varied phenomenon, ranging in instrumentation from solo instrumentalists, small trios, and quartets to large orchestras, in structure from collectively improvised free jazz to meticulously prearranged compositions, in context from popular dance music to avant-garde "serious" music. The differences between these subgenres are often greater than between what is classified as "jazz" and as "the blues." In fact, the blues form and many of its distinctive elements crop up repeatedly in virtually all varieties of jazz, as a form that fed jazz's development and yet continues to coexist alongside it. A survey of by now classic jazz performances of all genres reveals numerous titles including the word "blue" or "blues"—just one indication of how fluid the boundaries between these genres are.

Olly Wilson has argued for defining "black music" based on "a shared core of conceptual approaches to the process of music making" (99). He identifies this core as a set of six common tendencies: a particular organization of rhythm; a percussive style of playing any instrument, even the voice; the use of antiphony; a high density of musical events; a wide range of timbres used; and the incorporation of physical motion into music making (84). This broader definition would certainly include blues and jazz, as well as genres such as ragtime, gospel, R&B, reggae, and rap. I see a primary justification in grouping the two related genres of black music here in their shared origins and historical development. It remains a subject for future research whether other genres make use of similar features and are imitated in a like fashion in novels.

A further consideration are the extrinsic meanings both blues and jazz are assigned by musicians and authors, which overlap considerably. Both blues and jazz are associated with a particular social and cultural group, with African Americans. As such, these musical forms are often taken as embodiments of a particular ideology or as symbolizing a collective experience and history. African Americans have been characterized by leading black critics as "blues people" (LeRoi Jones) and their literature as employing a "blues matrix" (Baker) and "blues idiom" (Murray). At the same time, studies of jazz in African American fiction focus on many of the same literary texts, indicating that the two musical traditions play a similar role in literary production.

A jazz novel, as a translation of elements from one medium to another, depends on processes of esthesis and poiesis, as discussed in the theory of semiotics presented in part 1. The novel presupposes that a reception of jazz has taken place: the author's response as a listener of jazz music. In addition, processes of poiesis or artistic creation convert that listener's response to the music into another art form, as a text. Because the jazz that is being converted into text is already a single listener's interpretation, it is doubly mediated. In the following analyses I will compare musicological definitions of jazz forms and techniques with their imitation in the novels, but it is important to keep in mind that the jazz in these novels is always a particular listener's idea of jazz—as Jarrett pointed out, "what people say jazz is" (2). Not all elements of jazz music are equally salient for listeners, and thus it is only a relatively small group of elements that are in fact seized on as characteristic and imitated by the novels. Therefore, it is not the aim of this study to explicate what actual jazz music is, but to explore instead what it means for the novels, and what idea of jazz serves as a model for these texts.

Text Selection

The texts examined in this section date from the seventies—Albert Murray's *Train Whistle Guitar* (1975), Michael Ondaatje's *Coming Through Slaughter* (1976)—through the late eighties and nineties—Xam Wilson Cartiér's *Be-Bop, Re-Bop* (1987) and *Muse-Echo Blues* (1991), Toni Morrison's *Jazz* (1992), Christian Gailly's *Be-bop* (1995)—all the way up to the twenty-first century—Jack Fuller's *The Best of Jackson Payne* (2000), Stanley Crouch's *Don't the Moon Look Lonesome* (2000), and Albert Murray's *The Magic Keys* (2005). Most, but not all, were written by American authors (notable exceptions are the French author Christian Gailly's *Be-bop* and the Canadian Michael Ondaatje's *Coming Through Slaughter*), and of the Americans, only Jack Fuller is white. The dominance of African American authors in this corpus reflects the social significance of jazz, in which the music is frequently seen as representing black culture and traditions, as an art form indigenous to the United States. Because jazz is an American development, it is not surprising that American and specifically African American authors should be more interested in taking this homegrown art form as a model for writing as well as a symbol for their own culture. On the other hand, while a racial or cultural context is part of the extrinsic meaning jazz holds for many texts, it cannot be reduced to this meaning. Non-African American authors like Ondaatje, Fuller, and Gailly demonstrate that jazz and blues need not be connected to race or nationality. Accordingly, the analyses in the following chapters consider jazz novels and their readers independently of any ethnic or cultural affiliation.

Of these writers, several are also more intimately acquainted with the music they explore in their novels. Jack Fuller is a jazz critic; Albert Murray and Stanley Crouch have written nonfictional works on jazz as well as jazz novels; Murray and Crouch have, along with Wynton Marsalis, both served as artistic consultants to Jazz at Lincoln Center, actively influencing the development of mainstream jazz and its reception; Christian Gailly played jazz saxophone until the age of twenty-five. In all cases the author's perception of the music plays a key role in its treatment in the novel. These authors are also listeners and recipients of jazz music, which they interpret and adapt in their writing, and which can be seen as a response to that music. Thus both esthesic or reception-based processes and processes of poiesis or creation are intricately connected to the jazz novel, as both a creation of a textualized version of jazz and as a reception or interpretation of the jazz music that preceded it. Throughout my analyses of the jazz features in these texts, the question of how the texts perceive jazz and how that conditions both the selection of elements to be transformed into text and the means used in that imitation forms an important background to the formal analyses themselves.

In analyzing a novel's imitation of jazz music, it is essential to form a concrete picture of what exactly is meant by "jazz." These novels do not aim merely at a vague impression of musicality, but seek to evoke specific elements of what distinguishes jazz from other musical genres. These characteristics of jazz include elements from the three main levels of sound, structure, and of the performance situation. Chapter 2, "Elements of Sound in Jazz Novels," considers the role of rhythm and distinctive timbres or tone colors in jazz novels. Chapter 3 is devoted to "Structural Patterns in Jazz Novels," which includes the riff, an open-ended linear structure consisting of a series of choruses, the greatest hits album as a means of structuring the novel, and call-and-response patterns. Finally, chapter 4, "The Performance Situation in Jazz Novels," looks at the way the novels emphasize the performance situation over composition as the primary creative act, in part by assigning a central role to improvisation in both jazz and jazz novels. In each case, I introduce these features at the start of the appropriate sections with a discussion of their role in jazz music before proceeding to the text analyses that consider the imitation of these elements in the jazz novels. These analyses will show that jazz novels go beyond the widespread symbolic treatment of jazz to employ its structures and performance context on the level of their narrative construction.

Notes

[1] See Rice, "Finger-Snapping" and "Jazzing It Up," as well as Eckstein.

[2] See Murray, "Function of the Heroic Image." He also refers to the concept of the "blues idiom" in works such as *The Hero and the Blues*, *Stomping the Blues*, and *The Blue Devils of Nada*.

[3] An exception is Michael Borshuk's *Swinging the Vernacular: Jazz and African American Modernist Literature* (2006), which combines a focus on cultural contexts with detailed formal analyses of jazz literature from Langston Hughes to Albert Murray. His chapter on the latter writer will be relevant for my own analyses. Alfonso W. Hawkins, Jr. also provides close readings of jazz and blues techniques in Murray's novels in his study *The Jazz Trope: A Theory of African American Literary and Vernacular Culture* (2008), which overlaps with the techniques I identify in my own analyses. What is somewhat problematic is his retrospective application of the "jazz trope" to texts that pre-date the blues and jazz

as musical idioms (such as Booker T. Washington's *Up from Slavery*, published in 1901), so that it no longer refers to the imitation of jazz forms in literature but remains somewhat vague. For him, jazz becomes a metaphor for a large number of African American cultural strategies (including signification, masking or cloaking, adaptation, and inversion-conversion; see xvi), ignoring much of its specificity as a musical form.

[4] See also Yaffe's article "White Negroes and Native Songs."

2: Elements of Sound in Jazz Novels

OF THE MANY FEATURES that can be used to distinguish jazz from other varieties of music, two of the most immediately apparent are those of rhythm and timbre, both elements of sound. In contrast, structural elements only develop in time, over the length of a piece, while elements of the live performance such as improvisation can only be recognized by listeners as such by comparing the performance with other versions. A distinctive rhythm and tone color, however, can be perceived nearly instantaneously, thus providing an appropriate starting point for this discussion of jazz elements in musical novels.

In music the categories of rhythm and timbre, though both found on the level of sound, can readily be discussed independently of each other. A particular rhythmical pattern can be played with a rich tone or with one that is rather tinny, with a mute or without, with a generic sound or a very individual one.[1] The imitation of these two elements of jazz music, however, is accomplished by similar and overlapping textual means. This chapter will argue for the importance of poetry as a bridge between prose and music in the imitation of both elements: poetic meters, as well as other repetitive devices such as alliteration, assonance, rhyme, and syntactical repetition, help to establish and disrupt rhythmic expectations. Furthermore, poetic diction, such as the creative use of newly coined words or an innovative use of familiar words, contributes to an individual voice or timbre.[2] The overlap becomes even more apparent in the case of poetic compounds, which are a highly unusual and idiomatic stylistic element. At the same time, many of these compounds produce stress clashes, emphasizing the element of rhythm that traditionally receives little prominence in prose texts.

Because some of the same textual strategies are used to evoke both elements of jazz sound, I group the two together in my analyses. After brief discussions of rhythm and timbre in jazz music, this chapter will go on to consider textual strategies for evoking jazz sound. Because the texts put more explicit emphasis on rhythm—whether through references to poetic meters such as "iambic," "trochaic," and "anapestic" (all in *Train Whistle Guitar*, 5) or the prominence of trains as a metaphor for blues rhythms—the following analyses will focus on the imitation of rhythm, yet making reference to timbre wherever appropriate.

Rhythm and Timbre in Jazz Music

Rhythm

> There is no definition of jazz, academic or otherwise, which does not acknowledge that its essential ingredient is a particular kind of rhythm. . . . It is the distinctive rhythm which differentiates all types of jazz from all other music and which gives to all of its types a basic family resemblance. (Kouwenhoven, 128)

Rhythm, as numerous critics have observed, is one of the most distinctive features of jazz music. Attempts to define precisely what is so unique about jazz rhythm generally include reference to the polyrhythms inherited from African music, a nebulous concept known as "swing," frequent use of syncopation, and something Gunther Schuller has called the "democratization of rhythmic values" (Schuller, 6, 8).

African vocal and instrumental music is essentially polyrhythmic, making extensive use of multiple distinct rhythms played or sung simultaneously, creating complex interactions within the ensemble. Though early jazz drastically reduced this complexity, the tendency in jazz bands to play, for example, triplet patterns against $\frac{4}{4}$ time is directly descended from African musical models.[3] Other manifestations of this tradition can be seen in a much greater use of syncopation than in European music.[4]

Swing, "which is easy to feel but almost impossible to analyze or describe" (*The New Grove Dictionary of Jazz*, vol. 2, entry for "Jazz," 370), is a quality of playing with a rhythmic pulse that creates a sense of forward momentum. This can be done by anticipating the beat or lagging behind it, upsetting rhythmic expectations and creating tension between the fixed ground beat and the rhythms of the improvising instruments. The jazz musician Wynton Marsalis said of Duke Ellington, one of the greatest American composers and jazz bandleaders, that "if we are going to talk about Duke Ellington's rhythm, I think we have to talk about many rhythms, because swinging is about coordination. It's about attaining an equilibrium of forces that many times don't go together" (Marsalis and O'Meally, 143).

The phenomenon of swing is related to the "democratization of rhythmic values," by which traditionally underplayed notes on so-called "weak beats" are "brought up to the level of strong beats, and very often even emphasized *beyond* the strong beat" (Schuller, 8; italics original). A clear example of this feature is the practice in jazz of snapping on the offbeats two and four, rather than on the downbeat.

The beat, as the most basic element of rhythm, is also an example for the central role played by repetition in creating a sense of rhythm. G. Burns Cooper emphasizes the importance of repetition: "Repetition is crucial to our perception of rhythm, for only when we recognize sameness or at least parallelism between events can we organize them hierarchically. We arrange individual instances of an event into pairs or groups, and those pairs or groups into larger groupings" (19). This comment is significant also for the observation that rhythm is essentially a perceived rather than a purely objective phenomenon. Cooper cites Gerard Manley Hopkins's definition of rhythm as "any recurrent figure of sound" (12), which in language may be an element of phonology, syntactical structure, or of semantics. Cooper observes that it is the degree of repetition that allows any such figure to strike the listener as a pattern. This holds true not only of jazz rhythms, but also of rhythm in any variety of music, as well as in literature or many other realms of human experience, from biological rhythms such as the heartbeat or daily routines of waking, eating, and sleeping to repetitive motions in dance or manual work. James A. Snead argues for the central role of repetition (and an attending focus on rhythm) in black culture in general, citing examples in rituals, church rhetoric, jazz and blues music, and in African American literature. Snead is not alone in recognizing repetition's role in transcending any one art form or aspect of social life, as indeed some theorists have pointed out the overlap in rhythmic principles between music and literature, seeing shared origins in rhythms of the body that are essentially "organic" (Denise Levertov, cited in Cooper, 33).

Timbre

> Timbre is generally the least discussed musical element in jazz, and yet it is probably the characteristic more than any other that identifies something as jazz or non-jazz for the uninitiated. (Schuller, 54)

> There is a common approach to music making in which a kaleidoscopic range of dramatically contrasting qualities of sound (timbre) in both vocal and instrumental music is sought after. This explains the common usage of a broad continuum of vocal sounds from speech to song. (Wilson, 84)

When discussing the sound of jazz music, tone color or timbre is another very distinctive feature. Particularly when seen in contrast to European concert music, the variety of different sounds produced in jazz music, as well as their individuality, is quite striking. The jazz musician, regardless of his instrument, will often aim at a unique sound that is recognizable even when played in a jazz band or orchestra, something that is avoided in most forms of ensemble music in the European tradition. A musician such as Louis Armstrong (trumpet), Charlie Parker (alto saxophone), Thelonious Monk (piano), or Charles Mingus (bass) has a distinct and recognizable individual "voice," in the same way that singers like Bessie Smith, Billie Holiday, and Ella Fitzgerald do.

While jazz timbre is frequently referred to as "natural," in contrast, for example, to the nasal tone common to Islamic music,[5] Albert Murray points out the conventional and practiced nature of what seems to be second nature. Like the jazz rhythms that seem natural to the listener, jazz timbre is equally stylized and idiomatic (*Stomping the Blues*, 108).

The timbres used by jazz musicians also reflect a constant desire to push the limits of their instruments. For example, brass players experiment with different kinds of mutes or plungers, knock on their instruments, or explore other means of producing speechlike sounds and other noises. Michael Jarrett, in his study of jazz writing, refers to what he calls "charivari," or "the art of noisemaking," as a central aspect of jazz sound (Jarrett, 158).[6]

Imitating Jazz Sound in Prose: Rhyme, Alliteration, and Meter

Poetry as a Bridge between Prose and Musical Rhythm

While literature and music share the element of rhythm, not all forms of literature share music's strong emphasis on it. Any utterance contains rhythm of some sort, because an organization into stressed and unstressed syllables is characteristic of language in general. English, for example, has relatively complicated rules for grouping syllables into feet and determining which syllable will bear stress. The trochaic meter that applies to English noun stress and the iambic meter used in verbs and adjectives, however, are much less obviously apparent to a listener than the more rigid meters of lyric poetry. Prose writing is characterized by a lack of formal meter, and though rhythm is present it is typically a marginal feature in a novel.

Literary criticism has devoted remarkably little attention to the role of rhythm in prose, and where it has been explicitly examined, the word "rhythm" is often used as a synonym for structure or pattern in general. If one uses an extremely broad definition of rhythm that encompasses any pattern of repetition, then the division of a novel into chapters (Walker), the different levels of tension or calm on the level of the plot, and the pattern of temporal progression or alternation in the novel's structure can all be seen as elements of rhythm. Terence Wright, for example, explicitly excludes the type of rhythm I am concerned with here from his analyses, "rhythm in the stricter sense of language-rhythms," focusing instead on what he calls "rhythms which inform the whole shape of a novel" (1). While the elements he identifies are unquestionably central to the structure of these texts, I prefer to call them patterns or structures, as they lack the temporal element of repetition in the more local and constant manner generally associated with the word "rhythm."[7] Since this "stricter sense of language-rhythms" may also occur in the novel, I prefer to reserve the word for this use.

If, then, rhythm is a directly perceptible pattern of recurring units,[8] it would appear that this type of patterning is much less frequent in prose texts, such as the novel, than in music. What in the text, for example, can correspond to the continuing presence of the musical beat? Without this kind of a constant rhythmic pulse, it becomes difficult for a text to construct the breaches with rhythmic expectations—the anticipation or delay of the beat, the competing rhythmic patterns used by different players at the same time—that are characteristic for jazz music. This kind of play with rhythmic expectations becomes much more accessible for a text that builds a bridge between the relative lack of surface rhythm in prose and its paragon in music. Such a bridge is established through the use of poetry.

Poetry is distinguished from prose primarily through its removal from—some would say elevation above—everyday patterns of speech. This distancing of language, language made strange,[9] is of course made particularly visible through the division of the text into lines. Its rhythm is also accentuated through the use of meters, while its semantic content differs from common usage because of an idiosyncratic vocabulary and more frequent use of metaphor. I argue in the following that jazz novels employ poetic language and forms in order to emphasize the element of rhythm. This element of poetry that is even more prominent in music becomes striking in a prose context. The resulting "poet's novels"[10] are musical in their disproportionate emphasis on the rhythmic aspects of their writing.

These features can be linked fairly closely with those considered to define poetry in contrast to prose. Studies of free verse, for example, define elements of the poetic that can be identified both in free and in metrical verse.[11] G. Burns Cooper compares the poetry and prose of several modern writers (e.g., Robert Lowell, T. S. Eliot, James Wright) to present a useful list of key distinctions:

1. There is a higher incidence of adjacent stresses in the writer's poetry than in their prose.
2. The writers use more monosyllabic nouns and adjectives in their poetry than in their prose.
3. Lowell and Eliot make significant use of iambic patterns even in verse that is not basically iambic, but Wright does not. Therefore, although iambic rhythms may be typical of much free verse, they are not required by it.
4. The characteristic rhythms of each poet at levels higher than the foot involve repeated use of a limited number of syntactic figures. (189)

These features are united by their focus on aspects of meter and rhythm. Though Cooper also examines the prosody of the poets' oral performances, meter—even in supposedly nonmetrical free verse—plays a central role in identifying a text as poetry rather than prose. Cooper continues by distilling two principles from these results: "poetry is characterized by more compression and by more regular alternation than prose or other forms of discourse" (189).

It would be a mistake to conclude that only poetry, whether metrical or "free," contains rhythm. All language is of course structured by rhythms, though they are not generally the primary focus in prose discourse. As Charles Hartman points out, "poetry makes us especially aware of rhythm . . . rhythm in poetry generally *seems* more highly organized than in other uses of language" (14; italics original). It is thus not the presence of rhythm itself that distinguishes poetry from prose, but poetry's increased emphasis on its own elements of rhythm. By making a metrical pattern more regular, for example, a poem sets up expectations in its reader that this pattern will continue. Subsequent breaks with that pattern are thus more striking. Prose, on the other hand, generally plays down its rhythmic aspects, relying more closely on everyday speech rhythms that are not stylized or regularized to the extent that they are in poetry. When prose does foreground its own rhythm through the use of similar strategies to those outlined in Cooper's study of free verse—a higher density of stressed words, the prominence of alliteration, compounding, and metrical patterns—it is an unexpected breach with the conventions of prose writing. In fact as early as 1922, C. M. Lotspeich commented on rhythmicality as a distinction between poetry and prose, but one that should be seen as fluid rather than rigid: "Poetry which represents too much of the effort of thinking tends just to that extent to become unrhythmical; and prose which largely assumes the consent of the reader borders closely upon poetry and tends irresistibly to become rhythmical" (302). Though his analysis normatively argues that prose requires a conscious process of reflection whereas poetry should be apprehended directly, in part through its rhythmic aspect, the awareness that the two genres form a continuum rather than polar opposites is important for this examination of rhythm in the novel.

A burst of poetry and rhythmicality in the novel is characteristic of those texts labeled "poet's novels," but also and especially of those aiming at musicality. Indeed, the rhythmic element of poetry has often been seen as stemming from its musical roots. The poet Amy Lowell, for example, saw "the 'beat' of poetry, its musical quality, [as] exactly that which differentiates it from prose, and it is this musical quality which bears in it the stress of emotion without which no true poetry can exist" (cited in Hartman, 40). If this "beat" of poetry can be extended into not only the nonmetrical poem but also into the (poet's) novel, clearly the lyric is not simply a genre, but a mode that can be employed to differing degrees in different forms of literature.[12]

In fact, poetry's intermediate (and indeed, intermedial) position between prose and music was already noted by Lotspeich. His essay compares the respective functions of the novel and poetry, arguing that the "mental processes" of the novel "interfere with our natural rhythmical functioning" (308). In poetry, on the other hand:

> There is no obstacle to rhythmic functioning and a rather free play of the imagination, so that, in addition to the esthetic feeling which is produced by the poem as a whole, there is throughout its length a constant stimulating and intensifying, due to the reaction of rhythm and imagination on the esthetic feeling. Thus, poetry occupies a position midway between music and prose fiction; it represents a blending of sensational and intellectual elements; in its rhythm and tone effects it approaches music, in its intellectual content it approaches prose. (309)

What is new here is the conscious exploitation of poetic means, because of poetry's position between prose and music, in order to add a musical element to the novel. In order to evoke jazz rhythm, the novels make use of the poetic mode.

Rhyme, Alliteration, and Stress Clash: Rhythm in Cartiér's *Be-Bop, Re-Bop* and *Muse-Echo Blues*

I have claimed above that the novels under consideration in this chapter employ precisely those features of rhythm identified in free verse and indeed poetry in general. In this and the following sections, I will demonstrate this through several examples from the texts. Xam Wilson Cartiér's novels provide one of the most vivid examples of poetic techniques used to foreground the rhythm of the text. Nearly every page of *Be-Bop, Re-Bop* provides ample evidence of alliteration, assonance, and rhyme. Here are eight examples from four consecutive pages that are typical of the novel as a whole:[13]

1. our **f**ellow **f**ools (35)
2. behind the cr**ack**er's b**ack** (36)
3. bl**oo**d **m**ixed with **m**ud (36)
4. **D**ouble **d**ug his **d**reams (36)
5. *How you* l**and**, *how you* st**and**, *how you* balk at comm**and** (37)
6. the foodstore f**ight** and our consequent fl**ight** (37)
7. "the color of gr**ief** sent to bring back rel**ief**" (38)
8. **i**cy **e**yes (38)

In addition to the element of repetition demonstrated by alliteration and rhyme, some of these examples also employ readily apparent metrical patterns, as in the anapests of examples 5 and 7. Taken together, many such examples draw the reader's attention to rhythm in this novel, which corresponds to the frequent allusions to jazz music and sometimes even explicitly to the "curious rhythmic effect" (13) of black music. Other direct references to rhythm include the way bebop's beat "blows [the white folks'] souls outa socket" (26), the discord between the narrator and her husband as "rhythms now different, no longer in sync" (70), and a reference to the cliché that blacks have an innate gift for rhythm with *"topheavy right brain lobes (Rhythm&Artistry Division: shuffle shuffle tap tap, heeheehee)"* (93; italics original). A particular kind of rhythm is thus associated with black culture, specifically with black music, but this association is also revealed as a simplification, a cliché perpetuated both from within and outside the group in question.

Cooper, following Joan Boase-Beier, also identifies the more prominent use of compounds as a characteristic of poetry. Boase-Beier argues that certain categories of compounds are not possible in normal speech, but yet are commonly coined in poetry, such as verb-adjective compounds. She observes precisely this type of compound in Ted Hughes's poetry, however, for example, in the neologisms "sag-heavy" and "hover-still" (cited in Cooper, 29). She argues that "poetic principles interact with the rules of the standard grammar in well-defined ways to cause the relaxation of constraints such as the one against verb-adjective compounds" (Cooper, 29). Several examples of this type of "poetic" compound can be found in *Muse-Echo Blues*—"sense-happy" (35), "squirm-restless" (107), "screech-hollow" (146), "shimmer-surreal" (171)—and in *Be-Bop, Re-Bop*: "shine-coiffed" (123), "twist-minded" (126). As Cooper points out, "such compounds do sound 'poetic' to us, and . . . it is specifically their unusualness that makes them attractive to poets, and that also makes them prominent" (30).

The high concentration of compounds in poetic language contributes to the higher density not only of meaning—as a newly coined compound may replace a longer phrase that would otherwise be necessary to convey that meaning—but also of stresses. The prominence of compounds is a very noticeable characteristic of Cartiér's writing, which is full of familiar compounds like "hard-headed" (*Be-Bop, Re-Bop*, 86), "woodpile" (87), and the slang term "peckerwood" (94). Even more striking, however, is her coinage of new words like "yankeemythians," "oil-smiling," "lily-whiteland" (94), "what-else-but-need," and "back-throne driving" (95). Compounds often juxtapose two stressed syllables in close succession—"boot-splintered" (44), "to waypave" (47), "boil-downable" (48)—and if the compound is unfamiliar, there is a hesitation as to which syllable should receive prominence. Established compounds in English receive stress on the first syllable ("HOTdog," "the WHITE House"), which contrasts with the normal stress pattern of emphasizing the second item as the head of the phrase ("a hot DOG," "a white HOUSE"). When the reader encounters these new word formations, he or she is slowed down because there is a tendency to stress the head of the phrase (boot-SPLINtered), but the orthographic convention of writing it as a compound suggests a stressing of the first syllable (BOOT-splintered). The expectations of the reader are thus doubly upset by such neologisms: on the one hand, the word itself is unfamiliar and in some cases the meaning may not be immediately apparent. On the other, the play with stress patterns causes pauses in the reading tempo as a rhythmic alternation is established and then broken.

Within the context of a jazz-inflected text such as *Be-Bop, Re-Bop*, such a stress clash might remind the reader of jazz rhythms, in which the stressed beats are frequently not on the downbeat. This "democraticization of rhythmic values" (Schuller, 8) and the combination of different rhythmical patterns means that in jazz stresses are more likely to occur in close proximity than in classical music. This jerky rhythm—which yet remains quite danceable—is fittingly reproduced by the unusual stress patterns of Cartiér's compounds.

These compounds, of course, not only contribute to the prominence of rhythm in the novels, but also to the individuality of the writing style. The poetic nature of such compounds—not least *because* they violate restrictions on compounding in casual speech—is instrumental in creating a distinct and individual poetic "voice." In addition to the neologisms coined by Cartiér, further examples of such an idiolect can be seen in Murray's highly idiomatic use of the phrase "also and also" throughout the four novels of his "Scooter" series,[14] Ondaatje's poetic voice in the hybrid novel *Coming Through Slaughter*, and the individual voice of the nameless narrator in Morrison's *Jazz*.[15] Referring to poetic devices in Canadian "poet's novels," Ian Rae observes that "such formalized speech [in poetry] makes readers conscious of the musical properties of language" (Rae, 12). Poetic language, such as Cartiér's creative word formation, foregrounds the speaking "I" in such a way as to emphasize his or her individuality in the manner of a jazz musician's unique tone.

Another feature of both novels that gestures toward poetry is the recurring presence of backslashes to suggest revisions or alternatives in terms of the content of the phrases in which they appear, or line breaks in a formal sense. A passage in italics (italics are frequently used to represent not only the protagonist's thoughts but also passages that are particularly reminiscent of a solo improvisation in character and style) at the end of the second chapter could be re-lineated with the backslashes as line breaks, yielding a piece of free verse as follows:

> *Wait, Time, don't you see?*
> *At just 43 he was kicked into infinity by an off-the rack*
> *black*
> *heart attack*
> *and I was only*
> *I'm still trying to improvise*
> *to finishingtouch-up the rest of his life*
> *in the riffs and the runs*
>   *(BOPBOP*
> *A-REE BOP!)*
> *of the chase through the*
>   *(BOOGEDY*
> *BOOGEDY*
> *BOPBOPBOP)*
> *neo-blue*
> *everblack*
> *labyrinth life*
>   *of my dreams!*
>
>   (*Be-Bop, Re-Bop*, 14; italics and capitalizations original)

Alternatively, the backslashes could represent rests in musical notation, as this unexpected punctuation produces pauses in reading. In either case, they affect the speed and rhythm of the prose in these passages, which is underscored by the frequency of rhyme and syntactic similarity in the phrases set off by backslashes (*off-the-rack, black, attack; neo-blue, everblack*). The connection to improvisation is of course made explicit here ("*I'm still trying to improvise*"), and the flexibility and spontaneity of improvisation is reflected structurally by the lack of transition between "*and I was only*" and the following line "*I'm still trying to improvise*," which seems to be a new start. *Muse-Echo Blues* exhibits a similar use of backslashes, as in the following passage, which has also been re-lineated to interpret the backslashes as line breaks:

> Sweet release! The music whines for you
> croons to you with ease
> please! just don't stop
> op scrop *do* she-bop
> It hails you and soothes you
> then flails you
> but SCOOP! Diddley op
> it bounces you over your home in earth-hell
> lifts you two
> make it three broad crooked airtides to the side
> of mainstream straight-n-narrow
> to where sound becomes sight

and the gash-rent globe seems whole again
to long-range ears
and outlandish eyes—"

(*Muse-Echo Blues*, 191; italics and capitalizations original)

The re-lineation of the two passages presented here interprets the backslashes as indications of line breaks, perhaps as an allusion to the frequent disparagement of free verse as differing from prose only in its division into lines. A suggestion of line breaks can be a gesture toward poetry. Both these examples can of course also be read as prose passages with the backslashes as punctuation that interrupts the normal flow of the line,[16] yet the text remains choppy, not least because it contains further interruptions in the form of parenthetical asides or interjections. In both cases, these interruptions are nonsense syllables borrowed from scat singing, a further explicit musical reference.[17]

Scat singing is a case of the voice being used not for language, but as an instrument like any other in the jazz band. The nonsense syllables used are chosen for their sound rather than sense,[18] and in a verbal context it represents an instance of pure sound. Such scat syllables can also be seen in many other passages throughout both novels, but their presence here is particularly striking. The "music" evoked by the nonsense syllables interrupts or alternates with the text, suggesting the interplay between different musicians or the simultaneity of text and music. In the context of rhythm, the scat singing here serves to disrupt regular rhythmic expectations, with stressed syllables indicated in italics ("op scrop *do* she-bop") or capital letters ("but SCOOP! Diddley op"), rhymes between the text and the accompanying scat interjections ("stop," "she-bop," "Diddley op"), a high frequency of monosyllables, and changing rhythmic patterns. Finally, the inserted scat syllables also serve to evoke differences in timbre, as variations in the syllables chosen allowed scat singers in the bop period, such as Ella Fitzgerald, to imitate a wide range of instruments, "thereby greatly expanding the range of timbres and attacks in scat singing" (*The New Grove Dictionary of Jazz*, vol. 3, entry for "Scat singing," 515).

A related technique is the quotation of song lyrics, often with elongated syllables to suggest the phrasing of the sung version. There are many examples of this strategy in *Muse-Echo Blues* and *Be-Bop, Re-Bop*, ranging from quotation of songs that provide background atmosphere for the plot, such as the music issuing from a neighbor's door in *Be-Bop, Re-Bop*—"George Winsome's sensuous singing,... *before fools and kings... the greatest thing you could ever learn... is to love... and be loved... in return....*" (135; italics and ellipses original)—or the numerous songs cited in *Muse-Echo Blues* that are performed in concerts or heard on the radio. In most cases, the particular song thus thematized is relevant to the meaning of the scene in terms of content. Additionally, the lyrics are rarely simply printed as ordinary text, but nearly always involve the use of hyphens, irregular spelling, and ellipses to indicate the tempo or phrasing of the tune:

> Ladyday's croon trickled in then in a thin, haunting strain of meandering pain, each note a gnarled link in a seaweedlike chain. *"You doe-wan know . . . what love is . . . un-til you've learned the mean-ning of the blue-woo. . . .*
> Sound filtered up from the jukebox, the rasp of Ladyday's tired-teenage voice with its blunt edge of premature pain. *Why peo-ple tearr the seams of oth-thuh folks' dreams . . . is o-vah my head! . . .*
> Ladyday's voice sifted up like unruly sand. *Do nuth-thin til you hear from me. . . . Pay no at-ten-tion . . . to what's said. . . .* (*Muse-Echo Blues*, 107–10; italics and ellipses original)

In this example, Billie Holiday's songs play on the radio as Lena and her son Chicago are having an intensely personal conversation. It is punctuated by lyrics that are printed in such a way as to imitate Lady Day's pronunciation and rhythm, and which not only contribute to the blues-inspired tone of the passage but also call attention to the rhythmic nature of the prose overall.

Even more interesting are examples in which the surrounding text and the quoted song lyrics interact more directly, as in the reference in *Be-Bop, Re-Bop* to the song "Dixieland": "back in the Land of Cotton (*Look away!* You got that right)" (107; italics original). Here, the song is not playing in the scene presented but surfaces in the narrator's mind when remembering the story of her great-grandmother's past in the South. The term "Land of Cotton" evokes the following phrase of the song, "look away," causing the narrator to remark in an aside on how apt it is, considering both the context of her great-grandparents' flight from persecution and the general unwillingness to reflect on such dark episodes of the past. The result is a general impression that the music tells a story that is accurate, albeit in ways perhaps unintended by the original composer.

Another example of interference between the musical lyrics on the level of histoire and discours can be seen in *Muse-Echo Blues*, when the typographical conventions used to depict phrasing and techniques of song lyrics are extended to the narration of other passages as well. Listening to Cecil Taylor on her record player, the narrator relates: "Cecil T's jumping for joy on his keys, working the juice from each piano note with a stacca-to tease and then *longato* squeeeeeze . . ." (*Muse-Echo Blues*, 78; italics original). Here, the hyphens used to indicate notes in quoted song lyrics that are pronounced distinctly are mimetically applied to the word "staccato," while the lengthening indicated by "*longato*" is reproduced in the extension of the vowel in "squeeze."

Werner Wolf categorizes the citation of song lyrics in the text as "evocation of vocal music through associative quotation" (*Musicalization of Fiction*, chapter 4.5). He situates this variety of intermedial reference (covert intermediality, in his terminology) "between 'thematization' and 'imitation.'" It verges on imitation in so far as song texts . . . may be modeled in rhythm or in their general structure on the music they go along with. On the other hand, and this is perhaps the more obvious affinity, it verges on thematization by citing at least a part if not the entirety of one component of the 'source' medium" (69).

It is furthermore "an evocative introduction of parts of this other medium into the 'target' medium" (69). In the examples discussed here, Cartiér's novels use this form of associative quotation not only to evoke the medium of vocal jazz music but also to introduce rhythmic elements into her prose text. The melismas and lengthened syllables emphasize these rhythmic elements rather than merely referring to or thematizing the songs in question. What is more, the extension of such techniques of textual representation of music to other words—as in "*PROLONNNGED TENSION*" (*Be-Bop, Re-Bop*, 91; italics original) or "long blowing gale of a waillll. . . ." (*Muse-Echo Blues*, 46)—is less a case of evoking a recognizable song than of an attempt to turn the novel itself into rhythmic singing.

Poetic Meter

The stress patterns reflected in poetic compounds are a localized example of rhythmic patterns that can also be found on a larger scale as poetic meters. Meter is used in poetry to organize sound and movement, setting up expectations that may be fulfilled—if the meter is followed regularly—or upset—if the meter is disrupted or changed. Meter is a shared component of both language and music, and can be defined as "the basic structure of beats in time" (Cooper, 92). Prose generally does not emphasize the aspect of meter, though it may also be present, whereas much poetry—even free verse—is characterized by regular meter. The impact changes in meter can have on the reading experience is made clear in a statement by D. W. Harding: "an invitation to regular movement offered at one point, only to be withdrawn at another, brings stumbling and a disjointed line" (156). This is meant as criticism of unsuccessful free verse, which—normatively—should "avoid setting up a repetitive pattern in one part of a line and disrupting it in another" (ibid). Yet as he recognizes elsewhere, "smoothness" need not be the goal of all writing: "Deliberate interruptions, breaks in the flowing sentence structure and its rhythmical continuity, may serve the writer's special ends" (133). This is precisely the case in jazz-inflected prose, which seeks to reproduce a multitude of rhythmic patterns in the manner of its musical model. The use of poetic meters and especially their frequent variation is an important tool in the rhythmic repertoire of jazz novels.

Xam Wilson Cartiér's novels *Be-Bop, Re-Bop* and *Muse-Echo Blues* are striking examples of poetic meters used within the prose text to build a bridge to musical rhythms. Anapests are particularly common in both novels, often combined with rhyme, which adds to their prominence and rhythmic musicality. Both the phrases "How you land, how you stand, how you balk at command" (*Be-Bop, Re-Bop*, 37) and "The color of grief sent to bring back relief" (38), for example, exhibit a regular anapestic rhythm:

    -    -   /   -   -   /   -   -   /   -   -   /
How you land, how you stand, how you balk   at com- mand
          The co-   lor   of   grief sent to bring back re-   lief

whereas the phrase "the foodstore fight and our consequent flight" (37) is a combination of iambic and anapestic meters:

    -    /   -   /   -   -   /   -   -   /
the food- store fight and our con- se- quent flight

Alternatively, it could be pronounced with an additional stress on "store" in the compound "foodstore" (rather than just a secondary stress). If so, the close proximity of three stressed syllables would slow down the rhythm of the line for the "fight," which appropriately enough then accelerates when describing the "flight." This type of formal reflection of the content of the line is also typical of poetry rather than of prose.

The first "solo" in Albert Murray's *Train Whistle Guitar* (4–5) is notable in its introduction of music on the level of content, as the blues guitarist Luzana Cholly here makes his first appearance, but also on the level of sound. Rhythmically, the second paragraph not only employs different poetic meters to conjure up the polyrhythms of jazz and blues, but also names them explicitly, beginning with the "idiomatic iambics" (here used only in the word "iambic" and in Luzana Cholly's name). From there the meter switches to the "trochaic-sporty stomping-ground limp-walk," with trochees such as "picking," "plucking," "knuckle knocking," and "strumming." The anapestic meter is then demonstrated not only by the word "locomotive," but also in the quoted blues lyrics that end the solo: "Anywhere," "hang my hat," "prop my feet," "who could drink muddy water," "who could sleep," and "hollow log."

As discussed above, jazz novels may employ poetry as an intermediate stage in order to evoke aspects of the music.[19] In the case of musical rhythm, the text uses poetry's rigid meters to build a bridge between the prose text and music. Here, the emphasis on poetic meters—particularly the explicit naming of the meters used—draws the reader's attention to the aspect of rhythm that the text shares with music. Because the text proceeds sequentially in a single line rather than containing multiple parallel strands, it cannot actually use multiple rhythms simultaneously, playing them off one another in the manner of African polyrhythms. Instead, this passage names one meter after another—iambic, trochaic, and anapestic—in order to point out the interplay between the different rhythmic patterns that are not kept entirely distinct but overlap with one another. These rhythmic patterns are not only a gesture toward poetry, but are also explicitly linked with another source of rhythm, as exemplified by the phrase "anapestic locomotive" (5). The connection between the rhythm of trains and jazz or blues music will be examined in the following section.

The Rhythm of Trains

> Trains represent a certain type of freedom: they represent communication, and they represent the ability to get from one place to another with a group of people to see some other people. And also a train represents incantation and percussion; so you hear whoo-whoo, whoo-whoo, chug-a-chug-a, chug-a-chug-a, ca-junk, ca-junk, ca-junk. (Marsalis and O'Meally, 152)

> Swing is possible . . . only when the beat, though it seems perfectly regular, gives the impression of moving inexorably ahead (like a train that keeps moving at the same speed but is still being drawn ahead by its locomotive). (Andre Hodeir, cited as an epigraph to chapter 1 in O'Meally, 6)

As Wynton Marsalis asserts in the first quotation above, taken from an interview with Robert O'Meally about Duke Ellington's music, trains have something extremely rhythmic about them. The distinctive repetitive sounds of the wheels on the tracks, pistons pumping, and train whistles are evocative of an ideal of freedom of movement from place to place. Houston A. Baker points out the role of the train station as a crossroads or "juncture," one which he sees as central to the history of the blues (1–14). This place of transience is the setting, for example, for legends about the development of the blues as an art form, as in the story of W. C. Handy hearing a man sing a blues about railroad crossings while waiting for a train, which he later recorded as "Yellow Dog Blues" (Baker, 4). Numerous other blues revolve around trains as metaphors for escape, such as "Broke Down Engine Blues," "Statesboro Blues," "Trouble in Mind," "Goin' Where the Southern Cross the Dog," and others (McPherson, 15). Yet railroad imagery is not only important on this level of content, but especially for its particular rhythms. James McPherson, in writing about "train people," says of Wallace Saunders, who wrote the first ballad about Casey Jones:

To him [the locomotive] may have offered the same mobility and freedom it seemed to offer whites, and a belief in this promise was reflected in his spirituals. But after achieving a kind of freedom, he began contemplating what was suggested to the listening habits of his ear by the *motion* of the machine. He liked its rhythms: the regular, recurring beat of the train could sound like the patter of feet and the clapping of hands. He also liked its steady drive and thrust, its suggestion of unrestrained freedom and power, the way, in the right hands, a quilling whistle sounded. He became expert in reproducing this motion on a guitar by running his fingers rapidly along the strings, or by playing successive chords with a regularity and sound similar to that of a moving train. The lonesome sound of the whistle could be reproduced by blowing through a harmonica. (15)

The percussive or rhythmic aspect of railroad sounds finds its way into blues and jazz music in the form of onomatopoeic elements, from the "bell-like piano chorus" played by Count Basie in his "One o'Clock Jump" (Murray, *Stomping the Blues*, 124), to "a steady train-wheels-over-track-junctures guitar back beat" (Baker, 8) used by a number of solo blues guitar players.[20] Such sounds not only function as iconic signs imitating elements of the world outside of music, a rich source of inspiration to this musical tradition, but also provoke a comparison between the systems of the blues (or the blues "matrix," to use Baker's term) and the network of intersecting railroad tracks and stations. In addition to the aspects of transience, forward motion, and (perceived) freedom mentioned above, another element of a train that is relevant for music is its status as being simultaneously "one thing" and "a lot of things": "It sounds like a lot of things; it sounds like one thing. You hear a train, and you think of a whole bunch of things, but it's still one thing. . . . And this is how Duke [Ellington]'s music was, shuffling. You have trombones down there playing and the bass, the clarinets. You start with that sound, then something else comes in on top" (Marsalis and O'Meally, 152). Because a train is at once a whole unit and a collection of a number of smaller units (such as the many individual cars), like the skyscraper with its many floors, it provides a metaphor for the choral structure of the jazz song, as will be discussed in chapter 3. In addition, the fact that a train not only *consists of* many things but also *sounds like* many different things underscores the ability of music to say multiple things at once. As Marsalis says of Ellington's orchestration, many components combine to form the entire sound, whether different instruments in an orchestra or band, or different parts of the train, such as rumbling boxcars, clattering wheels, screeching brakes, ringing bells, etc. Furthermore, the frequency of such devices in blues and jazz music has caused them to take on symbolic aspects as a conventional marker of genre.

In the jazz novels considered here, depictions of trains are closely linked to jazz and blues on the level of content, such as when the guitar playing of Luzana Cholly is explicitly linked to the sound of train whistles in *Train Whistle Guitar*[21] or when the journey of cornet player Buddy Bolden to the insane asylum is made into a "*Train Song*" in *Coming Through Slaughter* (85). Trains in these novels also evoke jazz and especially blues music through common associations, as the critical comments on the relationship between trains and the blues discussed above demonstrate.

Most significantly in the context of this chapter, train imagery in these novels is used particularly to foreground rhythmic elements—not only of the trains but also of the music evoked by the text more generally. A few examples will illustrate this rhythmic connection between trains and jazz or blues music: In Toni Morrison's *Jazz*, two of the passages most striking in their use of repetition both include a train. The "clicking" and "tapping" that forms the rhythmic center of one of the narrator's "solos" toward the end of the novel is only audible "when the loud trains pull into their stops and the engines pause" (226).[22] Even more apparent is the connection between trains and rhythm in the "train-dancing" scene (30–32). On their trip from Virginia to the city Joe and Violet Trace experience the motion of the train as a kind of welcome dance, which emphasizes the association between trains and a rhythmic motion and sound.

The connection between trains and musical rhythm is stronger in Ondaatje's *Coming Through Slaughter*, in which the novel's title refers to the musician Buddy Bolden's literal train ride through the town of Slaughter, Louisiana, en route to the insane asylum. In addition to this prominent reference, the riff "passing wet chicory that lies in the fields like the sky," which appears three times in the novel, also refers to the same train ride.[23] This phrase not only describes the view from the train, but also imitates it rhythmically through a dactylic meter and phonetically with the sounds [tʃ] and [k] of the word "chicory" resembling the onomatopoeic representation of a train's sound as "chug-a chug, chug-a chug." What is more, the musical connection of this train motif is present from its second appearance, where it is presented in isolation as the highly repetitive "*Train Song*" (85).

The most significant use of trains occurs in Albert Murray's first novel *Train Whistle Guitar*. The title, even more obviously than in *Coming Through Slaughter*, associates the blues with trains, as Luzana Cholly's guitar playing is said to sound like a train whistle, as well as like an "anapestic locomotive" (5). The guitarist unites the figures of the freight-train-hopping vagrant and the talented blues musician and is one of the narrator's earliest role models and father figures. In addition, train tracks, train whistles, and people who work on or ride the rails provide a good deal of the atmosphere of the novel: there are, for example, the railroad lines that make up the geography of Gasoline Point,[24] the train whistles that Scooter feels he "had been born hearing and knowing about" (50), the quoted blues lyrics "*Anywhere I hang my hat anywhere I prop my feet*" (5) that portray the migrant lifestyle, and the way Scooter and his friend Little Buddy Marshall imitate "the L & N porter we liked best in those days" (38).[25] These various uses of train imagery together create the atmosphere of Scooter's childhood in rural Alabama, at the same time underscoring the connection between trains and blues music, as personified by Luzana Cholly, the "twelve-string guitar player second to none" (11). Cholly is the first of the many teachers and surrogate parents in the Scooter series, and one who prefigures a number of the many themes that will become important for the remainder of the narrative: the blues—Scooter later plays the bass in a jazz band; spatial mobility—though he doesn't ride the rails, he leaves home to go away to college, tours the United States with the band, and even visits France; the importance of education—Cholly extracts a promise from Scooter and Buddy to stay in school when he catches them trying to hop a train and follow him (30); and even storytelling, as Luzana Cholly's guitar playing included "sneak[ing] our names into some very well known ballad just to signify at us about something, and . . . mak[ing] up new ballads right on the spot just to tell us stories" (10). Significantly, Scooter also sees the train whistle with which the guitar is compared as a storyteller:[26] "Not to mention his voice, which was as smoke-blue sounding as the Philamayork-skyline-blue mist beyond blue steel railroad bridges. Not to mention how he was forever turning guitar strings into train whistles which were not only the once-upon-a-time voices of storytellers but of all the voices saying what was being said in the stories as well" (15). The trains in *Train Whistle Guitar* thus not only evoke the rhythm of the train as an influence on blues rhythms, emphasizing the musicality of the text, but also establish a nexus of meaning that forms the foundation of not only this novel but the remainder of the series as well.

Notes

[1] Though rhythmic qualities such as playing ahead of or behind the beat also contribute to an individual style, they can still be seen as distinct from aspects of timbre per se.

[2] Another textual strategy for imitating timbre that is not specifically poetic is the use of dialect to characterize the speaking voice. While African American vernacular English is used in many jazz novels, especially in quoted direct speech or dialogue, this technique is less prominent in the jazz novels considered than the creation of a more individual voice or "idiolect," the speech variety of an individual speaker rather than of a regional or social group. The difference between these two categories of speech could be compared to the difference between the individual tone of a player such as John Coltrane (=idiolect) and the sound of a saxophone in general (=dialect).

³ See e.g. this passage from Jack Fuller's *The Best of Jackson Payne*: "Jackson's rhythm. It was like an Afro-Cuban band, with ten different things going all at once, except this was just one man." A fellow soldier asks him what he is doing and he responds, "I'm just counting.... Three against four. Five against six. Different things" (15).

⁴ See e.g. Schuller: "the syncopation of jazz is no more than an idiomatic corruption, a flattened-out mutation of what was once the true polyrhythmic character of African music" (15).

⁵ See Schuller's claim that "African speech, singing, and playing are all marked by an open tone and natural quality. In this they are closer to European and Western tradition than to the Islamic, which is indeed characterized by a thin, nasal, wavering quality" (55).

⁶ Jarrett bases this trope on the common descriptions of (aspects of) jazz sound as wailing, cries, growls, etc.

⁷ See also Harding: "Beyond the paragraph it seems most unlikely that we get any direct perception of the unity and patterning of a long piece of writing.... Instead there is a reflective grasp of structure: observation and retrospective survey show that a large section of a work, possibly the whole work, has a unity of patterned divisions, recurrent points of tension or heightened speed, a succession of increasingly emotional climaxes, perhaps a post-climactic repose.... Although the pattern is analogous to a rhythm, and each phase is experienced by the playgoer in heightenings and relaxations of tension as the play proceeds, the total pattern is not experienced as an immediate perceptual whole—it has to be surveyed and thought about" (136).

⁸ On the definition of rhythm as consisting of "directly perceptible unit[s]," see Harding: "though there is no sharp dividing line [between units of rhythm and larger movement patterns in prose] the distinction remains valid and the extremes are readily discriminated—at one extreme the rhythm which is an immediate fact of perception, at the other the movement structure of a long section of prose which can be identified only when we reflect and look back" (154).

⁹ See the discussion of "literarische Verfremdung" (literary alienation) in Link, 100–120. In particular, Link distinguishes between the defamiliarization of the signifier (i.e., alliteration, assonance, rhyme), of the signified (i.e., metaphor, oxymoron), and of complex literary defamiliarization such as tropes and symbols. The present discussion of rhythm focuses primarily on aspects of alienation in the signifier, but the poetic quality of these texts is equally a result of their unusual treatment of the signifieds. See e.g. the idiomatic use of "also" by Albert Murray in his Scooter novels as an example of language "made strange" on both the level of the signifier ("the also and also of") and on the level of the signified (where "also" implies hybridity and membership).

¹⁰ Ian Rae's 2008 study of the "poet's novel" is to my knowledge the only attempt thus far to examine poetic novels as a distinct genre. Though a precise definition of the term "poet's novel" is still sadly lacking, he identifies a number of conventions that also characterize the musical novels I consider here, with their use of poetic devices to bridge the gap between prose and music.

[11] Prose poetry should also be listed in this context, as it is often defined as "a short composition employing the rhythmic cadences and other devices of free verse (such as poetic imagery and figures) but printed wholly or partly in the format of prose, i.e., with a right-hand margin instead of regular line-breaks," thus behaving in a manner very similar to the poetic prose of the jazz novels considered here (*The Concise Oxford Dictionary of Literary Terms*, 180).

[12] For the lyric as a "mode," see Daniel Albright: "lyric is a mode, discoverable in odes and dramas and novels and possibly the telephone directory," cited in Rae, 10. Similarly, on poetry and prose as differing in degree rather than kind, see Hartman, 45–46.

[13] In all eight examples the emphases are added. The underlined syllables represent rhymes, boldfaced letters are examples of alliteration or assonance, and the italics highlight an instance of syntactic repetition called epistrophe. Similar examples can be found throughout the novel; this group of four pages was chosen at random.

[14] The phrase "also and also" will be discussed as an example of a "lick" that structures the narrator's improvisation. See the section on "Improvised Breaks in *Train Whistle Guitar*" in chapter 4.

[15] The individuality of the narrator is also instrumental in establishing a parallel to the live performance situation. See the section on "The Narrator as Performer: Imitating Orality" in chapter 4.

[16] In other cases, the backslashes are used more sparingly, suggesting rather a spontaneous revision of the text than verse lineation.

[17] Scat singing, according to Gunther Schuller, is "a manner of singing employing nonsense syllables" (381), a technique for which Louis Armstrong was particularly famous. Other examples of such nonsense syllables can be found in *Muse-Echo Blues*, 25, 26, 34, 45, 46, 72, 124, and in *Be-Bop, Re-Bop*, 27, 47, 119, 148, among others.

[18] Langston Hughes's "Simple" presents the theory that the "nonsense syllables" of bop have their origin in "'the police beating Negroes' heads.... Every time a cop hits a Negro with his billy club, that old club says, 'BOP! BOP! ... BE-BOP! ... MOP! ... BOP!' That Negro hollers, 'Ooool-ya-koo! Ou-o-o!'.... That's where Be-bop came from, beaten right out of some Negro's head into them horns and saxophones and piano keys that plays it. Do you call that nonsense?" Cited as an epigraph to chapter 7 in O'Meally, 121.

[19] Another such intermediate stage will be discussed in chapter 4, in which oral storytelling links the written text to the live performance situation of jazz music.

[20] Though railroad imitation is most commonly associated with guitar players, pianists also developed techniques to produce similar sounds: "One new technique made more use of rising and falling chords. The bass, played with the left hand, was made to reproduce the rhythms and counter-rhythms of a high-speed train running smoothly against track. The right hand produced treble variations, perhaps the voice of the conductor, the puff of the smokestack, the moan of the whistle, which imposed a narrative over the rhythmic movement of the bass. The music was called 'boogie-woogie,' perhaps in commemoration of the American 'bogie trunk' invented by the engineer John B. Jervis" (McPherson, 16).

[21] See e.g. Murray, *Train Whistle Guitar*: "playing the blues on his guitar as if he were also an engineer telling tall tales on a train whistle, his left hand doing most of the talking including the laughing and signifying as well as the moaning and crying and even the whining, while his right hand thumped the wheels going somewhere.... Then there was also his notorious holler, the sound of which was always far away and long coming as if from somewhere way down under.... I myself always thought of it as being something else that was like a train, a bad express train saying Look out this me and here I come and I'm on my way one more time" (8).

[22] Over a length of one and a half pages the word "click" or "clicking" appears six times, "snap" or "snapping" five times, "tap" twice, and "ticking" once, for a total of fourteen occurrences; Many other present participle -ing forms are also used, adding to the prominence of this sound pattern.

[23] The phrase "passing wet chicory that lies in the fields like the sky" occurs on pages 60, 85, and 139 of Ondaatje's *Coming Through Slaughter*. See chapter 3 for a more detailed analysis of this phrase as a riff.

[24] Train tracks (identified by the train company or railway line that they belong to: AT & N, L & N, M & O, GM & O, GM & N, Southern; beginning on page 2, but also throughout the novel) are major landmarks near Gasoline Point (the township itself is connected with if not actually named for the train stop there: "that was also the name on the L & N timetable and the road map," 3). Furthermore, more distant places are identified as "express train destinations" (3).

[25] The call and response that results out of the boys' imitation of both the porter and a preacher's sermon, "as if I were moving along the aisle of a church and a train coach at the same time" (39), is analyzed in greater detail in the call-and-response section of chapter 3.

[26] James McPherson suggests that engineers' homemade train whistles have an affinity to the human voice, such that "railroad engineers were fathers to much of American music" and "pioneered in the creation of an art form" (14).

3: Structural Patterns in Jazz Novels

JAZZ'S ASSOCIATION WITH "FREEDOM" and its emphasis on elements of "improvisation, originality, [and] change"[1] may conspire to create the mistaken impression that it is formless. On the contrary, like any variety of music, jazz relies on several levels of structure.[2] Freedom must always be seen in relation to constraint, as the constraints of a form or structure are a prerequisite for experimentation. As a fellow musician says of Buddy Bolden in Michael Ondaatje's novel *Coming Through Slaughter*, "We thought he was formless, but I think now he was tormented by order, what was outside it" (37). Without expectations of a regular form—a source of order—deviations from it cannot be perceived as such. The relative freedom of improvisation in jazz, for example, is only possible because of structural patterns that provide a jumping-off point for the soloist, such as the repeating structure of the chorus with a set harmonic framework and a regular number of measures, the beat itself as a means of keeping time, repetitive melodic patterns such as riffs that produce familiarity, often occurring within a dialogic framework of call and response between members of the band. All these structural devices set up an expectation of continuity, provide a framework within which the soloist has an opportunity to anticipate the beat, modify familiar melodies, or engage in a conversation with another player. In each case, it is the upsetting of expectations that creates interest and excitement, but form and structure are required in order to establish those initial expectations.

This chapter considers several levels of structure within jazz music and the novels inspired by it. The most basic level of structural organization, the regular recurrence of the beat, has already been referred to in chapter 2 on rhythm. The present chapter argues that each level of structural organization may be adapted from a musical context to a textual one, whether repeated small melodic units such as the riff, larger structural units such as the chorus, the form of an album consisting of individual songs, or general patterns of antiphony or call and response.

The Riff

Let us define a riff as a relatively short phrase that is repeated over a changing chord pattern, originally as a background device, although it later came to be used as foreground material in the so-called riff tunes of the Swing Era.... In true riff tradition, the riff itself remains unchanged while the underlying harmony shifts.... The repetitiousness of the riff corresponds exactly to the repetitive structuring of African songs and dances, especially work and play songs. (Schuller, 48)

Jazz and other forms of music descended from African models make extensive use of repetition. James A. Snead has argued for repetition as a key feature of black culture more generally, and sees recurring motifs like the riff as exemplifying this tendency. A riff is a short phrase, usually two to four bars long, revolving around a central tone, and is played repeatedly with little or no variation. It is the contrast with a new harmonic situation that leads to an impression of change. This recurring phrase helps to structure many jazz pieces and anchor the collective performance.

In addition to the riff, there are several other instances of repetition in jazz music that should be distinguished from it. The most basic form of repetition is the constant presence of the beat, which establishes clear expectations as to the ongoing rhythm of the piece. In the blues, whole melodic lines are repeated in a regular AAB pattern and many jazz performances based on popular songs also employ a refrain or theme that is restated at regular intervals. There may also be smaller units that are repeated, such as in motivic improvisation, which will be discussed in more detail in chapter 4. Call-and-response patterns are also based on a regularly repeated exchange and frequently employ riffs as invariant responses.

A first point for clarification is exactly what can be seen as making up a textual riff. Can the "relatively short phrase that is repeated over a changing chord pattern" (Schuller, 48) be evoked through a recurring motif or idea, or is it better to restrict our consideration of textual riffs to (linguistic) phrases that are repeated in nearly identical form? The fact that both a musical and a literary phrase are called by the same name need not imply that they are comparable or in important ways similar. I first consider the possibility of a more general concept or motif as corresponding to a musical phrase like the riff.

In the "traindancing" example from Toni Morrison's *Jazz* cited by Alan Rice, the word "dancing" or "danced" occurs five times over a period of three pages (twice on page 30 and three times on 32; once more as "train-danced" on 36). To call dancing a riff, however, would suggest the concept rather than the word, which would seem to be too short to fill that role. Referring to the concept, Rice claims that dancing is a "riff that structures the passage, [in which] the dancers respond to the rhythm of the train and ... in which the City in a kind of antiphonal response to the migrants dances a welcome too" ("Finger-Snapping," 116). In a similar passage, Rice sees the use of words for sounds like "clicking" and "snapping" as "an extended riff on the compulsive, 'finger-snapping,' 'clicking' rhythm of African American life" (116). This description, however, demonstrates an ambiguity in terminology. If a riff, as musical definitions show, is a repeated short phrase, how can a passage be "an extended riff"? It would seem that Rice here means that the passage is a solo based on this riff or containing several riffs. "Clicking" and "snapping," however, can only be seen as the same riff if it is not the specific form that is repeated, but a more general idea or concept of noisemaking.

Alan Munton, in a vociferous attack on critics for "mishearing jazz" in Morrison's writing, objects to Rice's confusion of musical terms, as when Rice sees a passage in *Sula* as improvisation, riff, and call and response at once (239).[3] While it is conceivable that a jazz-inflected text could choose a motif as its equivalent for the musical phrase, Rice's lack of consistency weakens his analysis of this passage. I agree with Munton that it is a mistake to label either "dancing" or "clicking" riffs in the Morrison passages analyzed by Rice. A more precise description might be to see these short phrases inserted into a solo as "licks" rather than riffs. A formulaic improvisation uses previously formed material, short standardized phrases called licks, which are combined in such a way as to create something new. Unlike a riff, which is somewhat longer than a single word, formulaic licks do not call attention to themselves as recognizable units, but are recombined in such a way as to conceal the seams between them.[4]

What kinds of phrases can be called riffs, then, or is Munton right to discount the possibility altogether? I suggest a more rigid definition than Rice has used, while acknowledging that the type of jazz imitated in literature may vary from text to text, as it is based on that text's individual esthesic response to jazz. Because text and music share the ability to produce a linear phrase—a melodic unit in music, a linguistic phrase in text—it seems reasonable to look for textual riffs as short phrases or clauses, generally shorter than a full sentence, but longer than a single word. They can be repeated in nearly identical form, and like a musical riff, their changing context causes them to appear differently with each reiteration. In response to Munton's question of "where, for example, is the element of harmony in prose" (241), I suggest that the context within the paragraph or other textual unit corresponds to the changing harmonic context of a riff in jazz music.

The repetition of a phrase is an example of means shared by both music and text, while the textual context corresponds in an analogical way to the harmonic context in music, imitating foreign means. While the text is able to repeat phrases in the same way as music, exact repetition is a technique generally employed to a much lesser extent in text. The expectations of the reader require greater development and change, frequent presentation of new material, and much less repetition of what has already been said. Exact repetitions of whole phrases in the style of a riff, therefore, are quite striking in a textual context and contribute to the evocation of a musical model. As Snead points out, "Narrative repetition tends to defuse the belief that any other meaning resides in a repeated signifier than the fact that it is being repeated" (76). Repetition thus empties the signifier of its signified and the ensuing lack of referentiality evokes the musical sign. Because they are so readily apparent, such riffs may be used more sparingly than in many types of jazz. The novels considered here employ their textual riffs in varied fashion, whether nine[5] or twelve times throughout the course of the novel, as few as three times, or significantly more often. Where they do recur frequently, they may even be found irritating to the reader, seeming to belabor the point in a manner that may quickly become tedious.

"The Girl from South Dakota": Riffs in Stanley Crouch's *Don't the Moon Look Lonesome*

One such example is Stanley Crouch's novel *Don't the Moon Look Lonesome*. The story of the white female jazz singer Carla and her black trumpet-playing boyfriend Maxwell, the novel makes use of vernacular speech patterns—both African American vernacular and general American slang—and a few frequently repeated phrases used to describe or identify the protagonist. She is "the girl from South Dakota," a phrase that occurs several times in most chapters, either repeated verbatim or modified to "the South Dakota girl," "Miss South Dakota," or "the diva from South Dakota."[6] Upon first reading the novel, I found this repetition jarring, an excessive emphasis on Carla's origins in the Midwest that seemed at odds with her explicit desire to fit into the jazz community in New York and specifically with the African American friends and family of her boyfriend(s). Treating her home state as a riff[7] serves also to mark her as the "Other," a white girl in a predominantly black environment, a country girl in the city. The scenes in which it is missing are either in contexts where Carla is less actively involved in the proceedings (i.e., during the church service or while she is listening to her friends talking) or in her memories of her own family, in which a description like "the girl from South Dakota" is no longer sufficient to distinguish her from other South Dakotans.

The epithet is most often used as Carla's own self-definition, in the context of her sense of individuality, as well as her gumption and determination to succeed, though occasionally also by her black girlfriend Leeann ("my South Dakota buddy"). While its many repetitions over the course of the novel—thirty-six in part 1 and nineteen in part 2—make the motif highly recognizable to the reader, it does take on a different character as the context of its use changes. The tone is different when said or thought by Carla herself (the third-person narration is focalized through her perspective for most of the novel in the form of free indirect discourse) as opposed to the few times it is used by her friends, as for example when Leeann teases Carla about being a lightweight when it comes to drinking, telling her, "You better stick to the light stuff, *little Miss South Dakota.* The last thing I need now is a drunken white woman crying the blues about her and her black boyfriends" (322, emphasis added).

Its function also develops as the novel progresses. Originally a fairly banal form of characterization, later insights into Carla's position in the sea of race relations suggest that her own regional and ethnic view of herself is part of the difficulty she is encountering with her African American boyfriend. Believing herself to be free of prejudice and longing for a world beyond black and white, her racially constructed identity as "snow white," "Norwegian," and "from South Dakota" shows that she persists in seeing herself and others in racial terms, despite the wealth of positive associations she has with the African American community.

The many reiterations of this riff-like phrase also add up to so many uses of the first-person singular. As Carla slowly realizes,[8] she is very much absorbed with herself, tuning out when her friends are talking of their experiences and neglecting to take others' opinions or feelings into consideration. Carla essentially tells her story by constantly returning to a focus on "the girl from South Dakota"—herself.

"What I Remember When I Remember": Riffs in Albert Murray's *Train Whistle Guitar*

Another example of a textual riff can be found in Albert Murray's *Train Whistle Guitar*, the first novel in the Scooter series, published in 1974. Murray's other three novels—*The Spyglass Tree*, *The Seven-League Boots*, and *The Magic Keys*—continue the narrative of the protagonist known only by the nickname Scooter and were published in 1991, 1996, and 2005, respectively. Murray, a jazz critic and essayist as well as a novelist and poet, has written repeatedly on the importance of what he calls the "blues idiom"[9] for African American culture, and has confirmed its influence on his own writing. This first novel consists primarily of memories of the narrator's childhood, and the riff used prominently underscores the theme of memory, taking the form of "the X I remember when I remember Y." Used twelve times[10] over the course of the novel, this formula is like a refrain to which the narrator returns in his reminiscences of childhood. These memories are closely associated with sensual impressions, whether colors, sounds, or smells, and help to elicit more detailed memories of people from his past.

The first three appearances of this riff occur early in the novel and are focused on gradations of the color blue:

The color *you almost always remember when you remember* Little Buddy Marshall is sky-blue. . . . But the shade of blue and blueness *you always remember whenever and for whatever reason you remember* Luzana Cholly is steel blue. . . . But blue steel is the color *you always remember when you remember* how his guitar used to sound. (6–7; emphasis added)

Tying this memory-based motif in with sensual impressions of color, this passage also introduces the central theme of the blues—both evoked through the color blue, repeated eight times in these two paragraphs, and through the first reference to Luzana Cholly's legendary guitar playing.

Several occurrences of the riff also connect sound, color, and music, or evoke smells and tastes that set off a train of childhood memories.[11] The last four riffs are associated with memories of girls and the narrator's first sexual experiences. Continuing the strong presence of local trees and flowers that began with the view from the chinaberry tree on the first pages (which also becomes the "spyglass tree" of the second novel), the narrator associates his girlfriends from long ago with different flowers: Deljean McCray "is always the girl I remember when I remember dog fennels and dog fennel meadows" (139), whereas "the one I remember when I remember crape myrtle yard blossoms is Charlene Wingate" (157). These memories are also tied to musical impressions, whether of a Jelly Roll Morton tune played on the victrola or a flirtatious song the girl danced to.

Though the basic formula "the X I remember when I remember Y" is maintained (sometimes with the addition of "always" or in the second person instead of the first), the changing context yields different effects. What exactly is being remembered is different in each case, much as the tension between the riff and the chords played beneath it changes with each repetition in jazz music. The three repetitions in close succession at the novel's outset cause this formula to be very recognizable, while its varying context prevents monotony. It is also worth noting that this riff contains an element of internal repetition that is common throughout the novel. The two uses of "remember" within a phrase that itself is repeated as a unit makes it more compelling as an example of a riff than single words such as those identified as riffs by Alan Rice. A two- to four-bar melodic phrase contains smaller units that may themselves be repeated, particularly the central tone around which the riff revolves. Here, that central tone (or word, or concept) is "remember." The emphasis on remembering also suggests that Scooter remembers these incidents from his childhood not for the sake of the *memories*, but for the sake of the process of *remembering* itself. The content of the memory becomes a vehicle for the form of remembering rather than the reverse.[12]

The potential objection could arise that this formula could just as easily be seen as a theme and variations, not even necessarily a musical one. In response, I argue that the pervasive thematization of the blues and other musical forms (ragtime, honky tonk, boogie woogie, and stride piano) serves as an explicit marker of musical influence, which can then be used to explain technique as well as content. There is no reference in the novel to classical themes and variations, and thus less motivation for such an interpretation of this device than in the realm of the blues. For what it is worth, Murray has confirmed such readings extratextually, stating that the series of which *Train Whistle Guitar* is the first volume is "about the initiation and escapades of a blues-idiom hero. It is an attempt to create the literary equivalent of the blues" ("Function of the Heroic Image," 575). This can of course be seen on the level of content, as the Scooter novels together make up a *Künstlerroman* about the coming of age and artistic development of a blues bassist and writer. But the imitation of techniques such as the riff, the succession of choruses, and the improvisational breaks, as well as a foregrounding of rhythmic and other sound-related qualities of language, demonstrate a significant influence of the blues on the form of the novel as well.

"Passing Wet Chicory": Riffs in Michael Ondaatje's *Coming Through Slaughter*

A third example that uses the device of the riff as a means of evoking jazz music is Michael Ondaatje's novel *Coming Through Slaughter*, which is about the legendary jazzman Buddy Bolden, who was said to have gone berserk in a parade in 1907. In contrast to the previously cited examples, this textual riff appears only three times in the novel, but its exposed position contributes to a riffing function: "Passing wet chicory that lies in the field like the sky" (60, 85, 139). This rhythmic phrase seems to lack any referentiality on its first mention, in which it comprises the entirety of the text printed on that page. A context and referential meaning is not provided until its third and final appearance toward the end of the novel, when Bolden is on the train heading for the mental asylum:

> Am walked out of the House of D and put on a north train by H. B. McMurray and Jones. Outside a river can't get out of the rain. Passing wet chicory that lies in the field like the sky. The trees rocks brown ditches falling off the side as we go past. The train in a wet coat. (139)

In this scene, despite the surreal quality of Bolden's impressions, indicative of his confused mental state, the fields of wet chicory do have a concrete referent in the view from the train window. For the previous uses of this line, however, such a context is absent, which causes the imagery to be mysterious and nonreferential, foregrounding the sound rather than the sense of the words.

The rhythm of this phrase is predominantly dactylic, with an extra unstressed syllable in the middle of the word "chicory":[13]

```
 /    -   -   /  (-)  -   -   /   -   -   /   -   -   /
Pass- ing wet chi- co-  ry  that lies in  the fields like the sky
```

Converted into musical beats, the phrase consists of five measures:

```
 1    2   3   1   +    2   3   1   2   3   1   2   3   1
Pass- ing wet chi- co-  ry  that lies in  the fields like the sky
```

$\frac{3}{4}$-time is relatively unusual for jazz music, but the rhythm of this riff can be better understood in the context of the train ride. Even before this context is known, the phrase is explicitly associated with trains at its second use under the title "*Train Song*" (85). Its $\frac{3}{4}$ meter evokes less a jazz motif than the rhythm of a train on the tracks: **chug** chug chug **chug**-a-chug chug **chug** chug chug.

The musicality of the phrase at its first appearance is underscored by the preceding scene. Lying in bed with Robin Brewitt, Bolden taps his fingers on her back as if he were playing the cornet, "improving on *Cakewalking Babies*" (59; italics original). The phrase that follows is clearly not that early jazz tune (recorded, for example, by Louis Armstrong and the Red Onion Jazz Babies in 1923), which is played in a fast $\frac{4}{4}$ time and does not contain any of these images in its lyrics. Still, the juxtaposition of this musical context and the isolated phrase causes the reader to interpret "passing wet chicory" as a musical motif, particularly in the absence of a recognizable referential meaning.

The "*Train Song*" is reminiscent of riff-based improvisations, in which the riff is played repeatedly, before being modified:

Train Song

Passing wet chicory that lies in the fields like the sky.
Passing wet chicory that lies in the fields like the sky.
Passing wet chicory lies
like the sky,
like the sky like the sky like the sky
passing wet sky chicory
passing wet sky chicory lies (85)

The repetitions of parts of the phrase in new combinations in the last few lines lead to a breakdown of the regular rhythm of the initial riff, particularly the three stressed syllables "wet," "sky," and "chi" in close succession. Though riff-based improvisations were common in early jazz and were later avoided by bebop musicians, these irregular rhythms and experimentation are more suggestive of bebop than of earlier varieties of jazz with their predilection for danceable rhythms. Indeed, the postmodern techniques of the novel as a whole would seem to correspond more closely to bebop avant-gardism than to more conventional New Orleans jazz. Still, this is a modern perspective on a variety of jazz that was extremely innovative for its time, combining disparate strands of musical traditions such as marches, ragtime, the blues, and gospel. As Dude Botley says in a passage of *Coming Through Slaughter* largely quoted (although with modification) from Martin Williams's *Jazz Masters of New Orleans*, "He's mixing them up. He's playing the blues and the hymn sadder than the blues and then the blues sadder than the hymn. That is the first time I ever heard hymns and blues cooked up together" (81; cf. Martin Williams, 13–14).

This riff thus occurs only three times, but in three decidedly different contexts. The first time it is presented in isolation, without accompaniment, so to speak, and without a clear harmonic or narrative context. At its second appearance the riff forms the basis for a lyrical experimentation in the "train song," repeated and deconstructed as a solo—much like Coltrane's motivic improvisations on the phrase "a love supreme" on the eponymous album, in which the same motif appears repeated in different rhythms and in all the different keys (*The New Grove Dictionary of Jazz*, vol. 2, entry for "Improvisation," 319). Finally, it appears within a narrative context, embedded in a paragraph in which it stands out only because its previous iterations cause it to be immediately recognizable as a riff. The small number of occurrences need not disqualify the phrase as a riff, since they are striking enough to create the impression of repetition and varied enough to illustrate the riff's many functions.

Choruses

> Popular songs usually have two sections: a verse, which is often through-composed (i.e., having no repeated phrases) and ends on the dominant; and a refrain (also called a chorus). In jazz performances the verse is little used, if at all; in early jazz it was usually played only once, at the beginning of the piece, and after the 1920s it was generally discarded altogether and the refrain was taken as the sole material. (*The New Grove Dictionary of Jazz*, vol. 1, entry for "Forms," 823)

This section focuses on the chorus, a "musical form in jazz delineating a chord structure or progression which in its totality forms the basis for an improvisation" (Schuller, 375–76), which is the largest unit of musical structure within the jazz song. The lowest level of structure is of course the beat, which is then grouped into measures or bars of two or four beats per bar. Bars are in turn grouped into phrases, generally four bars long, and phrases are combined into chorus patterns such as AAB (twelve-bar blues form), AABA, or ABAC (both examples of sixteen- or thirty-two-bar popular song patterns).

The most common forms used in jazz are those based on the popular song or on the blues progression (*Jazz-Lexikon*, 823–24). As indicated in the definition above, the popular song's dual structure of chorus and verse are generally reduced to the chorus alone, however, with the source of contrast not between chorus and verse, but between different realizations of the chorus. Within a jazz band, the chorus can be orchestrated in a number of different ways, including, for example, a statement of the theme by the ensemble, solo variations on the theme by different instruments such as trumpet, saxophone, and trombone, and a return to the theme by the whole group at the end of the piece. The chorus is closely associated with improvisation, as indeed it grew out of the break, a "short rhythmic-melodic cadenza" (Schuller, 375) that interrupts the ensemble performance. This interruption of the accompaniment is an opportunity for the soloist to briefly stand alone before the regular chord progression resumes with the next chorus. With the advent of the great soloists from Louis Armstrong onward, this break was expanded to the point that soloists no longer were restricted to one to two bar breaks, but could instead improvise for the length of a twelve- or sixteen-bar chorus or longer. The use of the chorus as the unit of measuring larger blocks of time explains why a jazz musician refers to solo improvisation as "tak[ing] a chorus" (Schuller, 375–76). The number of choruses in a piece is not fixed, but may vary widely, depending on how many choruses players take for their solos. As John Kouwenhoven points out, this indeterminate length—in which "there is no inherent reason why the jazz performance should not continue for another 12 or 16 or 24 or 32 measures"—is quite different from European classical music, where "themes are developed [while] in jazz they are toyed with and dismantled" (129).

The resulting sense of forward momentum is what Kouwenhoven sees as the primary aesthetic effect of jazz music, which he connects to an American ideology of progress. It is also an effect that is not contingent upon a hierarchical structure of beginning, middle, and end, but one that can continue for an indefinite length of time:

> Once the momentum is established, it can continue until—after an interval dictated by some such external factor as the conventional length of phonograph records or the endurance of dancers—it stops.... And as if to guard against any Aristotelian misconceptions about an end, it is likely to stop on an unresolved chord, so that harmonically, as well as rhythmically, everything is left up in the air. Even the various coda-like devices employed by jazz performers at dances ... are often harmonically unresolved. They are merely conventional ways of saying "we quit," not, like Beethoven's insistent

codas, ways of saying, "There now; that ties off all the loose ends; I'm going to stop now; done; finished; concluded; signed, sealed, delivered." (129)[14]

This formal structure as a linear series of choruses producing an impression of forward momentum rather than a hierarchical structure with a clear beginning, development, and resolution or ending has been compared by Kouwenhoven and others to the structure of a skyscraper, the chorus unit corresponding to the steel cage that forms the individual floors of the building. In each case, additional units can be added indefinitely, without a preordained stopping point. Similarly, the character of each chorus can be quite different, though its structure remains the same as all the others, just as in the skyscraper "something very different goes on in each floor" (Marsalis and O'Meally, 145). Another metaphor that is appropriate to the description of jazz structure is the train, which also consists of a linear series of any number of possible cars. Wynton Marsalis speaks of a train as sounding simultaneously both "like a lot of things" and "like one thing" (Marsalis and O'Meally, 152). A train as metaphor for jazz structure has the advantage of containing associations of rhythm and mobility: "Trains represent a certain type of freedom: they represent communication, and they represent the ability to get from one place to another with a group of people to see some other people. And also a train represents incantation and percussion; so you hear whoo-whoo, whoo-whoo, chug-a-chug-a, chug-a-chug-a, ca-junk, ca-junk, ca-junk" (Marsalis and O'Meally, 152). Both the image of the skyscraper and that of the train serve to capture a key element of jazz structure, which is the linear series of discrete units of indeterminate number that combine to produce an impression of forward or upward momentum.

This structure of discrete units strung together is a feature of jazz music that literature is also capable of employing for its own purposes. Texts that take jazz as a structural model have no difficulty imitating the chorus structure, as its linearity and composition out of several individual units are examples of means that the two media can share. Indeed, Kouwenhoven also pointed out that this kind of episodic structure is characteristic not only of serial forms like the comic strip and the soap opera, but also of the writings of the American authors Mark Twain and Walt Whitman. The feature most often criticized in *Huckleberry Finn*, for example, is its lack of closure. This is not a failing of the novel, however, but intrinsic to the kind of story being told, namely, one of a series of adventures: "The real structure of *Huck Finn* has nothing to do with the traditional form of the novel—with exposition, climax, and resolution. Its structure is like that of the great river itself—without beginning and without end. Its structural units, or 'cages,' are the episodes of which it is composed" (132). Though Kouwenhoven cites *Huckleberry*

Finn in order to illustrate the Americanness of this pattern, such an episodic structure is of course not restricted to American literature, but can be found in classical texts such as Voltaire's *Candide* and even further back, in Cervantes's *Don Quixote*. The genre or mode of the picaresque comprises a series of adventures of the (anti)hero, which are presented as a sequence of episodes rather than as a single plot building toward a climax. The traditional novel form, however, has moved away from this linear and open-ended form to instead strive toward an Aristotelian progression from an exposition through a development to a climax and a denouement. When contemporary jazz novels thus draw on this shared episodic capacity, they are striking to a reader, situated as they are within the context of the traditional novel's development. An irregular sequence of episodes that could theoretically be reordered at will—thus emphasizing their discreteness—upsets readers' expectations about the novel form, causing them to seek other explanations for the source of this technique. Given the novels' many other indications of the role of jazz music in their construction, the chorus structure of jazz becomes a logical parallel.

The Picaresque Blues Hero: Choruses in Albert Murray's Scooter Novels

Albert Murray, in explaining the jazz- or blues-like episodic structure of his novels, makes reference to the picaresque as the corresponding literary category:

> My narrative structure is not geared to a tightly knit plot. It is a picaresque story, more a matter of one thing following another than one thing leading to another. To me, the "and then and then and also and also and next after that" of a picaresque reflects a sensitivity consistent with contemporary knowledge of the universe. (Scherman, n.p.)

If one considers the use of the term "picaresque" as often used to describe episodic novels that relate a hero's string of adventures,[15] this literary mode would appear to form a parallel with the episodic chorus structure found in jazz music. There is, however, significant debate over what constitutes the picaresque, whether that be a narrowly defined genre, restricted to a handful of classic texts from the Spanish sixteenth and seventeenth centuries, or a broader concept of a mode or "ahistorical narrative 'deep structure'" (Wicks, 26) that may occur in a much wider range of texts. Regardless of the precise definition used, a few central features seem to find general agreement among critics: (1) the protagonist is a *picaro*, or a rogue-like antihero, generally living in a low or poor milieu, but always with the status of an outsider in society; (2) picaresque novels are nearly always narrated in the first person or comprise a fictional autobiography, which presupposes the accompanying temporal contrast between the narrating protagonist and the actions of his earlier, experiencing self; and (3) the plot structure is chronological and episodic, encompassing a wide range of settings.[16]

Murray would appear to be adopting a loose definition of the picaresque such as that given by Wellek and Warren in *Theory of Literature* (1948): "In the picaresque novel, the chronological sequence is all there is: this happened and then that. The adventures, each an incident, which might be an independent tale, are connected by the figure of the hero" (215; cited in Wicks, 29). Murray's comments on the picaresque in his novel cited above emphasize aspects of sequence and a lack of causality, yet his view of the picaresque story consists not only in its episodic structure, but also involves a hero who is resilient and creative in dealing with what life throws at him. In Murray's case, that hero is Scooter, who emerges from humble origins in "the briarpatch" (a motif first mentioned on page 3 of *Train Whistle Guitar*) and narrates his own story as a progression from one remembered adventure to another.

The most striking difference between Scooter and the traditional picaro, however, is his overwhelmingly positive characterization. Scooter may be creative and resilient, but he is no rogue or trickster, and indeed he has no need to be, as life rarely throws him any curve balls, to use a metaphor from baseball, which provides one of his early influences. Scooter proceeds in picaresque fashion from one adventure to the next, particularly in *Train Whistle Guitar*, and from one setting to the next, as exemplified by his travels with the band in *The Seven League Boots*—but encounters nothing but well-wishers along the way. His future success in every venture is expected from the outset, as his teacher Miss Lexine Metcalf proclaims with the oft-repeated phrase, "Who if not you, my splendid young man, who if not you?"[17]

Formal education plays a central role in Scooter's life, beginning with his school days in Miss Metcalf's classroom, college in the South, and after a musical interruption as a bassist in a popular jazz band, progressing to graduate study in literature in New York City and finally a teaching job at his former college. This suggests that Scooter's story is less a picaresque novel in the strict sense of the word than it is the more positively connoted *Bildungsroman*. Christoph Ehland pointed out that the picaresque had a considerable influence on the *Bildungsroman* (92). He distinguishes them primarily through the former's "fragmented spatial discourse," whereas the series of episodes and settings in the *Bildungsroman* proceed in a "controlled sequence . . . each a further step towards the harmonious and meaningful integration of the juvenile individual into society" (92). This is an apt description of Scooter's story, as his journey is indeed harmonious. Though the question of his purpose in life remains open, there is never any doubt that he will do something meaningful and successful with his talents. Each episode can stand alone in the sense of a picaresque adventure, whether those adventures be sexual encounters, experiments in music or literature, or travels around the United States or to France, yet each episode is also a learning experience that has repercussions in shaping Scooter's perspective on life.

Indeed, by the last novel, *The Magic Keys*, it becomes clear that the seemingly random twists of his life were in fact carefully orchestrated events. When Scooter meets up with Hortense Hightower after returning to his old college campus and beginning work on a memoir project, she explains to him that she had earmarked him to help write the memoir from the time they had first met—his stint in the band, freelancing in LA, and graduate study in New York all serving as necessary preparation for that task. Indeed, Scooter's various father figures and confidantes along the way are generally aware of a sense of purpose in his path that only becomes clear to him much later.

This sense of linear purpose and even of fate guiding and protecting Scooter along his charmed path would seem to be at odds with the perception of the novels as a series of isolated episodes or choruses. This tension between different concepts of time in the novel—a linear progression versus a repetitive or cyclical concept of time[18]—can be explained through the other intertextual references in the novels. Scooter's path is compared to a "storybook hero's quest" (*The Magic Keys*, 220). Fairytale imagery permeates all four novels, from the "spyglass tree" that is his college education, and the "seven league boots" of his travels, to the use of the term "magic keys"—"Some gold, some silver, some platinum. Or how about some sharp, some flat, some natural?" (220)—for the various experiences that open doors in his future. The fairy tale or allegorical mode is one that makes use of repetition, as in the schematic use of three wishes, three dresses, three nights, and the like.[19] At the same time, these repetitions also represent progress toward a happy end, as in Scooter's case.

The other main intertextual parallel to Scooter's "quest" is Homer's *Odyssey*, as a letter from his college roommate at the close of the last novel makes clear: "Nor should you ever be unmindful of any of those slapdash—slapstick, nay, downright farcical escapades and labyrinthine misadventures old ever so jam-riff-clever Odysseus himself had to maneuver his way out of and back on course to and through the gateway to the remembered hometown boy blue bliss with the one for whom he had forsaken all others not only in Ithaca but everywhere else" (*The Magic Keys*, 242). Like Odysseus, Scooter travels around to many places and has many adventures (including a number of sexual encounters) before marrying his college sweetheart and returning to Alabama. The *Odyssey* could perhaps be considered picaresque avant la lettre, as indeed it does contain the elements of a trickster hero and a series of discrete adventures with variation in space as well as time. The Scooter novels clearly partake of this kind of the picaresque, with the important innovation of likening the episodic structure to the repeated choruses of jazz music. This dual approach of using structures taken from both jazz and classical literary paradigms, on the one hand, corresponds to the hybridity characteristic of both jazz and the jazz novel in particular, but also of intertextuality in general. On the other hand, it is also an example of the shared means of the two media of music and literature, which both make intertextual references to predecessors and are both able to structure their temporal progressions as a series of episodic units. Murray's texts are thus able to imitate the chorus structure of a jazz piece by foregrounding the elements of repetition and episodic form that are common to both media.

Fragmentation and Multiple Voices: Choruses in *Don't the Moon Look Lonesome*, *Coming Through Slaughter*, and *Jazz*

The structural divisions of *Don't the Moon Look Lonesome* occur on several levels. On the one hand, the novel consists of two main sections, *Part One: The You and Me That Ought to Be* and *Part Two: Back in the Apple*. Each contains twelve chapters, which may be a reference to the traditional twelve-bar blues form. Indeed, some chapters are left unnumbered or subdivided in such a way as to retain the overall number of twelve chapters per section: there is a "Prelude" before part 1 begins, part 1 contains both a chapter 11 and an "11A," and there is an unnumbered "Interlude" between chapters 23 and 24 in part 2. Additionally, the novel is structured by a division between the time of the narration and the time of remembered events, as in Murray's novels. Here, the free indirect discourse focusing on Carla's perspective loosely links the various passages set in the past and the present. The main narrative progression covers a period of several weeks, in which she first accompanies her boyfriend Maxwell to Texas to meet his parents and then returns to New York alone, as they struggle through problems in their relationship largely related to a clash of cultures between black and white. The bulk of the novel, however, takes place outside of this time period and consists of Carla's memories of her childhood, past relationships, and many conversations with friends.

The "present" of the novel and the events contained therein serve primarily as a jumping-off point for longer reminiscences and reveries, frequently set off by the use of italics, as when Carla lies awake brooding over conversations with Maxwell's parents and the many memories they trigger. The italicized passages of her memories in chapter 6 are considerably longer than those printed in normal typeface, sometimes just three sentences long, brief "interlude[s] between memories" (104). Elsewhere, the relative length of the main sections and italicized passages is similar or the proportions are reversed.

What is essential here is that the temporal stream of the novel is regularly interrupted by passages that occur at a different point in time and are interspersed seemingly at random. If these scenes can be combined without any temporal connection, they could just as easily be reordered, which emphasizes their discreteness. This is one means of imitating jazz's use of the chorus form, since a series of disconnected memories are strung along one after another, without a necessary order or a clear limit to their number.

A comparison with the Scooter novels discussed above shows that both make use of memories as interruptions of the narrative progression. This is a common device in jazz novels, also found in Xam Wilson Cartiér's *Be-Bop, Re-Bop* and *Muse-Echo Blues*,[20] as well as in Paule Marshall's *The Fisher King*. Alan Rice has referred to this kind of flashback as "as a continual cutting back to an earlier event as the musician returns intermittently to an old theme" ("Jazzing It Up a Storm," 430).[21] This interpretation has been criticized by Alan Munton for its lack of musical accuracy. He argues that "the 'cut' is a term unknown to jazz, but Snead's authority is such that Rice and others write as if it were an actual feature of the music" (245). While Snead's description of the "cut" can be usefully applied to the interruptions of narrative by memories, Munton is correct in pointing out that this flashback technique is not directly taken from jazz music. I argue instead that these interruptions of the narrative are significant as a means of undermining expectations of a continuous and causal progression of events. Of course, this can not be traced exclusively to a musical model, but combined with other factors this fragmentation in these novels does evoke jazz's use of choruses as discrete units connected primarily by their linear order rather than by an overarching Aristotelian pattern.

This principle of fragmentation is even more apparent in *Coming Through Slaughter*, which makes use of very marked breaks between narrative passages. Rather than divide the sections up into clearly delimited chapters, as in *Don't the Moon Look Lonesome*, Ondaatje's novel consists of three numbered sections, each of which contain pieces of narrative told from different perspectives, as well as interviews, lists of songs or bands, etc. These fragments are strung together in a disjointed order— "spread . . . out like garbage" (134)—in a manner that challenges expectations of causality and continuity.

The different bits of text are not only heterogeneous in terms of genre, but are also characterized by a variety of perspectives. Interviews present the first-person point of view of several band members and Bolden's friends, as well as that of staff from the mental hospital. Frequent use of dialogue allows further voices to be heard, and Bolden himself narrates an increasing portion of the second and third sections. The interviews can be compared to short solos by different voices, for the length of a break in early jazz, whereas the passages narrated in Bolden's voice correspond to the soloists who gradually took whole choruses as solos. The increasing length of narrative solos, especially by a famed jazz innovator—although the historical record does not substantiate Ondaatje's portrait of Bolden as a true soloist—thus corresponds to a historical development from the "multi-linearity" of early jazz to an emphasis on the soloist after 1920 (Schuller, 57–58). That Ondaatje anticipates this development in a novel set largely in 1907 is yet another example of his stated practice of modifying history "to suit the truth of fiction" (*Coming Through Slaughter*, 157).

Like *Coming Through Slaughter*, Toni Morrison's *Jazz* makes use of different voices to demarcate the borders between some of its chorus-like segments. The narrator takes the first few choruses herself[22] before handing the solo over to Violet. This is a shorter solo within the chapter, such that it can best be seen as an improvisation on the break.[23] Later solos by Joe, Dorcas, and Felice cover a longer period of time and alternate with the narrator to fill an entire chorus. This alternation of shorter solos by different voices or instruments is reminiscent of the practice in some jazz music of "trading fours." Soloists take turns playing for four bars each, in an atmosphere that may range from playful and encouraging to fiercely competitive. In *Jazz*, this is particularly pronounced in the seventh and eighth chapters. In the former, Joe's voice (set off by quotation marks) alternates with the narrator's. The narrator in this section talks about Joe's search for his mother, the mysterious figure called Wild, whom Joe tracks as if she were indeed a wild animal. Juxtaposed with this are Joe's comments on his search for Dorcas, whom he also tracks around the City. Dorcas's solos in the eighth chapter form another example. Here, the narrator's view of the party and Dorcas's relationship with Joe contrasts sharply with Dorcas's own description of it. The narrator looks for larger themes—war, romance—while Dorcas tells a story that is specific and individualized. In both cases, the two voices deal with the same topic, the search for a woman, on the one hand, and the romantic triangle of Joe-Dorcas-Acton on the other, though the specific realizations of their solos are quite different. This is very similar to the way a soloist will perform a set of variations on the given melody, as discussed in greater detail in chapter 4.

Saying that the units that form the jazz piece or the jazz novel are discrete segments of a number that need not be predetermined does not mean that there is no connection between the choruses or chapters, or that they could be cut up and reassembled in any other order. The order of the chapters in *Jazz* is by no means arbitrary (nor is that the case in the other novel considered), as the enjambement-like transitions between the chapters make clear. Each chapter ends with a pithy sentence from which a key word is taken as the starting point for the next chapter. In some cases the beginning of the chapter will extend the scene of the previous one temporally, as in the transition from the first to the second chapter. The first chapter ends by describing Violet's pet canaries, "One of whom answers back, 'I love you'" (24). The second chapter then responds, saying, "Or used to" (27). Other chapters pick out a single word that will be the jumping-off point for a discussion that goes in a different direction altogether. This is particularly pronounced when the voice of a character ends one chapter and the narrator begins the next, using a word from the character's solo. For example, Joe ends his solo by talking about how he reinvented himself seven times, concluding, "and let me tell you, baby, in those days it was more than a state of mind" (135). The narrator then seizes on the phrase "state of mind," but applies it to a completely different topic, her own attempt to read her characters and tell their stories: "Risky, I'd say, trying to figure out anybody's state of mind. But worth the trouble if you're like me—curious, inventive and well-informed" (137).

Similarly, a jazz musician may quote phrases from a solo that has gone before, picking up elements from it to vary and expand on. Both a series of choruses and a novel made up of individual chapters are linear progressions, and it is precisely this repetition with a difference that creates the sense of forward momentum that Kouwenhoven identified as central to the skyscraper-like aesthetic found in jazz.

The Novel as Greatest-Hits Album: Jack Fuller's *The Best of Jackson Payne*

In addition to structuring a novel around the form of an individual jazz piece, using an episodic structure to imitate jazz's use of choruses strung one after the other, novels may also choose the larger form of the jazz recording as a model. In such cases, units of the novel, such as chapters, correspond to individual songs, whereas the novel as a whole is likened to an entire album.[24]

A prime example of the novel as "greatest-hits" album is Jack Fuller's *The Best of Jackson Payne*. The title of the novel makes use of a common formulation from jazz and pop music albums, which frequently start with the phrase "the (very) best of," followed by the name of the artist. The twelve chapter titles also contribute to the overall reading of the novel as a greatest-hits album, as all but one are taken from the names of tunes Payne plays. Some are familiar standards, such as "Taps" (chapter 1 and chapter 12), "That's Why the Lady Is a Tramp" (chapter 5, based on the standard "The Lady Is a Tramp," though the full title of the chapter is not mentioned as a song in its own right) and "My Funny Valentine" (chapter 6).

Others are fictional songs or albums with no referent outside of the novel:[25] "Stormin' at the Point" (chapter 2), "Off the Bar" (chapter 4), "The Standard Form of the American Popular Song" (chapter 7), "Stuck in a Groove" (chapter 8), "The Kensington Sessions" (chapter 9; this is in fact one of Payne's albums, not a song), "Celestial Faith" (chapter 10; this, too, is an album), "Sweet Thing" (chapter 11). Though they refer to songs only within the novel, lacking a referent in the outside world, their referents within the novel are multiple. In addition to being the titles of songs or albums Payne wrote and recorded, they also refer to key events in his life or, in one case, to a person ("Sweet Thing" is the nickname Payne and Vera use for their daughter, Michelle). For example, "Stormin' at the Point" refers to the place on the coast where Payne practiced his saxophone alone for hours. Though "Off the Bar" was taken by critics "to be a musical wordplay referring to its odd syncopation" (84), it also marks a turning point when Payne had progressed musically to the point where he no longer would submit himself to the ritual for a horn player to "get up on the bar and wag his ass" (74). Payne saw walking the bar as a kind of prostitution of his art, and getting "off the bar" was an assertion of his musical virtue.

"The Shell Casing" is the only chapter title that is not explicitly taken from one of Payne's songs. Like the other titles, it evokes a significant event in his life and has overtones of word play. The phrase "the shell casing" is an allusion to the bit of metal Payne had clenched in his teeth when he became shell-shocked in the Korean War, and thus conjures up the atmosphere surrounding not only his injury but also his fear at the time that he might have gone deaf in the blast. One might speculate that this, too, is the title of a song Payne composed at some point, one that is simply not mentioned explicitly in the novel. However, Quinlan suggests that this is not the case, claiming that "many of Payne's compositions drew their titles from important experiences in his life, but none referred to the war" (51). It is thus appropriate that the one chapter title not taken from one of Payne's recordings is used for events in his life that he did not refer to in his music.

The "best of" formula used in the novel's title implies that the contents will be the highlights of an illustrious career in music, that there will be no attempt at completeness, but instead at selecting the "best" in a retrospective manner. This is particularly apt for Fuller's novel, which prominently features the fictional biography of the jazz tenor saxophonist Jackson Payne. Written by the musicologist Charles Quinlan (who is also fictional), the biography explores the connection between art and life, as he explicitly seeks insights into the man's life through his music and vice versa:

> Among his colleagues, of course, there was a raging debate over whether the music and the life had anything to say about one another. But by listening to Payne play, Quinlan felt sure he was able to divine things about the man that simply could not otherwise be known, because jazz gave the listener privileged and immediate

access to the inner state of the man playing it.[26] Perhaps the truths thus revealed did not meet the standards of scholarly proof. But hearing the scratchy, raw-edged recording, he pushed beyond the epistemological borders of the academic form, opened himself to leaps of improvisation, turned his own work into jazz. (5–6)

As this passage suggests and the progress of his research and writing further demonstrate, Quinlan's attempt to write the story of Payne's life is a parallel to writing music. The biography that can only elucidate the highlights or most significant moments in Payne's life—necessarily fragmentary because of the passage of time and unreliability or unavailability of witnesses—, conducted retrospectively, is like the reissuing of Payne's music in a selective collection. Indeed, a comment presumably made by Quinlan's publisher or a colleague makes it clear that Quinlan's work can be seen as a kind of "greatest-hits" album: "Are you looking for a title? I'd call it 'The Best of Jackson Payne'" (320).[27]

Because this suggested title for the biography is identical with that of the novel as a whole, questions of metafiction immediately arise. The novel as a whole imitates the form of the greatest-hits album with nearly all the chapter titles taken from Payne's songs, the biography Quinlan is writing is a case of life being used to explain music, and what is more, the novel and the biography would appear to be the same thing. This suggests that Quinlan's musical biography of Jackson Payne is highly unusual in form, in which he allows fragments of interviews, writing on music theory, conversations with his publisher and colleagues, and even his own story of his challenges and frustrations with his work and other personal issues to mingle with his narrative about Payne's life. Such interruptions emphasize the constructed nature of such a biography and Quinlan's role in interpreting and shaping Payne's life. This approach is akin to a jazz musician's use of a standard tune as a starting point for his own improvisation. The biographer takes his subject's story as the opportunity or jumping-off point to tell his own story, and Payne's life becomes the "call" to which Quinlan's writing "responds."

Call-and-Response Patterns

Call and response: The performance of musical phrases or longer passages in alternation by different voices or distinct groups, used in opposition in such a way as to suggest that they answer one another; it may involve spatial separation of the groups, and contrasts of volume, pitch, timbre, etc. The term (the equivalent of which in more formal analytical language is "antiphony") originates in descriptions of the singing of African-American work-songs, in which a leader and a chorus respectively sang verse and refrain or successive phrases in alternation. In jazz it is used for exchanges between instrumentalists, two sections of a big band, and even a singer and his own instrumental accompaniment. (*The New Grove Dictionary of Jazz*, vol. 1, entry for "Call and response," 373)

Call and response, also known as antiphony, is another central feature of jazz and related musical traditions. As a form of interplay between soloist and ensemble, between two soloists or sections of a band, or even between the band and its audience, this pattern contributes a conversational or dialogic element to jazz. The prominence of the call-and-response format in jazz has been traced to roots in African musical practice, where the interaction between a solo cantor and a chorus takes this form, or where even solo performance generally involves an antiphonal relationship between a verse and a refrain (Schuller, 27).

In early New Orleans jazz the response of the ensemble was often stylized in the form of a riff (Schuller, 28). A riff is frequently the collective response to a soloist's performance, echoing the interjected formulaic responses of a Baptist congregation to a sermon by a dynamic preacher. Call and response is thus not restricted to narrowly musical contexts, but is also found in a religious setting with the congregation answering the preacher (Schuller, 375).[28] In contrast to responsorial practice in Catholic church services, in which a church choir or assembled congregation waits for the cantor to complete his phrase before the set response is added, in African and African American contexts there need not be a temporal division between the call and the response (*Jazz-Lexikon*, 186). That is, the response may begin before the call has ended and vice versa, leading to overlapping of voices. Another main difference between these two types of antiphony is the relative spontaneity of call and response in both African American church services and in jazz music. While the responses are not entirely spontaneous but must accord with conventions, there is more room for improvisation in African American responses than in the invariable answers of the congregation to the cantor in a Catholic church. Albert Murray acknowledges the element of spontaneity even as he asserts the stylized nature of call and response in *Stomping the Blues*:

> Nothing is likely to seem more spontaneous than call-and-response passages, especially in live performances, where they almost always seem to grow directly out of the excitement of the moment, as if the musicians were possessed by some secular equivalent of the Holy Ghost. But as is no less the practice in the Sunday Morning Service, the responses are not only stylized (and stylized in terms of a specific idiom, to boot), but are almost always led by those who have a special competence in such devices. After all, no matter how deeply moved a musician may be, . . . he must always play notes that fulfill

the requirements of the context, a feat which presupposes far more skill and taste than raw emotion. (98)

The interaction of call and response clearly relies to a large extent on the tension between freedom and constraint—the ability to be spontaneous within a more or less rigidly defined framework of appropriate responses, as will be argued in chapter 4.

The link between call and response and dialogue has been commented on both in reference to jazz music and to the novels based on it. Mark Osteen points out several levels of dialogue in the context of improvisation: between musicians, a musician with himself (hearing what he plays and reacting to it as he goes), with the "text" or the piece he is improvising on, with previous improvisations (his own and by other players), as well as with the audience (12–13). Osteen is hardly alone in seeing dialogue in jazz performance, as indeed the metaphor of a conversation is one of the most widespread ways of talking about jazz. Jazz is "saying something," as Ingrid Monson puts it in her book on jazz improvisation, and musicians frequently refer to their performances as a conversation.[29] Describing the jazz song or jam session as a conversation is of course just another metaphor for the interaction of call and response.

Just as the call-and-response pattern can be found at various levels of the jazz performance—as a dialogue between two musicians or two sections of a band, between a soloist and an ensemble, between the band and its audience, and even between a band and its predecessors—antiphonal patterns are important at many levels of the jazz novel. Some of the most common uses of call and response are the depiction of call-and-response situations on the level of plot, especially sermons; the prevalence of direct speech, often in the form of dialogue; the alternation between different narrators; sections of text that contrast with one another, as in an alternation between different time frames of the novel such as the present day of the plot and a remembered past;[30] and the explicit involvement of the reader by the narrator or text. This section first considers the prominent role given to antiphonal sermons in the plot of *Don't the Moon Look Lonesome* and *The Best of Jackson Payne* before proceeding to the structural use of call and response in dialogue and larger antiphonal sections of the texts. The topic of the text's "call" and the reader's "response" is briefly touched on here and developed further in chapter 4 on the performance situation in jazz novels.

Sermons in *The Best of Jackson Payne* and *Don't the Moon Look Lonesome*

As so often with the imitation of musical forms, the thematization of call-and-response patterns helps to increase the reader's awareness of the musical parallel so that he or she may better recognize it on the structural level of the text. In *The Best of Jackson Payne* and *Don't the Moon Look Lonesome* this thematization occurs in the form of embedded sermons that demonstrate the call-and-response pattern in a church context.[31] In Crouch's novel, the church service that Carla attends with Maxwell's family extends over the majority of the longest chapter in the novel. Rather than merely describe the scene in the church or Carla's impressions of it, the novel uses thirteen headings with italicized explanations of what is to come in each section of the service. This commentary would appear to come from "the little program printed on a single sheet of folded blue paper that had the sign of the cross drawn at the top and a barely skilled drawing of roses with exposed thorns on the border" (182), which Carla reads as each portion begins. The antiphonal nature of the church ritual is made explicit with reference to the service as "the dialogue with the evidence of things unseen" (182).

The church service contains much that is musical, such as the humming of the deacons in the initial prayer, a humming that "contained the sound of invitation, the very same sound that Carla loved in jazz music" (183). This singing spreads to the rest of the congregation, including Carla herself, and later during the section "Praise and Worship" they all sing "songs that no one called," that is, that are spontaneously begun by different members of the group,

> in some kind of unpredictable antiphony ... boomeranging throughout the congregation, picking up one voice here, another there, leads and backgrounds rising into the air. Then, while one theme was being sung, someone would suddenly begin another song, which would create a round as it edged up into position and took over ... until some giant voice from somewhere in the church burst into yet another tune, demanding another modulation, other voices to reinforce the lead, another backup of chorus work that immediately broke into to parts, one stating, another answering, both underlining the direction. (187)

After this improvised and antiphonal musical interlude, the assistant pastor leads the congregation into a more meditative type of song, before the singing is replaced by announcements. The performance by the choir is another musical high point, and their singing of "Amazing Grace" (which is also the title of the whole chapter) accompanies the section "Offering" as well. Finally, the "Benediction" is also sung, rather than spoken, concluding the ritual (211).

In addition to all this actual music that occurs as part of the church service, there are also numerous examples of antiphonal patterns in the structure of this scene. This call and response in a verbal context provides a parallel to the call and response of jazz music. In the section labeled

"Litany" the assistant pastor reads from Hebrews 1:10 to 1:12 and the congregation repeats each phrase after him. In the section "Assistant Pastor" the speaker's announcements take the form of a conversation and elicit reactions from the congregation, who "responded with the emotion of students who had been told school would end a month early" with a good deal of "oohing and aahing" (188).

The sections that are most explicitly antiphonal are "Ministering," when the "*Pastor begins to talk about things that are on his mind*" (193, italics original), and the sermon itself. During the "ministering" the congregation interjects statements of agreement as the pastor speaks:

> "We see everywhere around us a sense of loss. The air is full of grief. Melancholy seeps from the leaves of the trees. There is sadness inside the water. Weevils of ill will walk through the food. Memory is rotting in the streets and everywhere around us. Men have forgotten how to be men—"
> "They sure have!"
> "Now ain't that the truth!"
> "—and women have forgotten how to be women—"
> "Trouble in the world, trouble in the world"
> "—and *both* have forgotten how to do the many things you *have* to do if you want to raise children up to be something other than savages."
> "Amen to that." (193; italics original)

In the sermon, the pastor actively encourages the congregation to respond, asking, "Does anybody out there hear that? Does any one of you hear what I'm saying up here on this clear Sunday in the house of the Lord?" (204). This elicits a clearly recognizable call and response between pastor and congregation:

> "Oh, yes, oh yes."
> "I hope so up here. But *you* better hope so."
> "You better *hope*!"
> "I said it and I mean it: you got to get ready."
> "Get ready now!"
> "You got to get *ready*."
> "Better!"
> "I'm talking about *ready*!"
> "Yes!"
> "Here it comes."
> "Bring it on down."
> "There was a king once upon a time, praise the Lord."
> "Amen."
> "This king, oh, my Lord."
> "Lord, Lord, Lord."

"He was known. Yes, he was known. He was known as Ethelred. He was known as Ethelred the Unready."
"Make it plain."
"Listen to that. I said, *'Ethelred'* I said, *'Un*ready.'"
"Tell it!"
"That's what I said: I said, *'Unready.'*"
"Mmmmmmmm." (204–5; italics original)

The pastor's style of speech addresses the congregation directly, involving them in a conversation about the subject of his sermon. They contribute to the unfolding of his message by picking up elements of the pastor's call, responding through repetition and expressions of agreement with what he has said. The formulaic nature of these responses is evident, with set phrases such as "Bring it on down," "Amen," "Make it plain," and "Tell it." In other cases, the pastor feeds the congregation key words that encourage a set response, such as his use of "oh, my Lord," and his own repetition in order to create emphasis and build up suspense. James A. Snead has called a preacher's interruptions of himself of this kind a "'social' beat," not "at all . . . denotative or imperative but purely sensual and rhythmic" (72).

This type of repetition is closely associated with a musical model, and is comparable to the music that is central to the context of the church service, as shown above. The repeated word or phrase is taken out of its context in a sentence, separating the signifier from its signified and allowing the word to approach the status of a musical phrase in its self-referentiality.[32]

The importance of the church service as a model for call and response in *Don't the Moon Look Lonesome* is made clear both in the length of its presentation and its position very close to the center of the novel. It comprises a turning point in Carla's and Maxwell's relationship, as they briefly grow closer together before separating on their return to New York. The call-and-response patterns represented here in such detail are also echoed throughout the rest of the novel, both through the widespread use of dialogue and conversations and the alternation between the "call" of memory and Carla's "response" in the present. Furthermore, the text's use of terms like dialogue, antiphony, and response serves to emphasize the role of antiphony throughout, as for example in a section of chapter 12 entitled "Blues treatise in dialogue tempo." This section of a remembered conversation about the blues is introduced with a characterization of the blues as "the religious power of the spirituals given secular form" (276). This linking of religion and spirituals with the blues encourages a reading both of the church scene as thoroughly permeated by music and of the blues in the rest of the novel as conditioned by a cultural environment that grew out of the black church and its rhetorical strategies. The use of these rhetorical strategies thus contributes to the jazzing of the novel as a whole, while this specific example also illustrates the way form and content unite to create textual meaning.

A similar connection between the church's rhetoric and blues or jazz music is made in *The Best of Jackson Payne*. There, the sermon that takes on central importance is entitled "The Song of Satan." Payne's local pastor, Reverend Corn, gives a sermon that builds on the musical scale to present a duality of the good and evil present in all things. Each note of the scale stands for both positive and negative images:

> There are twelve tones in the good Lord's scale, brothers and sisters.
> Twelve apostles to show the way.
> *Hallelujah.*
> But before you sing it, there's something you got to know.
> *Tell us, brother.*
> Satan's scale is exactly the same.
> *Save us.*
> *Have mercy.*
> *Amen.*
> Close your ears to the Devil's melody, my friends. And open your hearts to the Lord.
> *Tell us how.*
> The first note of the scale is C, the Christ child come down to redeem us from our sin.
> *Hallelujah.*
> But C is also the cross where they nailed Him. There has never been an evil greater than C.
> *Save us, brother.*
> And next to it is D, which can be delightful, for it is the dawn of eternal life.
> *Hallelujah.*
> But it is also damnation, waiting with the Devil's hundred fires.
> *Lord, have mercy.*
> And E is everlasting peace, an eternity of glory in the good Lord's loving eye.
> *Amen.* (24; italics original)

More stylized and less diverse in their responses than in *Don't the Moon Look Lonesome*, the congregation here varies just a few phrases—most often "*Amen,*" "*Save us,*" "*Have Mercy,*" and "*Hallelujah*"—in responding to the preacher's calls. This is partly because the sermon here presented is a transcript of a radio broadcast and represents a sermon that was given annually, thus possessing more the character of ritual than of novelty or spontaneous response.

In addition to explicitly dealing with music on the level of content, this sermon is distinctive in its use of a musical structural model, the twelve-tone scale. It is reminiscent of romantic concepts of the different tones of the scale as standing for different moods or emotions (see Haimberger, 36–41). In Reverend Corn's sermon, however, the character of each note is due to the words that begin with that letter rather than a sense of atmosphere created by the key itself. The scale forms a framework for metaphor, while the content assigned to each key or note is not directly connected to a musical model.

The influence of this sermon on Jackson Payne is evident in his use of the phrase "No Greater Evil Than C" as the title of a song he wrote much later. Fraught with associations, this title is variously interpreted by the biographer Quinlan, by other musical critics, and by Jackson Payne himself—though his own interpretation can only be deduced from contextual clues. While the "C" of the original sermon represents both Christ and the cross, critics interpreted it in the title of Payne's song as standing for cocaine, "reinforcing the prevailing myth of life corrupting music" (27). Quinlan uses the reference to the original sermon and its message of the proximity of good and evil to deduce that "the music was not only the victim of corruption but also its means" (27). Additionally, there is a musical meaning for "C" as a note in a scale, which in the context of this song is a major second away from the tonic of B-flat, making C a source of dissonance in the song. Another referent for "C" that the reader is able to infer soon after the text of the sermon appears is Reverend Corn, the preacher. He was Payne's first music teacher; he taught Payne to read music, but also gave him gifts of jazz records in return for sexual favors. The context of these incidents shows that jazz was associated with sinful pleasures early on for Payne, so that the music would indeed seem to contain both divine and evil elements.

The element of call and response in this sermon is emphasized by a passage of Quinlan's writing or lecturing on music theory that comes soon after the sermon:

> The first important structural principle of jazz is call and response. One can hear it in many different manifestations. The most obvious is when players "trade fours," that is, alternate four measure solos, each responding to the statement made by the previous player.
>
> Jazz drew this pattern from many sources. The gospel tradition, of course. But field recordings of prison work gangs, drill sergeants marching their troops, and auctioneers selling horseflesh all show the structure in its most rudimentary form. It is not too much to imagine that when a slave was traded, it was to the voice of call and response. (26)

This passage forms a clear link between the preceding sermon—in the gospel tradition—and the jazz that pervades the rest of the book. This definition of call and response is also significant in its introduction of the term "trading fours," which also recurs later in the novel. Quinlan, finding himself in uncharted territory in his new romantic relationship with Lasheen, dreams that "people were trading fours about [his] intentions" (229). As usual in this novel, the speakers are not explicitly indicated but can only be deduced by the style of their speech and subtle contextual clues. Here, the four soloists in the chase[33] seem to be Payne's fellow musicians Junior Leonard, Showon Tucker, and Red Sloan, concluding with Reverend Corn. All comment on Quinlan's desire for Lasheen, though each in his own distinctive idiom. After a longer passage of conversation between Quinlan and Lasheen, the call and response between musicians in Quinlan's mind seems to intensify, as they go down to trading just two measures. In this case, there are only three voices, presumably Quinlan's ex-wife, an unidentified black speaker, and finally Red Sloan again, recognizable by his tendency to speak in rhyme.[34] In a cutting contest or chase, musicians take solos of progressively shorter length, from whole choruses to half choruses, four measures and even two measures. The increase in intensity as the solos change more and more rapidly was a spectacle that drew in audiences and was a popular marketing tool for certain bands. Because Quinlan spends so much of his time thinking about jazz, his dreams—like his writing of Payne's biography—are modeled on jazz patterns like this one.

Further examples of call and response on the level of content[35] can be found in the inclusion of interviews, which add an element of drama to the novels by allowing characters to speak directly with an interviewer, whether that is a fellow character as in *The Best of Jackson Payne* or an extratextual jazz historian as in *Coming Through Slaughter*. Another example is a stylized schoolroom exchange between teacher and pupils in *Train Whistle Guitar*:

> *Good solo teacher talk morning dear children.*
> *Good unison-pupil response-chant morning dear teacher.*
>
> (52; italics original)

The interaction between soloist and unison ensemble response is made clear, while the lack of syntax—the phrases identifying the functions "*solo teacher talk*" and "*unison-pupil response-chant*" are simply inserted in the verbless greeting "*good morning*"—strips any specific content from the phrases and exposes their ritual significance as an example of the call-and-response pattern. Jazz novels' frequent reference to such dialogic patterns and their roots in various cultural contexts—whether in church, school, or conversations more generally—increases the reader's awareness of antiphony throughout the novels on a structural level as well, as indeed call-and-response patterns are visible in the frequent use of dramatized dialogue throughout the jazz novels.

Dialogue and Multiple Voices

Just as the discourse on jazz sees elements of dialogue in the music, discussions of jazz in literature have been quick to note the connection between call-and-response patterns shared with music and the use of dialogue in the novel. Gayl Jones, for example, notes that "in the literary text both dialogue and plot structure may demonstrate this call-and-response pattern: one scene may serve as a commentary on a previous scene while a later scene becomes a commentary or response to that one" (197). In the following discussion I pick up both these types of call and response, examining first some examples of the importance of dialogue and the related phenomenon of multiple voices in the narrative. I then conclude with a brief look at the call-and-response relationship between text and reader.

Direct speech or dialogue between characters is extremely widespread in novels based on jazz. Often this speech is made even more direct by the omission of introductory material such as "he said," or even of quotation marks. The many lengthy conversations rendered verbatim in Carla's reminiscing in *Don't the Moon Look Lonesome* generally do not indicate speakers explicitly, but do use quotation marks. *The Best of Jackson Payne* does use quotation marks and descriptive information to indicate speakers during passages conducted in third-person narration, but sections spoken by different characters in the first person are not labeled in any way other than contextual clues or style of speech.

In *Train Whistle Guitar* and the following Scooter novels quotation marks are not used, whereas speakers are occasionally marked explicitly, as for example in this dialogue between Scooter and his friend Little Buddy Marshall while playing hooky along Chickasabogue Creek:

> Talking about Chickasaw, Little Buddy said and looked at me, and I pulled my cap all the way down square and looked straight ahead and walked rocking dicty with my shoulders rounded and my arms dangling as if I were moving along the aisle of a church and a train coach at the same time.
> Oh will there be one, I said looking neither to the right nor the left.
> Stand up, Little Buddy said, with his cap square too, Step down.
> And give me your hand for Chickasaw Bend, Alabama, I said and held my arms out palms up and then let them fall.
> Chickasaw Bend, Mobile County, Aladambama United Tits of a Milk Cow, one time, Little Buddy said.
> Been long hearing tell of it.
> And ain't but the one.
> Oh but will there be one?
> Oh stand up step up step down.
> Oh whosoever will.

Let him come and give me your hand.
And give God your heart, brother.
One for Chickasaw.
I thank you, praise be, I thank you.
Two for Chickasaw Bend.
Amen Amen Amen Amen. (*Train Whistle Guitar*, 38–39)

Here, the speakers are initially indicated by phrases like "Little Buddy said" and "I said," but these are not repeated with each utterance, instead giving way to a series of comments that are divorced from contextual information. There is an impression of simultaneity, as it is no longer clear who says each line, such that they could also be overlapping.

This passage is distinctive in its use of at least two different models of call and response, both that of a train porter calling out the station— "Chickasaw, Chickasaw, he said, calling it out like the L & N porter we liked best in those days" (38)—and the rhetoric of a preacher in church. Several of the individual utterances are ambiguous, fitting in with both of these contexts, especially lines like "Oh will there be one" (39), which can refer to either a passenger buying a ticket or a heathen being converted, as the rest of the dialogue makes clear. A further referent in this call-and-response passage is that of the "Pledge of Allegiance" recited in school, mentioned just before this passage. Scooter, "schoolboy that [he] already also was even then" (38), is aware of being "call[ed]" at just that very moment by his teacher Miss Lexine Metcalf, who will be surprised when he fails to respond. The passage thus reflects on some of the sources of the call-and-response pattern and embeds them in a scene of antiphonal direct dialogue.[36]

This passage is also striking in its dramatization of the practice of Signifyin(g), most famously theorized by Henry Louis Gates, Jr.[37] Primarily an African American verbal practice in which participants demonstrate linguistic virtuosity in subverting statements made by others, Signifyin(g) includes various types such as parody, formal revision, but also homage (see e.g. Gates, xvii). Here, the boys' "performative interaction" (Borshuk, 177) is in part a parody of the form of a church sermon, in part a homage to the train porters they admire.[38] In also signifying on the practice of attending school—"We got your goddamn school right here" (39)—Scooter finds himself in a somewhat ambivalent position, caught between Little Buddy Marshall's rejection of school and his own proclivity for school learning, reinforced by the praise and expectations of Miss Tee, his teacher Miss Lexine Metcalf, Sawmill Turner (who promised to "stake [him] to all the ink and paper [he] needed as long as [he] stayed in school," 74), and many others. Signifyin(g) on conventions thus also serves as a means for Scooter to work through ideas about what is expected of him and to assert his individual power to choose his own path.[39]

In *Jazz* the thematization of dialogue on the level of content prepares the way for antiphonal interaction between the narrator and other characters. For example, Dirk Ludigkeit (180) points out the call-and-response aspects of Violet's conversations with her hairdressing customers, in which she responds to their "stream of confidences" with "'Ha mercy' at appropriate breaks" (*Jazz*, 16). An example of this kind of antiphony on a larger scale is the interaction between the narrator and other characters who take turns telling their own version of the story. It is most apparent where the voices alternate in short succession:

> The narrator juxtaposes Joe's voice in alternating paragraphs with the story of Joe's search for his mother. The practice is again strongly reminiscent of call-and-response patterns, this time between a soloist and a band, or even between two soloists in a "cutting contest": a soloist responds to, complements or contests the band's or another musician's statement, adding his own personal voice and interpretation to the performance. (Ludigkeit, 178)

As mentioned above in the context of *The Best of Jackson Payne*, one of the most distinctive forms of call and response can be seen in a chase, when musicians trade fours. This is an apt description of the changing narrative voices in this section of *Jazz*. On a larger scale, the changing narrative perspectives in the novel—from the main narrator to Joe, Violet, Dorcas, and Felice—also allow for a call-and-response interaction between the various voices. Their narrations do not exist in a vacuum, but elicit responses from one another, most notably when the main narrator admits to having "misread" her characters and being surprised by what they say and do. This kind of call and response on the level of multivocal narration can best be described as an alternation between soloists who take turns taking solos, as discussed in greater detail in chapter 4.

Like that of other jazz novelists, Morrison's use of call and response partakes of what Eckstein has called "the dialogic nature of a jazzthetic narrative scope, in which each solo call demands a response" (280). That response may come from another narrator-soloist, but it may also be from the reader, who is addressed by the text and encouraged to participate actively in the construction of its meaning. Sylvia Mayer points out the relevance of Wolfgang Iser's reader-response theory for any interpretation of Morrison's work. Morrison's goal of having "the reader work with the author in the construction of the book"[40] is merely an explicit statement of Iser's location of the work between text and reader (see *The Act of Reading*, 21). Mayer connects this statement of reader-response theory back to a jazz context, arguing that the literary work comes into being when the act of reading becomes a call-and-response relationship (6).

Eckstein, among others, emphasizes the importance of the audience in the performance of black music (279). As he argues for Morrison's novel *Beloved*, jazz novels assign their readership the role of the "collective chorus" in a "culture of antiphony" required for the interactive performance of art and meaning (280). Thus call and response is emblematic of a larger focus by jazz novels on the situation of performance, the relationship between the performer and his or her audience, as will be the focus of the next chapter.

Notes

[1] Toni Morrison, "Foreword" to *Jazz*, xviii. See also Morrison's statement in an interview with Alan Rice (Edinburgh 1988) that "the point in black art is to make it look as a jazz musician does, unthought out, unintellectual as it were. So the work doesn't show. . . . Because black people are very interested in making it look as though no thought went into it." Cited in Rice, "Finger-Snapping to Train-Dancing and Back Again," 114.

[2] Even free jazz, which rejects any strict orientation toward traditional structures such as song forms or fixed chord changes, is not completely "free," but may still include regular elements such as a rhythmic pulse, call-and-response patterns, or alternating soloists (see *The New Grove Dictionary of Jazz*, vol. 1, entry for "Free jazz," 848–49). The following analyses—like the novels they draw on—focus primarily on other varieties of jazz, however, which make greater use of recurring structural patterns.

[3] See Mark Osteen, who points out that "while Munton's attack rightly targets some of these critics' assumptions, some of the exaggerations are more his own than those of his critics" (39).

[4] For a discussion of the lick and other improvisational strategies, see chapter 4.

[5] Jack Fuller's novel *The Best of Jackson Payne*, though not analyzed in this context, also makes use of a textual riff. The phrase "One. Two. One two three four" is taken from the context of a bandleader counting off the beats before the group commences playing. This riff appears nine times over the course of the novel, often with commentary suggesting its varied meanings, which often focus on the tension between freedom and constraint in jazz music and in the protagonist's life. The tempo indicated by this counting motif provides an orderly rhythmic framework for the flexibility of the soloist's improvisation. This order is something against which Payne continues to struggle, even as he comes to accept its necessity.

[6] I counted occurrences of the riff "the girl from South Dakota" and its variants in Crouch's *Don't the Moon Look Lonesome* and found five in chapter 1, two in chapter 3, three in chapter 4, five in chapter 6, four in chapter 7, two in chapter 9, two in chapter 10, four in chapter 11, five in chapter 11a, two in chapter 12. It seems to become somewhat less frequent over the course of the second half of the book, though it is still used. It then occurs three times in chapter 13, once in 14, four times in 15, once in 16, once in 17, once in 19, once in 20, twice in 21, once in 22 ("the two Norwegian girls"), once in 23, and three in 24 (one of which is in quotation marks: "the diva from South Dakota").

[7] Because a riff in jazz music occurs within the framework of a particular rhythm, the objection might arise that the riff in this novel does not relate to any meter, but is itself prose and occurs exclusively in prose contexts. Though some of the other jazz novels considered do incorporate this rhythmic element (see especially the analysis of riffs in Ondaatje's *Coming Through Slaughter*, below), I do not consider this a necessary feature for a given phrase to function in a manner similar to a riff. The recognizable quality of the repetitions in *Don't the Moon Look Lonesome* yields a similar effect to a jazz riff, even divorced from the rhythmic component.

[8] See e.g. Crouch, *Don't the Moon Look Lonesome*, 462: "Could she have been so self-absorbed all these years that such elements of the emotional mix that was Ramona padded by unnoticed because the little sister had headphones on blasting her narcissism so loudly that she *never* heard the spiritual limp of her big sister?" and 475: "*Uh-oh: she had lost her place in the conversation and now had to catch up, having turned the dial to station ME while everybody was so busy amening the birthday girl*" (italics original).

[9] See e.g. Albert Murray, "Improvisation and the Creative Process," 112. More in-depth treatment of the blues idiom can also be found in *The Hero and the Blues, Stomping the Blues*, and *The Blue Devils of Nada*.

[10] The twelve instances of this riff could be seen as evoking the twelve-bar blues pattern: "I define the jazz musician as one who approaches or creates or plays all music as if improvising the 'break' on the traditional twelve-bar blues tune" (Murray, "Improvisation and the Creative Process," 112).

[11] An obvious intertext is Marcel Proust's *Swann's Way*, in which the protagonist's memories of childhood are triggered by the taste of a madeleine. An important difference, however, is the relative lack of a trigger for memory in Murray's novel. Scooter does not describe a sensation in the present that inspires the memory, but connects that memory to a particular sensation that serves as a symbol for the experience—or person—as a whole.

[12] I am grateful to Simone Paulun for this observation (personal communication).

[13] Alternatively, the unstressed middle syllable in "chicory" could be omitted in speech, yielding a pronunciation like "chic'ry." In this case, the meter is strictly dactylic throughout.

[14] On the lack of closure in the jazz ending, see also Toni Morrison's statement that "jazz always keeps you on the edge. There is no final chord. There may be a long chord, but not final chord. And it agitates you. . . . There is always something else that you want from the music." Cited in Rubenstein, 153.

[15] See e.g. *The Oxford Concise Companion to English Literature*, 454: "Nowadays [the term "picaresque"] is commonly, and loosely, applied to episodic novels . . . which describe the adventures of a lively and resourceful hero on a journey."

[16] See e.g. Wicks, Ehland, Dunn, Miller, Göbel.

[17] The motif "who if not you" is first mentioned in *The Spyglass Tree* on page 19. "My splendid young man" first appears in the same novel on page 21.

[18] Another example of this cyclical time or repetition is the way Scooter's various father figures are collapsed into one father type. In *The Magic Keys* the dancer

Daddy Royal, whose paternal role is evident in his name, refers to himself in terms that echo Scooter's memories of other father figures: "Then he said, You noodle and doodle and jive and connive to my segue *and here I come with my rawhide stride and my sporty, syncopated limp walk just like along any patent-leather avenue mainstem anywhere on the circuit, chitlin or caviar, transcontinental or intercontinental*" (234, italics original). In *Train Whistle Guitar* the phrases "rawhide" (7) and "trochaic-sporty, stomping-ground limp-walk" (4) are used to describe the itinerant guitar player Luzana Cholly, while "patent leather" (e.g., 99) evokes the stride pianist Stagolee Dupas, fils.

[19] The Russian Formalist Vladimir Propp studied the recurring plot elements in the variety of the folktale that he called the "wondertale," which he labeled "functions."

[20] In *Muse-Echo Blues* the flashback scenes are actually dream sequences with a different speaker rather than memories, but yield a similar structural result.

[21] Rice goes on to cite James A. Snead's definition of the "cut" in "Repetition as a Figure of Black Culture."

[22] Though it is never explicitly stated in the novel, the narrator is often presumed to be female, in part because of her diction and partially also through the stereotypical association of women with gossip. If extratextual information is taken into account, Morrison's assertion that the narrator is female can confirm this assumption: "Toni Morrison sprach bei einer Lesung in Amerikahaus Köln (13.5.1993) vom weiblichen Geschlecht der Erzählinstanz" (Toni Morrison spoke during a reading in the Amerikahaus in Cologne [13 May 1993] of the female sex of the narrative instance; Fritsch, 176n203). Although later in the novel it would seem that the narrator is not a "person" at all, but a personification of the novel or its discourse, the narrator's opening emphasis on her role as an observer suggests that she may be a neighbor or other witness to the events related. I use the female pronoun for the narrator, with the caveat that this is more out of convenience than narratological necessity.

[23] The phenomenon of "improvising on the break" is dealt with at length in chapter 4.

[24] A related phenomenon can be seen in Peter Wild's anthologies of short stories inspired by popular bands. See e.g. *Perverted by Language: Fiction Inspired by The Fall*; *Noise*, inspired by Sonic Youth; and *Paint a Vulgar Picture: Fiction Inspired by The Smiths*.

[25] The reference to or description of pieces of music can be fruitfully compared with the practice of ekphrasis, though this term is usually applied to the description of works of visual art. Claus Clüver has argued for a more expansive definition of the term that would also encompass descriptions of works of music: "The verbal representation of real or fictitious texts composed in a non-verbal sign system" ("Quotation," 49). Since this music does not exist outside the world of the novel, these descriptions can be categorized as "notional ekphrasis," a term credited to John Hollander (Heffernan, 7).

[26] Of course, Quinlan himself questions the premise that one can know the character of a musician through his music at various points throughout *The Best of Jackson Payne*, though it is initially accepted as a given. See e.g. 271: "It is a

towering romantic fallacy to think that jazz gives privileged access to a player's being. How can a deceptive, manipulative man make music that seems to have the clarity of the greatest truth? The same way a man with palsy can do precise work with his hands. A bad man can do beautiful music because the ability does not extend beyond the task."

[27] Statements in the first person in *The Best of Jackson Payne* are never explicitly labeled by speaker, such that a definitive identification here is not possible.

[28] As Bakhtin's concepts of heteroglossia and polyphony in "Discourse in the Novel" demonstrate, music is far from the only possible source of such dialogism. His work on the polyphonic novel, i.e., by Dostoevsky, shows that multi-voicedness need not be derived from music, but is a trait that can frequently be identified in novelistic prose. However, it is hardly a coincidence that Bakhtin uses a musical metaphor for this concept, and the marking function fulfilled by representations of and explicit references to jazz within the novels I am examining here makes it quite logical to relate these patterns to a musical model rather than other possible sources. In this context, the distinction in my theoretical model of intermediality between means shared between the two media and cases in which foreign techniques are imitated by literary means is an important one. The novel employs its own nonmusical means in order to evoke musical features such as call and response. While dialogism as such is certainly not solely derived from music, in combination with other devices and especially with the explicit marker function of jazz's thematization in the text, it does serve to evoke effects similar to those associated with jazz.

[29] See e.g. Wynton Marsalis, who talks about the members of a band participating in a "group dialogue," in Marsalis and O'Meally, 149.

[30] Jazz novels make frequent use of the contrast between present narration and past memory, as has been discussed in the analysis of choruses in *Don't the Moon Look Lonesome*, above.

[31] Another example of a sermon in a jazz-inspired novel is "The Blackness of Blackness" in the Prologue of Ralph Ellison's *Invisible Man*. Indeed, James Snead cites Ellison as saying "he modeled this sequence on his knowledge of repetition in jazz music" (72).

[32] See e.g. Snead, 76: "Narrative repetition tends to defuse the belief that any other meaning resides in a repeated signifier than the fact that it is being repeated."

[33] See *The New Grove Dictionary of Jazz*, vol. 1, entry for "Call and response," 373: "the most characteristic forms of call and response in jazz occur when musicians trade fours . . . and take part in a chase."

[34] This character's rhyming speech is reminiscent of the signifying practice known as playing the dozens, "a game of exchanging, in contest form, ritualized verbal insults, which are usually in rhymed couplets and often profane" (Peters, "Dozens," 56). There are strong parallels between the dozens—which is also referred to as "cutting" or "chopping"—and the cutting contest in jazz music.

[35] Katharina Gutmann discusses the importance of community in Toni Morrison's novels as an ensemble in a kind of call-and-response pattern between the individual

and society, although she does not extend this analysis from the level of content to that of structure (89–93).

[36] Borshuk observes that forms of call and response in *Train Whistle Guitar* go beyond dialogic conversation to "function . . . as affirmations of black community: a signal call is made by one speaker, demanding a response from another that performs their shared experience," an experience that is not only shared by the characters, but is also "extend[ed] to the reader, creating at once community and historical consciousness" (174).

[37] Borshuk also discusses this passage as an example of Signifyin(g), 177–78.

[38] Gates refers to the type he calls "unmotivated Signifyin(g)" as constituting not necessarily critique, but also "homage. . . . This form of the double-voiced implies unity and resemblance rather than critique and difference" (xxvii). Borshuk echoes this when discussing the boys' mimicry of Luzanna Cholly and other local heroes as well as their "celebratory naming ritual," both examples of "Signifyin(g) tributes [that] solidify community through vernacular expression and enable an emerging self-definition through association" (178).

[39] This path is of course characterized by hybridity, by what Murray called the "mulatto" character of America (Scherman, n.p.). In Scooter's case, this has a lot to do with the fusion of different strands of American experience, from African American music and sports achievements to a European American literary tradition. "In fact, what Murray does is offer a vision of hybridity, by juxtaposing the vernacular performance of the blues with the traditional academic performance at which Scooter excels. The boy's facility with the fixed texts of American history is as much a part of his subject formation as is his ability to respond to the classic blues. Murray, I would argue, intends the two to be interdependent, complementary. Neither constitutes a product of discrete blackness or whiteness. . . . Rather, both represent the organic process of exchange always at work in American culture" (Borshuk, 181).

[40] Morrison, "Rootedness: The Ancestor as Foundation," 341, cited in Mayer, 6.

4: The Performance Situation in Jazz Novels

> The centrality of improvisation in the jazz aesthetic means that jazz performance always has an evanescent quality, and such evanescence comes from jazz's status as an oral art form. (Rice, "It Don't Mean a Thing," 170)

> Whereas we are interested primarily in the *Eroica* and only secondarily in someone's performance of it, in jazz the relationship is reversed. We are only minimally interested in *West End Blues* [*sic*] as a tune or a composition, but primarily interested in Armstrong's rendition of it. Moreover, we are obliged to evaluate it on the basis of a single performance that happened to be recorded in 1928 and are left to speculate on the hundreds of other performances he played of the same tune.... (Schuller, x)

A GENRE OF MUSIC LIKE JAZZ that relies so fundamentally on improvisation is by necessity different from one performance to the next. The transient nature of music in general is further emphasized by this practice in jazz. Jazz has been described as "defying notation" (Schuller, x), as much of the music is played without the aid of a score and its wide range of timbres, for example, is difficult to capture in conventional musical notation. Together with the central role of improvisation, this lack of notation helps to create "an aesthetic of sheer presentness" (Rice, "'It Don't Mean a Thing,'" 170) in jazz music to an extent that is not found in most other genres. Of course a performance of classical music is also evanescent, but there is not the same emphasis on presence as in jazz, since a performance is perceived as being to a much greater extent repeatable. Classical musicians generally aim to reproduce an idealized version of the music, rather than to make it completely new; a dress rehearsal allows the coordination of tempi, dynamics, and other features that can thus be reproduced in essentially the same way in the performance. The difference between performances of classical music and jazz lies primarily in a culture that emphasizes the transience, changeability, and newness of jazz, as opposed to fidelity to a score in classical music. A comparison of jazz recording practice with that of classical music is also revealing in this context. Jazz musicians often record and release several different takes of the same piece—such as Charlie Parker's multiple versions of "Ornithology"[1]—as each performance is seen to be essentially different. Similar overlaps among performers of classical pieces are much rarer, in which a given pianist, for example, will generally record (or release) Bach's *Goldberg Variations* only once.[2]

This reflects a fundamentally different ideology and approach to musical performance in these two traditions. Where the classical musician most often aims at a faithful reproduction of the composer's ideal as indicated in the score, a jazz musician places the emphasis on a creative and innovative treatment of a starting tune or harmonic framework. The idea of the composer is thus secondary to that of the performer, who is expected to display not only technical proficiency but also originality and individuality. The jazz performer and his or her individual style take precedence over the content of the piece—*how* he or she plays is more important than *what* is played, the *process* of performing is privileged over the *product* of composition.

While much classical music of the European tradition assumes the existence of an ideal version of a given piece of music—as represented by the score and as intended by the composer—jazz gives pride of place to the performer rather than the composer. In some cases these two figures are of course identical,[3] but where that is not the case, the main interest is on the performer, as in the example of Louis Armstrong's rendition of "West End Blues" cited above.

Another distinctive aspect of jazz performance is its interactive character. Unlike concert music of the European tradition, jazz audiences are often actively involved in the performance. Much early jazz from New Orleans was performed at dances, funerals, or parades, in which the audience participated in an event rather than listening passively.[4] Dance was intimately connected to jazz music for at least the first few decades of its history; musicians like Duke Ellington claimed to be inspired by the movements of dancers, who would thus help to set the tempo and achieve the desired swing: "It's a kick to play for people who really jump and swing. . . . You start playing, the dancers start dancing, and they have such a great beat you just hang on!" (cited in Malone, 287). Wynton Marsalis had a similar experience with dance: "Also, the jazz musician gets inspiration from dancers. I can remember when I was growing up in New Orleans playing the street parades. When I would play them, you could look at the dancers and you'd see rhythms to play on your horn" (Marsalis and O'Meally, 144).

Reactions of listeners—whether dancing or calling out encouragement—also gave bands important feedback, allowing them to modify their playing in ways that are not as significant in classical performances. Erika Fischer-Lichte emphasizes the unpredictability of what she calls the "feedback loop" of live performance, in which listener's reactions can never be fully anticipated but always contribute an element of change and variety to each performance (see e.g. 43). This can also be seen as an example of the call-and-response pattern on a larger cultural level, in which the musicians engage in an antiphonal pattern with the dancers or listeners.

This chapter considers various aspects of the performance situation in jazz music and their evocation in the novels, beginning with the relationship between the performer and composer, which is reflected in the novels by tension between dramatized narrators and implied authors. I argue that elements borrowed from oral storytelling are used to link text and music, with orality as an intermediate stage. Several oral devices are imitated in jazz novels, from aspects of language and deictic references to the speech context to topics and styles reminiscent of gossip, to a strong focus on the figure of the narrator with an individualized voice. In my discussion of first-person narration I also examine the tenses used to convey immediacy. Since not all jazz novels restrict themselves to a single narrator, I consider the phenomenon of "collective improvisation," or texts that employ multiple narrators to evoke an ensemble performance, whether those different voices are complementary or competitive in the manner of a jazz cutting contest. The particular case of the early jazz performance within the setting of a New Orleans parade provides an example of a specific type of performance situation, and in this context I will look at the fragmentary nature of performance as represented in *Coming Through Slaughter*. The chapter concludes by considering the role of improvisation in jazz novels as one of the most salient features of the live performance. This section consists of analyses of the narrators' "solos" in *Train Whistle Guitar*, *Jazz*, and *Be-bop*, and the way they attempt to "improvise on the break."

The Narrator as Performer

Imitating Orality

The role of the performer and his or her relationship to the composer is mirrored in the relationship between narrator and implied author in a text. Indeed, the "composer" here should be understood as the "implied composer," as his or her intentions can only be inferred from the piece of music. The Bach of the *Goldberg Variations*, like the Ellington of "Mood Indigo," is a construction distinct from the historical person of either J. S. Bach or Duke Ellington. A primary means of emphasizing performance aspects in a jazz novel is thus the foregrounding of the narrator role. A prominent narrator function, often with a highly individualized personality and voice, is common in jazz novels. Rather than relating events from the perspective of an omniscient and anonymous narrator, these novels frequently draw attention to the individual who fills that narrator role.

This often occurs through the use of the first person, whether as an autodiegetic (I-protagonist) or heterodiegetic (I-witness) narrator (Genette, *Narrative Discourse*, 245 and passim). The main thing is for the narrator's voice to be distinctive and individual, not discreet and anonymous.

In those jazz novels that do not make use of a first-person narrator, the third-person narration is still prevented from appearing anonymous, taking on an individual flavor through strong internal focalization (Genette, *Narrative Discourse*, 189–94). In such cases, though the character is described in the third person, the perspective is overwhelmingly that of the individual character, and the style of language used corresponds to that of the character in the manner Gordon Collier has called "subjectivized third person narration" (cited in Richardson, 9), "in which the discourse of the narrator is infiltrated by language typical of the character being described" (Richardson, 9). Christian Gailly's *Be-bop* is such an example. Told predominantly in the third person,[5] it is yet so strongly focused on the consciousness and perspective of Basile Lorettu and Paul in their respective sections of the text that it can best be described as free indirect discourse. Many expressions appear to be the characters' own thoughts and the wording that would be typical for each character, and only the pronouns and names indicate an outside perspective.

I claim that a powerful strategy for evoking the performance situation—and especially for privileging the role of the performer over that of the composer—is the use of a distinct voice by the narrator, either in the first person[6] or as focalized through a character's perspective.[7] Yet a third means of employing narrative voices can be seen in novels that explore the limits of genre boundaries. Through the inclusion of various types of texts—such as interview transcripts (another way of giving voice to characters directly), archival material, or excerpts from a text on a higher diegetic level—novels like *Coming Through Slaughter* and *The Best of Jackson Payne* emphasize the multitude of voices over a single dominant voice. Even so, both make use of voices in the first person as one of their narrative strategies.

In addition to frequently being told by homodiegetic narrators in the first person, there are several other devices that contribute to the individual voice and spontaneous feel of these texts. These include dialect or slang, informal or conversational sentence structure and punctuation, deictic expressions that emphasize the importance of context, noticeable use of the present tense, and attempts to draw in the reader, whether through direct address by means of the second person pronoun or through metafictional devices that challenge the reader to participate actively in the production of textual meaning. These techniques combine to produce the impression of a story that is embedded in a performance situation, unfolding as it is told, just as a jazz solo is developed and modified during the process of improvisation.

Oral storytelling provides jazz novels with an important link between language and music, narration and improvisation. The following section examines jazz novels' strategies for evoking aspects of musical performance, focusing on the imitation of oral storytelling as a means of privileging the narrator/performer and his or her relationship to the reader/audience over the author/composer, who recedes into the background. The imitation of oral techniques thus forms an intermedial bridge connecting the jazz novel with the jazz performance.

Though distinctive narrative voices in the first person are hardly restricted to novels based on jazz,[8] this is one means of evoking the performer's role that is quite common in jazz novels. In these cases, the prominence of the narrator's personality and the relative absence of the implied author serve to evoke the dominance of the jazz performer over the composer. Indeed, these narrators often seem to usurp the author's role, claiming to determine or produce the text themselves, as in Xam Wilson Cartiér's novels *Be-Bop, Re-Bop* and *Muse-Echo Blues*, in Albert Murray's Scooter series from *Train Whistle Guitar* to *The Magic Keys*, and in Toni Morrison's *Jazz*.

From the opening line, the narrative voice of *Jazz* conveys an aura of immediacy, intimacy, and above all, orality. Her language is that of gossip as discussed by Esther Fritsch in her study of gossip in ethnic American writing. In addition to evoking oral rather than written language, this gossipy style creates closeness, combating the distance associated with writing (Fritsch, 39). Language of closeness[9] presumes a shared context in place and/or time, in which more emphasis can be placed on the means and process of communication, in contrast to language of distance, which privileges a higher density of information and focuses on the product or results of communication rather than the process itself.[10] In the following, I argue that the use of gossip and other oral forms of storytelling in *Jazz* and other jazz novels serve as a bridge between the traditionally static written novel and jazz music as embedded in the performance situation and the process of improvisational artistic creation. Jazz novels use linguistic means to imitate a musical context, as both media—literature and music—share the distinction between process and product. An evocation of oral language by the written text is thus a linguistic imitation of a generalized performance situation.

There are many means of evoking orality in literature, and numerous studies have examined this field in great detail. For our purposes, it will suffice to name Walter Ong's *Orality and Literacy* (1982); Ruth Finnegan's *Literacy and Orality: Studies in the Technology of Communication* (1988); Suzanne Fleischman's 1990 study of *Tense and Narrativity*, which considers the influence of oral storytelling on romance prose texts from the late Middle Ages to postmodernity; and articles by Paul Goetsch, such as "Fingierte Mündlichkeit in der Erzählkunst entwickelter Schriftkulturen" and "Der Übergang von Mündlichkeit zu Schriftlichkeit," which reviews the contributions of McLuhan, Goody, and Ong to the study of orality and literacy. A less conventional approach to the role of orality in literature is Irene Kacandes's *Talk Fiction* (2001), which considers the phenomenon of texts "talking" to their readers not through speech-like language, but through challenges to readers to "do something" as proposed by the text.

Critics such as Esther Fritsch, Justine Tally, and Gayl Jones, to name just a few, have analyzed the role of oral and folk storytelling idioms in Morrison's oeuvre, and similar studies exist on orality in the work of other African American authors. To my knowledge, however, there has as yet been no connection made between this imitation of oral forms and black music. Where blues or jazz are mentioned, they are simply listed as further examples of oral traditions rather than considered as a separate medium. It is quite a different matter to tell a story in the style of a spoken tale than to imitate jazz. Analyses such as those by Gayl Jones are thus unnecessarily simplistic.[11] Still, she is right to consider both blues and oral storytelling, but the direction of imitation is different: by imitating oral storytellers, the texts succeed in evoking an atmosphere of performance, in which the artistic product—whether story or music—is produced at least partially spontaneously and in which the primary focus is on the process rather than product of creation.

Some of the oral devices used in Morrison's *Jazz*—as representative of the jazz novel written in the first person—include informal language and slang, as well as shorter or incomplete sentences typical of speech; frequent use of deictic expressions that emphasize the role of context in communication; choice of topics and style typical of gossip; prominence of the speaker/narrator, who may also employ the present tense to convey immediacy; and active involvement of the listener/reader. Informal language and speech-like syntax clearly evoke an oral communicative situation, while their emphasis on rhythm and sound more generally serve to imitate aspects of musical sound and rhythm, as has been discussed more fully in chapter 2. Deixis is "any term or expression which, in an utterance, refers to the context of production of that utterance" (Gerald Prince, cited in Kacandes, 30),[12] and can be seen both in pronouns and in the use of temporal expressions like "then," "now," and "later," spatial expressions like "here" and "there," as well as demonstrative pronouns like "this" and "that,"[13] which draw their meaning from their relation to the particular time and place of their utterance. Taken out of the context of direct oral communication, that time and place must be reconstructed in a novel. Instead of clearly establishing that situation as a particular place in time, remote from the time and place of the reader, jazz novels evoke the closeness between speaker and listener by using many deictic expressions—although the reader must still construct that oral situation for him- or herself, the use of deixis encourages one to do so, to imagine a situation in which the narrator is speaking to the reader directly.

Fritsch has examined in detail the characteristics of gossip as a form of oral communication: the situation requires physical and temporal closeness, intimacy of the conversational partners, and direct interaction, and gossip is characterized by nonverbal aspects such as intonation, pitch, eye contact, gestures, and spontaneity (39). She goes on to identify aspects of *Jazz* that correspond to these elements of gossip, beginning with the implication of intimacy in the first line:[14] "Sth, I know that woman" (3). The narrator establishes herself[15] as someone with inside information due to sharp observation. As gossip, this information is both privileged and uncertain. Fritsch emphasizes the potential unreliability of gossip (181), which of course becomes central to this novel. Indeed, the narrator later puzzles over the mistakes she made in "misreading" the characters and their motivations. This unreliability also contains an element of changeability and revision, one that gossip shares with jazz and other improvised music.

Spontaneity and change during performance are also characteristic for other forms of oral storytelling, as pointed out by Justine Tally and Katharina Gutmann. In Gutmann's chapter on the sense of hearing, she begins by arguing for the influence of the oral tradition on both the content and form of Morrison's fiction, listing a wealth of first-person narrators as storytellers in the novels, including the "disembodied narrator" of *Jazz*, whom she sees as "the book itself" (71).

Tally examines the way storytelling and its dialogism—speaker and addressee interacting with each other—structure the novel's diegesis. She identifies four "storytelling strategies" used by the narrator of *Jazz*: "the slow, teasing divulging of information, ... the continuous repetition of terms and phrases,[16] ... the interruption into the narrative of personal observation, and ... a narrative line based on free association and circularity that brings the narrative back to where it started" (85). She sees jazz in the novel as a "metaphor for stories" (63), corresponding to Bakhtin's notion of carnival with its attendant heteroglossia, democracy, and hybridity (71–79). In the following section I examine the role of first-person narration in *Jazz* as an element of oral storytelling that evokes the performance aspect of jazz music.

The first-person narrator in *Jazz*, as indicated above, establishes herself from the outset as a source of information. She claims to know the characters, to know their histories, and to be reasonably well informed as to their motivations. Even her speculations, while serving as warnings that not all of this information is certain, lend an air of authenticity to what she does claim to know: "Whether she sent the boyfriend away or whether he quit her, *I can't say*. ... *But I do know* that mess didn't last two weeks" (5; emphasis added). The logical assumption on the part of the reader is that this gossipy, intimate voice belongs to that of a neighbor or other witness to the events she describes, and that we as readers are privileged recipients of this inside information. The narrator thus seems to inhabit the same diegetic level as the characters in the novel as an intradiegetic narrator, while the implied reader is also drawn in as a listener rather than as a reader. As a character herself, then, the narrator's point of view is expected to be limited to her observations and opinions, as she speculates on what she does not know for certain.

The narrator slowly and unobtrusively extends the boundaries of what she tells, however, going beyond her own observations to relate events she could not have witnessed as well as the thoughts of other characters. The intradiegetic first-person narrator thus seems to have morphed into an omniscient, presumably extradiegetic narrator, though this role also remains in flux. She continues to intrude herself on the story, expressing her opinions and preferences and inserting hints at her own unreliability and the impossibility of knowing anyone else's mind.[17] By the end of the novel, her apparent omniscience has been revealed as a fraud, as she admits to having "misread" her characters. Indeed, they are not the objects of her observation, but have been watching the narrator instead:

> I thought I'd hidden myself so well as I watched them through windows and doors, took every opportunity I had to follow them, to gossip about and fill in their lives, and all the while they were watching me. . . . I was so sure, and they danced and walked all over me. Busy, they were, busy being original, complicated, changeable—human, I guess you'd say, while I was the predictable one, confused in my solitude into arrogance, thinking my space, my view was the only one that was or that mattered. . . . I was watching the streets . . . so glad to be looking out and in on things I dismissed what went on in heart-pockets closed to me. . . . It never occurred to me that they were thinking other thoughts, feeling other feelings, putting their lives together in ways I never dreamed of. (220–21)

The narrator has thus shifted diegetic levels. No longer on the same level as the characters, observing them as a fellow resident of the City, no longer with a claim to omniscience on a diegetic level above the story being told, the narrator is now seen and observed by her own inventions. She is no longer in control of the story but is controlled by it. In fact, the narrator seems to have become not the creator of the story but the story itself,[18] as becomes clear in her appeal to the reader—reminiscent of Wolfgang Iser's reader-response criticism[19]—to "make me, remake me. You are free to do it and I am free to let you because look, look. Look where your hands are. Now" (229). Not only has the role of the narrator changed, yielding what is quite literally a "speakerly text,"[20] but the narratee/implied reader/reader role has also become ambiguous. While the narratee had been addressed earlier (the pronoun "you" is first used to draw in the listener/reader on page 4), the actual reader is now explicitly involved, whose hands are literally on the book, with "*fingers on and on, lifting, turning*" (229; italics original) the pages while reading these lines.

By claiming that the actual reader is the same as the narratee, the text/narrator collapses diegetic levels in a distinctly postmodern fashion. This use of second-person address corresponds to Brian Richardson's category of the "autotelic": "the direct address to a 'you' that is at times the actual reader of the text and whose story is juxtaposed to and can merge with the characters of the fiction. It is a narrativization of a form of address, and as such appears in relatively 'pure' instances only in extremely short texts.... In more extended works, it alternates with third or first person narration" (Richardson, 30).[21] In this case, the majority of the novel is narrated in the third person, in which the narrator relates the events surrounding the characters, or in the first person, either in the narrator's own voice or in the voices of Joe, Violet, Dorcas, and Felice speaking for themselves. It is only in the transition of the narrative voice to that of the text itself at the end of the novel that the autotelic function becomes significant.

This unusual transformation from narrator to speaking text suggests a model of artistic creation in which the art "product," the text, creates itself with the help of an audience.[22] It is constantly in a state of coming into being rather than already existing. This is yet another way of suggesting the model of oral cultures, in which a story unfolds only as it is told or a piece of music comes into existence only as it is being played. There is no recourse to the "original," as there is "'no concept of a 'correct' or 'authentic' version' . . . but the text is variable and dependent on the occasion of performance" (Gutmann, 63).[23]

The idiosyncrasies of the narrator in *Jazz* become even more pronounced when compared with other examples of first-person narration such as those in Albert Murray's Scooter novels *Train Whistle Guitar*, *The Spyglass Tree*, *The Seven League Boots*, and *The Magic Keys*. In contrast to *Jazz*, the narrating voice remains fairly constant. All four novels are told in memoir form, in the voice of the adult "Scooter" relating stories and memories from his youth. While this narrative form is quite conventional,[24] the developing personality of the narrator is in fact the main subject of the novels, and there is a blurring of boundaries between the narrator and the implied author. Though the musician Scooter is of course not equivalent to the writer Murray, the numerous parallels in their biographies encourage an identification of Scooter's ideals and attitudes with those espoused by Murray in his nonfiction works. Also, these parallels encourage the reader to view comments on music and on literature in a similar light, as the two are seen as sister arts and related forms of expression. Such an association of the narrator and author—like that of the jazz performer and composer—is reinforced on the level of content in

The Seven League Boots by images of jazz musicians like Scooter and The Boss Man who are both composers and performers.

The first-person novels by Morrison and Murray thus present two different models of narration. On the one hand, the narrator merges with the text to form a text that speaks for itself, a product that is also process, a piece of music that is always developing, never completed. On the other hand, the narrator merges with the implied author, or the performer with the composer, to suggest creation in performance in a manner that is typical both of the oral storyteller and the jazz musician.

This second model of creation in performance is also typical for Xam Wilson Cartiér's *Muse-Echo Blues*, in which the primary first-person narrator is in fact a jazz composer. In this novel, as well as in her earlier novel *Be-Bop, Re-Bop*, the first-person narrators provide the individual point of view or consciousness that filters the story, even when they relate the stories of others. In *Muse-Echo Blues*, for example, Kat's consciousness so colors the events of the novel that even the stories of Kitty (told in Kitty's voice in the first person), her musician boyfriend Chicago, and his mother Lena are presented as Kat's dreams of an imagined past, which interrupt her present life. Her search for meaning and significance in 1940s Kansas City in her failed attempts to compose in 1990 San Francisco represents a desire for roots in a blues and jazz tradition from which she has become alienated. Disgusted at what she sees as the BUPs' oreo-like behavior and denial of black culture,[25] she seeks inspiration in her own muse, a version of herself in 1945 Kansas City, one of the birthplaces of hot jazz (Berendt and Huesmann, 18).

Similarly, the narrator of *Be-Bop, Re-Bop* attempts to deal with her failed marriage and other problems by reliving the experiences of her father, Double, who as his name suggests is a kind of doppelgänger for the protagonist. While music colors the whole novel, it is through writing—her journal—that she is able to express herself, though not for an intended audience, but for herself. Her journal, and indeed her past, is in a constant state of revision. Rereading old journal entries triggers memories and new analyses of those past events, such that the journal and the history it embodies are not a finished product, but an ongoing process of reinterpretation.[26]

The Present Tense and Tense Switching in Performed Texts

In addition to person, another relevant aspect of the narrative situation that conveys a sense of performance is the tense used. While Murray's novels and Stanley Crouch's *Don't the Moon Look Lonesome* are rather conventionally related in the past tense, several other examples use the present tense as part of their dramatization of the storytelling situation. Christian Gailly's *Be-bop* is narrated entirely in the present tense, which suggests spontaneity in the relating of events only as they unfold. Other jazz novels use tense switching between past—telling the story—and present—acting it out. Fleischman's detailed study of oral patterns in literature elucidates the influence such orally conveyed stories have had on written texts. She cites studies on "performed narratives" in which the use of the present tense is a marker for performance:

> Tense switching is virtually always a mark of orally performed narratives of the type Nessa Wolfson . . . has labeled performed stories, on the basis of certain features that such texts share with theatrical presentations. These features include direct speech, asides, repetition, expressive sounds and sound effects, and motions and gestures. Not all but at least some of them must be in evidence for a narrative to constitute a performed story and not merely an oral report of past events. . . . The more fully a story is performed, Wolfson asserts, the more likely it is to exhibit tense switching. . . . In her data, tense switching occurs only in those narrations in which the speaker "breaks through" into performance. (8–9)[27]

Muse-Echo Blues is a clear example of this practice of switching between stories told in the past tense and the use of the present tense to lend immediacy and an air of "showing" to the "telling" of the tale. Within the same paragraph or even the same sentence, the narrator switches between the past and the present tense. Fleischman argues that this tense switching is "linked to a particular 'style' of narration, . . . the 'performed story'" (Fleischman, 68).[28] Though the present tense is used, it relates events that are clearly contiguous with those related in the past tense. It has thus been classified as the "historical present," the "narrative present," the "diegetic present," or "dramatic present," "a neutral tense which behaves like a P[ast]," or a "device for introducing the 'present of the living speaker' into the past story-world (and thereby ostensibly collapsing the distance between the two)" (Fleischman, 78).[29] The present tense thus evokes a storyteller who ceases merely to report events, but instead acts them out for the audience in the present tense.

In *Be-Bop, Re-Bop*, too, some events are presented in the past tense, as having already occurred, while others begin to be told in the present tense, sometimes alternating between the two tenses within the space of just a few sentences. In other cases, the narration is conducted primarily in the past tense, but sudden bursts of present tense lend immediacy and drama to the tale, very much as Fleischman observes in oral storytelling:

> There *was* strange restless silence before Vole replied. "Is that what's scaring you to death? What have you got to lose?" She *stopped* for a while, then *threw* out in a rush as if dammed up too long with a gush of her feelings now at high tide. . . . [= past tense]

With this last, *I'm* aghast; *I've* never heard Vole talk like this before—something*'s* up here that*'s* new and it*'s* out of control—but wait, listen up, Double*'s speaking* again—[= present tense] (21; italics added)

In this example, the narrator's sudden use of the present tense places her back at the scene of the events she relates, much as someone telling a story orally will use expressions like "So then he says. . . ." or "and I go. . . ." to dramatize or act out the scene rather than simply giving a factual report. In this way, the listeners seem to witness the events rather than merely hearing them secondhand. Of course, in an actual oral situation there would also be nonverbal elements like facial expression, tone of voice, and gesture to support this dramatization, which can only be implied in a written text. The use of tense switching is thus a crucial device for indicating this oral situation in the absence of other such oral means.

In Morrison's *Jazz*, a similar practice occurs. In the first chapter the narrator uses the past tense to refer to events that have already happened and the present tense to talk about characters' attributes, suggesting that these events are not far in the past and that these characters are still around and have not changed much. Violet, for example, "is awfully skinny" and "is mean enough and good looking enough" (4). The other uses of the present tense are the passages in which the narrator inserts her opinions, as if going off on a solo in the here and now. For example, "I'm crazy about this City" (7), she begins and proceeds to paint an upbeat portrait of the City's optimism in 1926. When she returns to the story proper, she uses the past tense—"Armistice was seven years old the winter Violet disrupted the funeral" (9)—but very soon the urge to "perform" the story takes over:

> Veterans on Seventh Avenue *were* still wearing their army-issue greatcoats, because nothing they *can* pay for *is* as sturdy or *hides* so well what they had boasted of in 1919. Eight years later, the day before Violet's misbehavior, when the snow *comes* it *sits* where it *falls* on Lexington and Park Avenue too . . . people *knock* on each other's doors to see if anything *is* needed or *can* be had. A piece of soap? A little kerosene? Some fat, chicken or pork, to brace the soup one more time? Whose husband is getting ready to go see if he can find a shop open? Is there time to add turpentine to the list drawn up and handed to him by the wives? (9–10; italics added)

The "performance" of the story gains an additional dimension as the narrator uses the voices of the people knocking on each other's doors. In fact, the narrator seems to enjoy the telling of the story so much that she remains in the present tense for much of the rest of the story, reverting to the past only to reveal previous incidents like Violet sitting down on the sidewalk or stealing the baby, or Joe and Violet meeting and moving north. The narrator's apostrophes, too—"Maybe she thought she could solve the mystery of love that way. Good luck and let me know" (5)—serve to add immediacy to the telling, as she addresses absent characters in a dramatic manner.[30]

Ensemble Performances: Multivocal Narration

In addition to the use of strong narrator roles as a means of inscribing the solo performer into the jazz novel, several of these texts allow multiple performers to take the stage together. There are a variety of different ways of presenting several voices within a text, whether through the prominent place of dialogue, the use of more than one narrator, or the inclusion of speeches or texts by other speakers within the narrator's main text, such as letters or interview transcripts. These other voices may differ not only in the degree to which they contribute to telling the tale, but also in their relative agreement or disagreement with one another. In a jam session in jazz, the musicians may be more or less in sync with one another. On the one end of the spectrum is the ideal of collective improvisation, in which the various voices or instruments develop their material as a group and the dominant mood is one of harmony.[31] On the other hand, such jam sessions can also be the setting in which fierce rivalries are carried out, as in a so-called cutting contest, or battle between rival soloists.[32] Here, clearly, the mood is one of competition and one-upmanship.

In jazz novels the relation between the various voices present can vary considerably, and in fact, these two opposing poles mask a wide range of middle ground, in which the relation between the voices is much more ambiguous. Even in the process of collective improvisation, musicians retain their individuality and it is utopian to believe that they completely submerge their own ambition and unique style in the collective performance. Indeed, some of the greatest soloists emerged from ensemble performances, as they gradually earned more frequent and longer individual solos, such as Louis Armstrong, who soon left his role as second cornet in King Oliver's Creole Jazz Band to become a featured soloist in his own right (Schuller, 77–78, 90).

Multiple Narrators: *Muse-Echo Blues*, Christian Gailly's *Be-bop*, and *Jazz*

An example of multiple narrator roles is Xam Wilson Cartiér's novel *Muse-Echo Blues*, in which the story runs on parallel lines in 1990s San Francisco, narrated by the jazz composer Kat, and 1940s Kansas City, narrated by Kitty, whose primary role is that of a "muse" to a jazz musician named Chicago. Though this second voice is identified as a dream or musing of Kat's, the two narrate alternating chapters in the first person. Because of the strong similarity between the two characters, who differ primarily in their locations in time and space, these voices can be seen as playing in harmony, telling different stories, but in the same style and in the same register.

In novels told in the third person multiple voices are also possible. In Gailly's *Be-bop* the focalization changes after the first of the three parts, such that Lorettu's thoughts are presented in the first and Paul's in the second section. In the third section, the focalization is more variable, encompassing these two characters as well as Jeanne and Cécile, albeit to a lesser extent. The use of free indirect discourse allows Lorettu's and Paul's voices to emerge clearly, recognizably distinct from each other, with only occasional intrusions of another, unidentified narrator. The use of Lorettu's and Paul's voices in this novel corresponds to solos taken sequentially, Lorretu in the first section and Paul in the next. In the final section the two play together, both in terms of the narrative perspective that migrates from one character to the other and, indeed, in terms of content, as the scene depicts a jazz concert in which Paul is invited to jam with the band after a long hiatus from playing the tenor saxophone.

A more striking use of multiple narrators can be found in Toni Morrison's *Jazz*. In addition to the chameleonic primary narrative voice discussed above in the section on the narrator as performer, several characters also seize the opportunity to speak in their own voices: Violet, Joe, Dorcas, and Felice. The first shift in narrative voice occurs in a lengthy passage that relates Violet's thoughts. Initially in the third person (though clearly focalized through Violet's perspective), the text on page 94 becomes the words of Violet's thoughts, dealing with her jealousy over Joe's affair with Dorcas, for a long time without a pronoun that refers directly to Violet, but after page 95 increasingly using the first person.

> Whenever she thought about *that* Violet, and what *that* Violet saw through her own eyes, she knew there was no shame there, no disgust. (94; italics original, underlining added)
> ... and he bought her underwear with stitching done to look like rosebuds and violets, VIOLETS, don't you know, and she wore it for him thin as it was and too cold for a room that couldn't count on a radiator to work through the afternoon, while I was where? ... Wherever it was, it was cold and I was cold and nobody had got into the bed sheets early to warm up a spot for me. ... (95; underlining added)

Then on page 97, still in the first person, the text no longer seems to be Violet's direct thoughts, but refers to her sitting in the drugstore as an event in the past tense. After one paragraph of Violet's narration, the pronoun returns to the third person. Though Violet's thoughts are still accessible, the narrative perspective has moved outside of her consciousness:

> I got quiet because the things I couldn't say were coming out of my mouth anyhow. I got quiet because I didn't know what my hands might get up to when the day's work was done. The business going on inside me I thought was none of my business and none of Joe's either because I just had to keep hold of him any way I could and going crazy would make me lose him.
>
> Sitting in the thin sharp light of the drugstore playing with a long spoon in a tall glass made her think of another woman occupying herself at a table pretending to drink from a cup. Her mother. She didn't want to be like that. (97; underlining added)

The narration by other characters takes various other forms. In the case of Joe, the narrator introduces his monologue as speculation on her part as to what his own version of the story might be: "if he had stopped trailing that little fast thing all over town long enough to tell Stuck or Gistan or some neighbor who might be interested, who knows how it would go?" (121). Joe's story that follows covers fourteen pages and is set off by quotation marks, as if he were really relating it to "Stuck or Gistan or some neighbor." As it turns out, Joe could not talk to his friends or neighbors, and the addressee for this story is initially ambiguous, though by the end of the monologue Joe no longer refers to Dorcas in the third person but has begun to address her directly, concluding by telling her that "I *chose* you. Nobody gave you to me. Nobody said that's the one for you. I picked you out. Wrong time, yep, and doing wrong by my wife. But the picking out, the choosing. Don't ever think I fell for you, or fell over you. I didn't fall in love, I rose in it. I saw you and made up my mind. My mind" (135; italics original). This echoes Violet's insistence in her own "solo" that she had chosen Joe as well: "Mine. I picked him out from all the others wasn't nobody like Joe" (96). This emphasis on choice and individual will is something that returns in a varied form in Dorcas's speech (again, set off by quotation marks), when she talks about leaving Joe because Acton was the one she wanted: "What I wanted to let him know was that I had this chance to have Acton and I wanted it and I wanted girlfriends to talk to about it" (189).

Felice's solo at the end of the novel rounds out the quartet (quintet, with the main narrator), again bringing up the subject of individual will, though somewhat differently. In her conversation at the Traces' house, Violet asks her, "What's the world for if you can't make it up the way you want it?" (208). It is appropriate that Felice's solo concludes the novel's performance, as her story is less a monologue like the others than a series of conversations that she relates verbatim to the unidentified listener. Her voice thus incorporates the voices of the three other characters and rounds out the picture that has emerged through the other perspectives, bringing those other voices together in a kind of ensemble performance. The initial narrator's final chapter thus has the character of an epilogue or coda, particularly in its direct appeal to the audience, as discussed above.

Multiplicity and Hybridity: Embedded Interviews in *The Best of Jackson Payne* and *Coming Through Slaughter*

The famed hybridity of jazz—with roots in African and European musical traditions, played by blacks and whites, containing elements of folk, entertainment, and art musics—finds expression in novels that blur the boundaries of conventional genres. The emphasis on the materiality—the sound image—of language is often seen as having a highly poetic quality. At the same time, the prominent place of dialogue alludes to drama and some texts also experiment with the use of different text categories such as interviews, letters, journals, and documentary material. Two of the most striking examples of this tendency are Michael Ondaatje's *Coming Through Slaughter* and Jack Fuller's *The Best of Jackson Payne*, both of which make extensive use of interviews, whether based on actual archival interviews or fictional.

The Best of Jackson Payne is the story of a (fictional) musicologist, Charles Quinlan, writing a biography of the (fictional) jazz saxophonist Jackson Payne, and his interviews with people who knew Payne are juxtaposed with his own writing, as well as the story of his search for the truth about the mysterious jazz legend told in the third person. The first pages of the novel, in the chapter "Taps,"[33] are related in the first person, but without any identification of the speaker until three pages in, near the end of the interview. This technique is maintained throughout the novel, yielding a hybrid text that allows multiple voices to speak, including but not limited to the protagonist Charles Quinlan. In many cases, the reader cannot identify speakers precisely, and quite often such identification is only possible retrospectively. This becomes somewhat more straightforward as the novel progresses, as the distinct style of some of the speakers becomes recognizable. Red Sloan, for example, is a musician who knew Payne early on and his comments are punctuated by short bits of rhyme, something that is disparaged by another character as "those fool poems of his" (45). Other characters use slang and African American vernacular English to varying degrees, though with quite a bit of overlap, as several characters hail from similar social milieus. They contrast sharply, though, with Quinlan's standard American English, which is the same variety as that of the third-person narration of his own story. There too, though, a contrast remains between the written, often quite academic style of Quinlan's book in progress and the sections that represent spoken dialogue.

The multiple voices presented as snatches of interviews constitute a plot element, as they serve to illustrate Quinlan's process of researching Payne's life.[34] In terms of the narrative of *The Best of Jackson Payne*, they relativize Quinlan's own voice as they contradict him and each other, presenting different perspectives on any given event. Yet it is important to recognize that the narrators of the individual stories told in the interviews are not on the same diegetic level as Quinlan's own text. As the biographer, he compiles the information received in the interviews he has conducted and acts on it to obtain additional information. He also interprets his sources and speculates on what cannot be known conclusively, occupying a superordinate role. In fact, the entire book can be read as Quinlan's own work, as not only a biography of Jackson Payne but as his story of the process of writing it as well.[35] This reading is supported by the conversation between Quinlan and an unidentified interlocutor, who suggests the very title for Quinlan's book that the novel as a whole bears: *The Best of Jackson Payne* (320).

In *Coming Through Slaughter* the interviews are less clearly fictional than in Fuller's novel. Here, the protagonist is a jazz musician who actually lived, as are several of the main characters. Some of the embedded interviews are taken from the William Ransom Hogan Jazz Archive,[36] while others are freely invented. The fictional interviews are not marked in any way as different from those based on historical fact, however, and a comparison of the "historical" interviews with those in the archives demonstrates that they have been modified, expanded on, reworded, and so on (see Petermann, "Unheard Jazz"). This illustrates Ondaatje's postmodern approach to history, which is seen as fragmentary rather than continuous and multiple rather than singular. In his "Acknowledgements" at the end of the text he clarifies: "While I have used real names and characters and historical situations I have also used more personal pieces of friends and fathers. There have been some date changes, some characters brought together, and some facts have been expanded or polished to suit the truth of fiction" (157). While the novel is not merely a biography but a story in part about how to write a biography, it demonstrates that there is not merely one version of a life. Like the story of Jackson Payne, who deceives people with his "jungle genius jive" (19), Bolden's life can only be partially assembled through the testimony of those who knew him. As his friend Webb searches for him both literally and figuratively, he consults all who knew him and is still at a loss: "Webb had spoken to Bellocq and discovered nothing. Had spoken to Nora, Crawley, to Cornish, had met the children—Bernadine, Charlie. Their stories were like spokes on a rimless wheel ending in air. Buddy had lived a different life with every one of them" (63). The different voices are necessary to construct the story of Buddy Bolden, but they do not yield a conclusive well-rounded whole, to use the wheel imagery in the quote given here. Instead, each version remains distinct. They coexist rather than negating one another. This kind of paradox is precisely what interests Bolden in his desire to escape from the structured, arching order of his rival's music. This is also a musical understanding of life, in which multiple versions—as represented by the various instruments of a jazz band—are simultaneously present and yet remain distinct from one another, they play together but can still be heard individually.

This also reflects the ideal of collective improvisation that characterized the early form of jazz that Buddy Bolden was credited with initiating. This novel does represent a kind of hero worship, an idolization of the individual genius, which was not yet central to jazz at the time but reflects the legends surrounding Bolden as the "father of jazz."[37] Still, the presence of multiple voices is a nod to the ensemble performances that were much more typical of the period.

The Role of the Audience: Second-Person Address in Albert Murray's *The Magic Keys*

Albert Murray's *Train Whistle Guitar* and the other three novels that make up the Scooter series make prominent use of the second-person pronoun "you." Though the narration is overwhelmingly conducted in the first person, the frequency of the second-person form of address is worth closer consideration. This "you" is not a specified addressee of the dramatized listener type, is not identified as "dear reader" or any more specific role.[38] Instead, the use of "you" often seems to correspond to the less common impersonal pronoun (in English) "one," as seen in this example from the fourth novel in the series, *The Magic Keys*: "So yes, on the outskirts of Mobile, Alabama, where I come from, you were indeed weaned from the home to be bottle-fed by teachers, but from these same teachers you also learned that you had to prepare and also condition yourself to assume total responsibility for yourself, *because once you graduated and went out into the world, you were on your own*" (20; italics original). In other cases, however, the generality of this form of address is lacking, and the "you" corresponds much more closely to "I": "You could feel it as soon as you arrived, just as you had anticipated you would. But before there was time to begin to really get with it, as you had gradually become used to being a college freshman and then sophomore and eventually and upperclassman on the campus down in central Alabama, you were back out on the road again, getting used to not being used to being somewhere else" (13–14). If the pronoun "you" were replaced by "I" here, or indeed throughout the novels, the narrative voice would be fairly conventional. Brian Richardson discusses this type of second-person narration in connection with Jay McInerney's *Bright Lights, Big City*: "We may note that this paragraph, if written in the first person, would sound rather ordinary; its second person form, on the other hand, both invites an identification, however tenuous, between the protagonist and the reader, and introjects a ludic element of self-consciousness that makes the theme less bland" (25). This ambiguity in the pronoun "you" is crucial,[39] as the reader tends to interpret it as "one," in a general usage, and yet is repeatedly confronted with examples that are much more specific. By using the second-person address to relate his own individual experiences, Scooter both draws in his listener and proclaims the universality of his story. Though the events of the plot mark him as a unique character, this generalizing tendency in the form of address allows the reader/listener to participate in his picaresque adventures.

This kind of reader participation is another means of dramatizing the telling of the tale, making past events seem present and collapsing the distance between the teller and his audience. Taken together, these effects all serve to evoke the situation of a live performance, in which an audience occupies the same time and place as the performer or performers. The reader's identification with Scooter through this pronoun you-that-means-I is a way of placing him or her in the present of the events related, sharing the scene of the performance by the storyteller Scooter.[40]

Jazz Performance as a Parade:
Coming Through Slaughter

In the earliest days of jazz, even before the style was known by that name, the music was most frequently performed in dance halls and in parades (Marquis, 33–35), two distinct performance situations that had a strong impact on what was played and how it was played. Many musicians saw dance as integrally related to their own art, as dictating the tempo and kind of beat used, helping to create that distinctive jazz element known as swing. Parades, on the other hand, reflect one of the roots of jazz music in the brass marching bands that performed at different events, whether celebratory or muted, on a holiday or at a funeral (Marquis, 32–33).

Ondaatje's concept of Bolden's music is fundamentally based on the parade context. From that one line that supposedly spawned the entire story—"Buddy Bolden who became a legend when he went berserk in a parade...." (134; ellipsis original)—the novel is based on an ideal of jazz as fragmentary and fleeting. The discussions of Bolden's music in the novel generally focus on this point, making this aesthetic explicit, as in the passage in which Bolden listens to his rival John Robichaux's music on the radio.

In contrast to the clear progression from beginning to ending as perceived in Robichaux's waltzes—"every note part of the large curve, so carefully patterned that for the first time I appreciated the possibilities of a mind moving ahead of the instruments in time and waiting with pleasure for them to catch up" (93)—Bolden rejects what he refers to as a "mechanistic pleasure." Instead, he aims at music in which each moment can be isolated from the rest:

> But I don't believe it for a second. You may perhaps but it is not real. When I played parades we would be going down Canal Street and at each intersection people would hear just the fragment I happened to be playing and it would fade as I went further down Canal. They would not be there to hear the end of phrases, Robichaux's arches. I wanted them to be able to come in where they pleased and leave when they pleased and somehow hear the germs of the start and all the possible endings at whatever point in the music that I had reached *then*. Like your radio without the beginnings or endings. The right ending is an open door you can't see too far out of. It can mean exactly the opposite of what you are thinking. (93–94; italics original)

Here explicitly connected to the context of parade music, his playing at any given moment must imply the endings that could come afterward. It is an aesthetic of the present, music that must be enjoyed *now*, independently of the past and future. In the novel, Bolden's friend Webb describes the music in much the same terms, realizing that "he was showing all the possibilities in the middle of the story" (43). For the fictional characters Webb and Bolden, the music is explicitly a "story," and as their other comments about it show, music can be said to have a "plot," to be "about" various subjects, and to consist of "sentence[s]" (37).

Theoretically, the novel *Coming Through Slaughter* could be read in much the same way. The chronology is not strictly linear, but moves around in time from the first scenes set in the 1970s to various points between 1900 and 1907, taken out of order, and back to 1976. Thus each moment must imply the possibilities before and after it, rather than proceeding in a clear arch, like Robichaux's music or a more conventional novel, from a single beginning to a single ending. Bolden's music, like Ondaatje's postmodern novel, does not believe in just one beginning or ending. Both are multiple, and history/the story becomes fragmentary.[41]

In addition to the lack of continuity in Bolden's parade performances, they are also remarkable for their transitory nature. In a fictional interview[42] Frank Lewis elaborates on the impermanence of Bolden's playing:

> If you never heard him play some place where the weather for instance could change the next series of notes—then you *should* never have heard him at all. He was never recorded. He stayed away

while others moved into wax history, electronic history, those who said later that Bolden broke the path. It was just as important to watch him stretch and wheel around on the last notes or to watch nerves jumping under the sweat of his head. (37; italics original)

The cult of the present that surrounds jazz is here depicted as a conscious choice, part of Bolden's aesthetic program. Were he to be recorded and played on the radio, he would need a different kind of music, or perhaps those circumstances would turn his music into something different. His accomplishment as a musician is presented in this novel as his spontaneity and his relentless pursuit of innovation and the limits of art, aspects that would be hampered by the time allowed for reflection, repetition, and polishing in a recording situation. Significantly, though Bolden almost certainly did read music (Marquis, 38, 105–6), Ondaatje's version claims that the trombone player Willy Cornish was "the only one able to read music" (112). Written music would be too permanent for Bolden's kind of composition in performance, in which he "wouldn't let [Cornish] even finish the song once before we changed it to our blood" (112). This type of impermanence, thus, is closely connected to improvisation and innovation, freedom from the constraints of a written or recorded "official" version, and is mirrored by Ondaatje's approach to the historical record—"the thin sheaf of information . . . a desert of facts" (134)—that formed the basis of the novel's plot. Because so little is definitively known about Bolden, Ondaatje takes the sparse data as the basis for his own improvisation, in which "some facts have been expanded or polished to suit the truth of fiction" (157). The transience of Bolden's music thus corresponds to the transience of history, his improvisations on standard tunes brought by William Cornish to Ondaatje's reimagining of the little historical information available.

The other aspect of the parade situation that is exploited in *Coming Through Slaughter* is the role of the audience as dancers and active participants. At the parade in which Bolden "went mad into silence" (108), related in Bolden's voice in the first person, a dancer appears out of the crowd[43] and mirrors his playing with the motions of her body. Initially he is in control and pulls the dancers to him with his music, but as the parade progresses the dancer becomes more active and Bolden finds himself reacting. Taking up the mirror metaphors that permeate the novel, as his mind begins to collapse, he can no longer hear himself playing, but sees her "hitting each note with her body before it is even out so I know what I do through her" (130). Their roles merge to the extent that he plays through physical movements that are like dancing: "hardly hit the squawks anymore but when I do my body flicks at them as if I'm the dancer till the music is out there" (130). His music then becomes truly interactive in a way that he sees as the culmination of his career. He has surrendered control, such that now his listener can manipulate him instead: "this is what I wanted, always, loss of privacy in the playing, leaving the stage, the rectangle of band on the street, this hearer who can throw me in the direction and the speed she wishes like an angry shadow" (130).

While this extreme depiction of the musician-audience interaction is rooted in Bolden's mental breakdown, it is significant for its dramatization of the audience's role in creating music. The many metafictional aspects of *Coming Through Slaughter* and the challenges of its fragmented, dissonant structure—like the direct address of the reader at the end of *Jazz* and the use of the present tense and tense switching in several jazz novels—are means of assigning the reader the audience's interactive role in creating the artwork in performance.

Solo Performances: Improvising on the Break

> Improvisation is generally regarded as the principal element of jazz since it offers the possibilities of spontaneity, surprise, experiment, and discovery, without which most jazz would be devoid of interest. Almost all styles of jazz leave some room for improvisation—whether a single chorus or other short passage during which a soloist may improvise over an accompaniment, a sequence of choruses for different soloists, or the entire piece after the statement of a theme—and some jazz is spontaneously created without the use of a predetermined framework.... Improvisation is the defining characteristic of much of New Orleans jazz and its related styles, some big-band music, nearly all small-group swing, most bop, modal jazz and free jazz, and some fusion. (*The New Grove Dictionary of Jazz*, vol. 2, entry for "Improvisation," 313–14)
>
> Improvisation is the heart and soul of jazz. (Schuller, 58)

While other genres of music may also allow room for improvisation, it is in jazz that improvisation plays the most central role. From the earliest jazz in turn-of-the-century New Orleans to bop and free jazz, improvisation in some form or another has been a nearly constant presence in the jazz tradition. In addition to the improvisations of great soloists over a background accompaniment, some varieties of jazz are also characterized by collective improvisation, in which not just a single soloist but several musicians or the whole ensemble improvise at the same time.

Of course, improvisation should not be mistaken for complete freedom, or "making things up out of thin air" (Murray, "Improvisation and the Creative Process," 112), as this would yield chaos rather than art. Instead, the jazz musician works within clearly delineated boundaries and draws on knowledge of his musical predecessors. The length of an improvised solo is generally established in advance, whether for the duration of a chorus or restricted to four bars, and the chord changes may also be rigid. Likewise, familiar material is used for a solo, whether pieces of a refrain or riff from the song itself, or standard licks and other patterns borrowed from other pieces. The great achievement of the improviser is to combine familiar material in unfamiliar ways, setting up expectations before tearing them down: "The essence of improvisation in jazz is the delicate balance between spontaneous invention, carrying with it both the danger of loss of control and the opportunity for creativity of a high order, and reference to the familiar, without which, paradoxically, creativity cannot be truly valued" (*New Grove Dictionary of Jazz*, "Improvisation," 322).

There are three main techniques for improvisation: paraphrase improvisation, formulaic improvisation, and motivic improvisation. In the first type, the melody or theme is paraphrased or modified in the improvised solo. This might be restricted to minor embellishment, or might stray further from the melody itself, to the point that it is barely recognizable as the same theme. Formulaic improvisation builds on musical fragments or ideas called "licks" (*New Grove Dictionary of Jazz*, "Improvisation," 317, 319), combining many formulas and licks from a whole repertoire of pieces. The melodic theme is adhered to less closely than in paraphrase improvisation, and the challenge is to hide the individual building blocks, creating a coherent whole out of a variety of disparate pieces. In motivic improvisation, just a few motifs form the basis of the improvisation, but unlike the formulaic type, these motifs draw attention to themselves and connect the various sections of a piece through their repetition and variation (315–21). In all these approaches, the improvisation oscillates between fidelity to a predetermined basis in a theme or harmonic and rhythmic structure and imagination or creativity.

Jazz pieces very often are based on previous music, such as "standards" or popular songs. The mode of improvisation allows for thorough reinterpretations of such pieces, creating new meanings in a manner similar to the technique of "signifying" as examined by Gates in *The Signifying Monkey*. Signifying "disrupt[s] the signifier by displacing its signified in an intentional act of will. Signifyin(g) is black double-voicedness; ... it always entails formal revision and an intertextual relation.... Repetition, with a signal difference, is fundamental to the nature of Signifyin(g)" (51). Indeed, Gates points out the similarities between jazz improvisation and signifying, using the example of John Coltrane's 1960 version of "My Favorite Things" (104).

Though most jazz involves at least some improvisation, not all jazz music is improvised. A good deal of big band music, such as that of Duke Ellington and his orchestra, was orchestrated in advance. Furthermore, some musicians were more disposed to risk-taking in their improvisations than others. While Charlie Parker was known for his brilliant improvisations, different with each performance, Louis Armstrong tended to perfect a single version of a solo that he would repeat at further performances (*New Grove Dictionary of Jazz*, "Improvisation," 322).

Improvisation also reflects an interest in process rather than product. Jazz is seen as constantly evolving, changing from one performance to the next, rather than aiming at a finished product. Kouwenhoven regards this quality as typically American, "a concern with the manner of handling experience or materials rather than with the experience or materials themselves," and connects it to the sequential, skyscraper-like structure of jazz (133). There are a number of different ways that a jazz novel can attempt to create the impression of improvisation, corresponding to different levels of the text's construction. A particular style of emphasizing the sound of language as well as inventiveness in forming new words and compounds can yield a playful effect, as discussed in chapter 2 on jazz sound. A narrator's use of oral elements (i.e., imitating the style of gossip, use of speech patterns, and direct address of the reader) can create the impression of spontaneity, of a story that is being made up as it is told. Jazz narrators also revise their stories as they tell them, inserting comments like "pourquoi ai-je dit qu'il avait envie de parler?, sans doute parce que j'avais envie de parler, non, il n'a pas envie de parler" (why did I say he felt like talking?, doubtless because I felt like talking, no, he doesn't feel like talking; Gailly, *Be-bop*, 22), or acknowledging that their story has turned out differently than expected, as in *Jazz*.[44]

The most striking imitation of improvisation, however, has to do with the structural device of the "break," which Albert Murray explains as follows:

> Another technical device peculiar to blues music is the break, which is a very special kind of ad-lib bridge passage or cadenzalike interlude between two musical phrases that are separated by an interruption or interval in the established cadence. Customarily there may be a sharp shotlike accent and the normal or established flow of the rhythm and the melody stop, much the same as a sentence seems to halt, but only pauses at a colon. Then the gap, usually of not more than four bars, is filled in most often but not always by a solo instrument, whose statement is usually impromptu or improvised even when it is a quotation or a variation from some well-known melody. Then when the regular rhythm is picked up again (while the ensemble, if any, falls back in) it is as if you had been holding your breath. (*Stomping the Blues*, 99)

The break provides an opportunity for a soloist to improvise. Such interruptions of the choral progression in jazz can be seen in passages that "break" the flow of narrative in a novel. The action of the plot is suspended for a few pages, while the narrator goes off on a tangent, develops a theme, or inserts other material. Such passages have a pronounced air of playfulness and often strike the reader as a free play of associations. Wordplay is often prominent, serving yet again to foreground the sound of the words used and remind the reader of the auditory element of language, which it shares with music. These improvised breaks range from solos of several pages as in *Train Whistle Guitar* and *Jazz* to short repetitive interludes in *Be-bop*.

Improvised Breaks in *Train Whistle Guitar*

Train Whistle Guitar is a memoir-like jazz novel notable for its use of poetic passages that interrupt the flow of the protagonist's reminiscing to evoke an improvisatory solo. The first such passage comes early in the novel and is graphically set apart from the main narrative by being printed in italics. After the first short chapter introduces the place of the protagonist's childhood and concludes by calling it "the briarpatch" and introducing his nickname Scooter, the first "solo" takes up the theme of naming and its connection to home. I quote this passage in full, as it exemplifies several features of the improvised solo:

> *I used to say My name is also Jack the Rabbit because my home is in the briarpatch, and Little Buddy (than whom there was never a better riddle buddy) used to say Me my name is Jack the Rabbit also because my home is also in the also and also of the briarpatch because that is also where I was also bred and also born. And when I also used to say My name is also Jack the Bear he always used to say My home is also nowhere and also anywhere and also everywhere.*
>
> *Because the also and also of all of that was also the also plus also of so many of the twelve-bar twelve-string guitar riddles you got whether in idiomatic iambics or otherwise mostly from Luzana Cholly who was the one who used to walk his trochaic-sporty stomping-ground limp-walk picking and plucking and knuckle knocking and strumming (like an anapestic locomotive) while singsongsaying Anywhere I hang my hat anywhere I prop my feet. Who could drink muddy water who could sleep in a hollow log.* (4–5; italics original)

Much as a solo may be structured around a preexisting melody, this passage picks up the themes of name and place from the previous section, introducing the nickname of "Jack the Rabbit," which is a product of place—"because my home is in the briarpatch"—, as is "Jack the Bear," whose home is "nowhere and also anywhere and also everywhere." This passage does not merely restate the theme, however, but experiments with it and strings it out, using a series of licks to connect the various ideas. The first repeated phrase is "I used to say My name is," which appears with a slight variation three times in this first paragraph. Ironically, the reader never learns Scooter's actual name in this novel,[45] so this emphasis on introducing oneself and determining one's own identity strikes a slightly strange note, either as seemingly disingenuous, or, more likely, as a claim that heroic self-naming is more important than official or legal names. Indeed, Murray regards Scooter's self-naming as early evidence of his skill as an improviser: "In the very first book, he tries to name himself. He says, 'My name is Jack the Rabbit and my home is in the briar patch,' which means that he has to be nimble or nothing. He's got to be resilient. In other words, he's got to be a swinger. He's got to be able to improvise on the break" (Rowell and Murray, 407–8). The many repetitions of the word "also," particularly in the unusual combination as a noun phrase "the also and also," are further examples of such a lick. The plethora of uses in this passage serves to sensitize the reader to this word, such that it becomes much more striking throughout the remainder of the text(s). Murray's use of "also and also" is highly idiosyncratic, and it forms a piece of his individual vocabulary that makes connections with his uses of it in other contexts. For example, in an interview with Tony Scherman that appeared in 1996, Murray used the phrase in discussing the picaresque plot structure of his Scooter novels:

> My narrative structure is not geared to a tightly knit plot. It is a picaresque story, more a matter of one thing following another than one thing leading to another. To me, the "and then and then and also and also and next after that" of a picaresque reflects a sensitivity consistent with contemporary knowledge of the universe. The connection between that and the requirements of ongoing improvisation in the jam session should be easy to see. (Scherman, n.p.)

Here, "also and also," like "and then and then," has nonhierarchical or noncausal implications. He aims at a plot that is serial or episodic rather than causal or climactic. The word "also" can thus be seen as a renunciation of formal structure, or more accurately, a demonstration that such formal structures are imposed from the outside on material that is inherently chaotic. Elsewhere, Murray refers to the "ultimate actuality of entropy (repeat, entropy) *of the void*, upon which we impose such metaphorical devices as AND, as in (andoneandtwoandthreeandfourand)...." (*The Magic Keys*, 237–38; emphasis original). "And," like "also," conjoins two or more entities, whether those are people or things, attributes, or actions, proclaiming their simultaneous existence. In *Train Whistle Guitar* there is a passage where Scooter is learning the parts of speech, in which Uncle Jerome "had his own special introduction to the principles of grammar: A noun is someone or something; a pronoun is anything or anybody; a verb is tells and does and is; an adverb is anyhow, anywhere, anytime;[46] an adjective is number and nature; a preposition is relationship; and *conjunction is membership*; and interjection is the spirit of energy" (71; italics added). The conjunction *also* is thus suggestive of Murray's concept of the United States as a "mulatto society," made up of "composite" identities,[47] but it also corresponds to his ideal of the blues idiom, in which a piece of music can say multiple things at once. The lick "and also" thus alludes to elements of the wider episodic structure of jazz at the same time as it functionally serves to link elements of an improvised solo.

Improvised Breaks in *Jazz*

The interruptions of the plot in *Jazz* include at least three solos that take the City—1920s Harlem, though only ever referred to as "the City"—as a primary theme or starting point for improvisation. They also include some of the most direct depictions of musicians and quotations from jazz and blues songs in the novel as a whole, such as when a "colored man floats down out of the sky blowing a saxophone" (8). Another such example is the following passage:

> Young men on the rooftops changed their tune; spit and fiddled with the mouthpiece for a while and when they put it back in and blew out their cheeks it was just like the light of that day, pure and steady and kind of kind. You would have thought everything had been forgiven the way they played. The clarinets had trouble because the brass was cut so fine, not lowdown the way they love to do it, but high and fine like a young girl singing by the side of a creek. . . . The young men with brass probably never saw such a girl, or such a creek, but they made her up that day. On the rooftops. . . .
>
> That's the way the young men on brass sounded that day. Sure of themselves, sure they were holy, standing up there on the rooftops, facing each other at first, but when it was clear that they had beat the clarinets out, they turned their backs on them, lifted those horns straight up and joined the light just as pure and steady and kind of kind. (196–97)

This passage, ostensibly only peripheral to the plot, is one of several that characterize the setting and tone of the novel. The City is presented almost as a protagonist, as a place that makes these events possible, and the music of this particular time and place colors the perceptions of all the characters involved, most prominently the narrator. Morrison's City is a place where music is in the air, on the rooftops, and on the streets, where drums incite political protest and lowdown music is held responsible for love affairs. And what is more, the music is undeniable—even Alice Manfred, who heartily disapproves of the questionable morals she associates with jazz, cannot escape the powerful presence of the drums on

Fifth Avenue (57–60). As an undercurrent to the events and motivations of the novel, jazz as a theme can be seen to fulfill a similar function to a key or mode in music. These solo passages that delve more deeply into the theme thus emphasize the key and anchor the reader's expectations of the framework of the novel.

In the following passage, the narrator's solo picks up the phrase "blues man," initially possessing a concrete referent in the blues guitarist sitting on the sidewalk, and modifies it through word play and typical blues refrains:

> Blind men thrum and hum in the soft air as they inch steadily down the walk. They don't want to stand near and compete with the old uncles positioning themselves in the middle of the block to play a six-string guitar.
> Blues man. Black and bluesman. Blacktherefore blue man.
> Everybody knows your name.
> Where-did-she-go-and-why man. So-lonesome-I-could-die man.
> Everybody knows your name. (119)

Not only are the phrases themselves—"where did she go and why," "so lonesome I could die"—suggestive of blues lyrics,[48] but the verse pattern also loosely echoes the typical blues form AAB, in this case repeating A not exactly, but in general form and rhyme, with the B phrase—"Everybody knows your name"—providing a contrast in form and content.

With the line "Joe probably thinks that the song is about him" (119), the end of the solo segues back into the main plot of the characters' story, as when a bandleader or drummer gives a signal that a break is over and that the ensemble should resume playing. And indeed, the narrator's comments on Joe's situation quickly lead into the next solo, this time by Joe himself.

Motivic Improvisation in *Be-bop*

Christian Gailly, a former jazz saxophonist, allows jazz to permeate his novel *Be-bop* in a variety of ways. In what has been described as "inimitably rhythmicized language,"[49] Gailly's novels employ aspects of rhythm, structure, and narrative techniques—the present tense, an informal, spoken style of free indirect discourse, as well as metafictional "revisions" of the story as it unfolds—that evoke a live performance and imitate the improvisational side of jazz music. I consider first his use of licks in building up individual passages in the style of motivic improvisation before considering the function of improvisation for *Be-bop*.

One of the most striking features of the language used in *Be-bop* is its high degree of repetition. Individual lexical items are often repeated with a surprising frequency within a short passage of text, as when the phrase "dit Cécile" (says Cécile) occurs seven times in a single paragraph (*Be-bop*,

76). Another example is this passage, soon after Paul and Jeanne arrive at the house they have rented for the summer:

> Venez, je vais vous faire visiter.
> Paul a horreur de visiter quand il est crevé. Même quand il n'est pas crevé. Il aura tout le temps de visiter. Et quand il aura fini de visiter, il commencera à s'ennuyer. Il s'ennuiera même en visitant. La plupart du temps, il s'ennuie même en visitant. Il s'ennuie déjà. S'il n'était pas si crevé, il s'ennuierait déjà insupportablement. Il a envie de leur dire visite sans moi mai Jeanne lui dit : Alors, tu viens?
> Visite guidée. (91)
>
> [Come, I'll give you a tour.
> Paul hates tours when he's exhausted. Even when he's not exhausted, actually. There will be plenty of time for a tour. And when he's done with the tour, he'll begin to be bored. He'll even be bored during the tour. Most of the time he's bored on tours. He's already bored. If he weren't so exhausted, he'd already be unbearably bored. He'd like to say, take the tour without me, but Jeanne says to him: So are you coming now?
> A guided tour.]

As in many such passages, Gailly here picks up just three lexical items—"visiter," "crevé," and "s'ennuyer" ("visit," "exhausted," and "to be bored")—and repeats them with slight modification several times. The overall impression of such a passage is that of someone reconsidering a thought, revising it, taking it to its logical extreme. From the initial idea—whether Paul's or the unidentified narrator's—of hating to take a tour while exhausted, this passage progresses to the reflection that he hates tours in general, that he will be bored afterward, that he will be bored during the tour, that he is already bored, and that he would be even more bored if he were not so exhausted. This is an example of taking a few key ideas or terms, like jazz licks, and combining them in slightly different ways that still allow them to remain highly identifiable. Their repetition allows the ideas surrounding them to be extended, modified, and varied, as a jazz soloist improvises using a repertoire of motifs ready to hand.

This technique of motivic improvisation occurs throughout the novel, though most prominently in the passages in which Paul is the focalizer, rather than Lorettu. This is no accident, but reflects the different musical models each is associated with. Paul's performance on the tenor saxophone is compared to John Coltrane's style, while Lorettu on the alto sax reminds Paul of Charlie Parker, whose solos he has actively memorized. One of Coltrane's most influential recordings is *A Love Supreme*, and the first movement of this suite, "Acknowelegement," prominently features a motivic improvisation on the four-note phrase that Coltrane both plays on the saxophone and sings: "A love supreme." Charlie Parker, on the other hand, was praised for never repeating a solo, due in part to his skill at formulaic improvisation, in which the building blocks of the solo are concealed and recombined to form something new. As Barry Kernfeld puts it in *What to Listen for in Jazz*: "The greatest formulaic improviser in jazz was Charlie Parker. . . . Parker brought to any musical situation a well-rehearsed body of formulas, which he then embedded into his lines in a fluid and frighteningly effortless manner" (138). The narrative style employed for the sections focalized by each of the protagonists thus corresponds to the improvisational style for which their musical models were renowned.

Though both men are (amateur) jazz musicians, Paul has not played in years and it is only at the end of the novel when Lorettu encourages him to join in a jam session that he picks up a saxophone again. Though Lorettu's life revolves around jazz, he does not see himself as improvising at all, but instead memorizes and reproduces Charlie Parker's solos:

> Lorettu, lui, ne voit pas le rapport, il n'a rien à jouer, n'invente rien, copie, imite, reproduit par coeur Charlie. Tout ce qu'il sait, c'est que souffler dans son alto lui fait du bien, et encore, seulement pendant, dès qu'il s'arrête ça va plus mal, et ça dure comme ça depuis le commencement. (76–77)

> [Lorettu, he doesn't see the connection, he doesn't have anything to play, he doesn't invent anything, copies, imitates, reproduces Charlie by heart. All that he knows is that blowing into his alto makes him feel good, but then that's only while he's playing, when he stops, he feels worse, and it's been like that from the beginning.]

A particular aspect of jazz that Gailly picks up here and makes fruitful for the novel as a whole is the tension between imitation and innovation. The alto sax player Lorettu sees himself as copying Charlie Parker rather than creating in his own right, Paul's playing is modeled on John Coltrane, and other musicians are similarly presented as playing in the style of Johnny Griffin, Gerry Mulligan, and Thelonious Monk. Lorettu would prefer to be a copy of a genius than to risk being a "nobody" on his own:

> peut-être il vaut mieux copier un très grand comme Charlie, (Parker), plutôt que d'essayer d'être un grand moi-même sans y arriver, continue, et rester petit, autrement dit ?, mieux vaut être le sosie d'un grand que personne soi-même. (17)

> [perhaps it's better to copy someone really great like Charlie (Parker) than to try to be great yourself and never get there, go on, and stay small, in other words, better to be the double of somebody great than a nobody yourself.]

When Paul listens to Lorettu's solo he recognizes Parker in his style and technical proficiency but hesitates to say so because he himself hates to be compared with Coltrane:

> Paul aimerait dire à Lorettu combien il admire son jeu, si proche de celui de Parker, mais, se dit-il, je vais forcément en arriver à lui parler de Parker, ça va peut-être lui déplaire, moi j'avais horreur qu'on me parle de Coltrane en me parlant de moi, mais c'est toujours comme ça, on ne sait pas quoi dire, on ne sait parler que par comparaison, autant se taire, mais, n'en pouvant plus de se taire, il attaque Lorettu sur le jeu du ténor. (179)

> [Paul would like to tell Lorettu how much he admires his playing, so like that of Parker, but, he tells himself, I would inevitably end up talking to him of Parker, he might not like that, I always hated when people would talk to me of Coltrane when talking of me, but it's always like that, you never know what to say, you can't speak except in comparisons, you might as well keep quiet, but unable to keep quiet any longer, he talks to Lorettu about the tenor's playing.]

Though Paul recognizes Coltrane in his own style and admits as much when asked what kind of tenor sax he plays (183), he yet yearns to be individual and admired for his playing in his own right and projects this disparity onto Lorettu. Ironically, in both cases, the players they imitate and reproduce so faithfully were known for their innovation and improvisational skill, albeit in different idioms and techniques. The same is true of Johnny Griffin, whose style is imitated by the tenor saxophonist who plays before Paul takes over:

> Il joue bien, même très bien, d'un style plus classique que Trane, rappelant plutôt à Paul Johnny Griffin, en moins bien, parce que Griffin, question invention, dans le genre improvisateur sans limites, on n'a jamais fait mieux, et on fera jamais mieux. (175)

> [He plays well, very well even, in a style more classical than Trane, rather reminding Paul of Johnny Griffin, though not as good, because Griffin, in terms of invention, the kind of limitless improviser, no one has ever done better and no one will ever do better.]

These talented musicians who so expertly reproduce their idols' solos succeed in creating an atmosphere of excitement, of inspiring their audience and one another, despite the flaw of being unable to improvise themselves but only to reproduce the improvised solos of other (greater) musicians. Though Paul cannot praise Lorettu's playing without speaking of Charlie Parker, he still admires it. Similarly, Lorettu thinks Paul plays "un peu trop coltranien" (a little too much like Coltrane) (187), but wants to thank him for the pleasure of hearing Coltrane again and is impressed in spite of himself with Paul's technical ability. In a musical culture in which individual accomplishment, as epitomized by improvisation, is valorized, Lorettu, Paul, and the others with imitative styles find themselves in a dilemma. They are technically proficient, such that they are able to masterfully reproduce complex solos by Charlie Parker and John Coltrane, yet not imaginative or ingenious enough to create their own solos. This may be related to the novel's setting in France, where musicians may see themselves as adopting a form of jazz that is not native to their own culture but imported from America. If so, Paul and Lorettu's ambivalent position between individual talent and rote memorization may relate to a larger awareness of or concern with a lack of authenticity. On the other hand, it can also be read as a reflection on the contemporary jazz scene more generally, as generations of young musicians are growing up in the shadow of the great improvisers who went before them. With access to recordings that make solos by Bird and Trane permanent, they can study and memorize what was originally (at least partially) spontaneous and transient.

In the novel *Be-bop*, the paradox of repeated improvisation offers another point of reflection on the jazz novel itself. Despite its many devices for evoking elements of a live performance—the present tense narration, the use of repeated lexical items as licks in a motivic improvisation, the narrator's revision of the story as he is telling it—it yet remains an artwork fixed on paper rather than an evanescent and momentary performance. Lorettu's and Paul's repetition of earlier solos in a manner that is virtuoso but no longer improvisatory thus mirrors Gailly's self-reflexive imitation of improvisation in his novel, in which he evokes, but can never actually achieve, spontaneity.

Notes

[1] Charlie Parker recorded "Ornithology" a total of twenty-seven times between 1945 and 1954 with different ensembles ("Charlie Parker Discography").

[2] Glenn Gould's two recordings of *The Goldberg Variations* in 1955 and 1981 form a significant exception, which provide a rare opportunity to compare different interpretations of the piece by the same performer at different times.

[3] One could indeed argue with Gunther Schuller that "*all* jazz players can be considered composers since they are in effect composing extempore" (134; italics original). See also Levine: "If jazz didn't obliterate the line between composer and performer, at the very least it rendered that line hazy" (433).

[4] This setting—like predecessors of jazz such as work songs and field hollers—can be seen as exemplifying an African ideal of art as embedded in a functional or utilitarian context, in contrast to the (relatively recent) Western ideal of "pure art" (Wilson, 87).

[5] The narrator does intrude himself on the story in the first person in a few instances, such as: "pourquoi ai-je dit qu'il avait envie de parler ?, sans doute parce

que j'avais envie de parler, non, il n'a pas envie de parler" (why did I say he felt like talking?, doubtless because I felt like talking, no, he doesn't feel like talking, 22) or "Mais si la scène vous gêne, on peut très bien la supprimer. D'accord, je la supprime. Elle a pourtant eu lieu" (But if it embarrasses you, this scene can easily be skipped. Okay, I'll skip it. But it did take place; 60). As Genette points out, all narratives are necessarily told in the "first person," yet those generally classified as "third-person narration" are told by narrators who do not include themselves as a character in the story they relate (*Narrative Discourse*, 244). There is also a comment on page 74 of *Be-bop* that seems to be in the voice of the narrator—"Oui, je sais, je suis vulgaire" (yes, I know, I'm vulgar)—, but which Cécile responds to as if Lorettu has actually said it aloud. This blurring of roles could suggest that Lorettu is in fact the narrator, who chooses for unexplained reasons to tell his own story and thoughts in the third person, only intruding in his own voice very rarely. If this is taken to be the case, Lorettu's narrative parallels his improvisational performance.

[6] Examples of jazz novels told in the first person include *Jazz* by Toni Morrison, *Train Whistle Guitar*, *The Spyglass Tree*, *The Seven League Boots*, and *The Magic Keys* by Albert Murray, *Be-Bop, Re-Bop* and *Muse-Echo Blues* by Xam Wilson Cartiér, and *Invisible Man* by Ralph Ellison.

[7] Other examples of jazz novels written in the third person but focalized on individual characters include *Un soir au club* by Christian Gailly, *The Fisher King* by Paule Marshall, and *Don't the Moon Look Lonesome* by Stanley Crouch.

[8] For example, all the novels based on the *Goldberg Variations* also make use of first-person narration in all or part of the narrative. It may seem problematic that these novels based on classical music employ the same kind of narrative perspective as do jazz novels, but in the conclusion I will examine the way similar techniques yield different results.

[9] Like Deborah Tannen before them, Peter Koch and Wulf Österreicher propose replacing the distinction between orality and literacy with differentiations in features that are traditionally assigned to the one or other pole. A graphic representation of their categories of language of distance and of closeness is printed in Goetsch, "Fingierte Mündlichkeit," 209.

[10] Justine Tally observes: "That the 'whole' story is set out on the first page of *Jazz* immediately signals that the 'facts' of the event (which will be repeated and elaborated upon throughout the novel) are much less important than the nature of the telling" (85). The importance of process over product in jazz is more explicitly thematized in *Be-bop, Re-bop*: "his passing, like his music, is more process than product by nature—that Double's demise has the matrix-free flow of an on-the-spot bop change" (9).

[11] Jones consistently lumps jazz and blues in with verbal forms of oral traditions. See for example her assertion that "*Invisible Man* is a multistructure of oral traditional forms—jazz and jazz solos, blues, oral storytelling, sermon, oratory, ballad" (150).

[12] Kacandes sees deictic expressions as literary correlates to "corporeal resources" used in speech, such as "touch, gaze, and/or inbreath."

[13] See for example the opening line of *Jazz*: "Sth, I know that woman" (3). The word "that" is an example of deixis, as it forms a kind of pointing, dependent on context for the identity of "that woman" to be made clear.

[14] In her essay "Unspeakable Things Unspoken" Morrison comments on the effects of the "whisper" that begins *The Bluest Eye*: "suggestion of illicit gossip, of thrilling revelation, there is also, in the 'whisper,' the assumption (on the part of the reader) that the teller is on the inside, knows something others do not, and is going to be generous with this privileged information. The intimacy I was aiming for, the intimacy between the reader and the page, could start up immediately because the secret is being shared at best, and eavesdropped upon, at the least" (386). Fritsch is correct in noting the applicability of this discussion to *Jazz* as well (169).

[15] For a justification of my use of the female pronoun with reference to the ambiguous figure of Morrison's narrator in *Jazz*, see note 22 in chapter 3.

[16] Repetition is typical of oral literature, in part as a mnemonic device for the benefit of both teller and listener. This use of "formulas" in oral storytelling, as noted by Walter Ong, is also reminiscent of repetition in music. Thus a single feature of the text—formulaic repetition—can simultaneously evoke an oral or a musical context. Walter Ong, *Interfaces of the Word*, 108; cited in Gutmann, 60.

[17] See e.g. Morrison, *Jazz*, 137: "Risky, I'd say, trying to figure out anybody's state of mind. But worth the trouble if you're like me—curious, inventive and well-informed. . . . So he didn't know. Neither do I, although it's not hard to imagine what it must have been like."

[18] "If jazz is a music the performer composes himself, then this novel she calls *Jazz* is a book that composes itself" (John Leonard, cited in Gutmann, 71). A more precise parallel, of course, would be a book that the narrator composes herself.

[19] See e.g. Iser, "Reading Process" and *Act of Reading*.

[20] Henry Louis Gates, Jr. defines the "speakerly text" as "a text whose rhetorical strategy is designed to represent an oral literary tradition," appropriating a definition of the Russian Formalist concept of *skaz* with its "illusion of oral narration" (181).

[21] One of the most distinctive examples of autotelic address given by Richardson is Italo Calvino's *If on a winter's night a traveler*, in which both the actual reader and the implied reader are addressed at different points, blurring the borders of diegesis.

[22] See Iser: "three important aspects that form the basis of the relationship between reader and text: the process of anticipation and retrospection, *the consequent unfolding of the text as a living event*, and the resultant impression of lifelikeness" ("The Reading Process," 290; emphasis added).

[23] The embedded quotation is from Ruth Finnegan, *Literacy and Orality*, 89.

[24] The novels clearly situate themselves within the *Bildungsroman* tradition, even down to the division of *The Seven League Boots* into sections labeled "The Apprentice," "The Journeyman," and "The Craftsman."

[25] "BUP" stands for "black urban professional" and is constructed on the model of the term "yuppie," derived from "young urban professional." "Oreo," named for the chocolate cookie with a white cream filling, is a derogatory term suggesting that someone looks black on the outside but is actually white inside.

[26] See Iser, "Reading Process": "one text is potentially capable of several different realizations, and no reading can ever exhaust the full potential, for each individual reader will fill in the gaps in his own way. . . . This is borne out by the fact that a second reading of a piece of literature often produces a different impression from the first" (280).

[27] Fleischman here summarizes findings from Wolfson, "A Feature of Performed Narrative: The Conversational Historical Present" and "The Conversational Historical Present Alternation," and in the embedded quotation cites Dell Hymes, "Breakthrough into Performance."

[28] Fleischman attributes the term "performed story" to Nessa Wolfson.

[29] Fleischman includes a detailed overview of philological and linguistic work on tense usage, 78.

[30] See Ellen Zyroff on the role of apostrophe in epic narration: "An author's apostrophe in epic is a rhetorical figure in which the poet turns away from his third person narrative to address some entity. It is perhaps the poet's most bold means of interjecting himself into his narrative. Each time he turns to address his own literary creations he commits a deliberate, self-conscious act which asserts the verisimilitude of the characters and actions and his personal involvement with them" (ii).

[31] See e.g. *New Grove Dictionary of Jazz*, "Improvisation": "The use of the term 'collective improvisation' is related to the concepts of soloist and accompanists. Where these functions are sharply differentiated the term is not normally used, even though all or most of the players may be improvising more or less freely. It is commonly applied in contexts where some or all members of a group participate in simultaneous improvisation of equal or comparable 'weight,' for example New Orleans jazz . . . it does not preclude the presence of a soloist but it implies a degree of equality among all the players in the ensemble" (314).

[32] See e.g. *New Grove Dictionary of Jazz*, vol. 1, entry for "cutting [bucking, carving] contest," which defines a cutting contest as "a competition between bands or soloists (often players of the same instrument) to determine which has superior skill, stamina, virtuosity, etc. The musicians play successive pieces or (especially in a contest between soloists) successive choruses in a single piece. Such a trial might take place spontaneously, during a performance or jam session, or, in early New Orleans jazz, when two bands, each engaged in its own publicity, met by chance on the streets" (545).

[33] All but one of the twelve chapters bear the names of tunes Payne plays, some familiar standards, others fictional with no referent outside of the novel: "Taps," "Stormin' at the Point," "Off the Bar," "That's Why the Lady Is a Tramp," "My Funny Valentine," "The Standard Form of the American Popular Song," "Stuck in a Groove," "The Kensington Sessions," "Celestial Faith," "Sweet Thing," and concluding with a reiteration of "Taps." The correspondence between chapters

and songs is part of the larger concept of the novel as a greatest-hits album, as reflected in its title.

[34] The same is true in Ondaatje's *Coming Through Slaughter*, as the interviews with jazz musicians, whether real or fictional, dramatize the biographer's search for the "real" Buddy Bolden.

[35] Quinlan's biography, as the product of his research on Payne, is extraordinarily interested in the processes that led to its existence, whether in the sense of Payne's life as a process of development or of Quinlan's research and writing process, even down to revisions of individual text passages: "One has to conclude that in his final musical phase, Jackson Payne was a towering failure. He pursued his end so furiously that it left him with nothing more to say. // Jackson Payne was the last towering colossus of jazz. Listening to his late works is like being in touch with an element as pure and reactive as free oxygen. // One has to conclude that Payne in his final musical phase was toweringly possessed. He reached for the voice of the deity upon his tongue, and from the sound it must have been a terrible God, indeed. // It is a towering romantic fallacy to think that jazz gives privileged access to a player's being. How can a deceptive, manipulative man make music that seems to have the clarity of the greatest truth? The same way a man with palsy can do precise work with his hands. A bad man can do beautiful music because the ability does not extend beyond the task" (270–71).

[36] See Ondaatje's "Credits" in *Coming Through Slaughter*, 157.

[37] See e.g. the subtitle to Marquis, *In Search of Buddy Bolden*. As Marquis points out in the appendix to the 2007 revised edition, this title is not his own claim, but reflects a popular view of Bolden promoted by the publisher.

[38] See Richardson, 18: "the familiar authorial colloquy in which a heterodiegetic narratee ('gentle reader') is directly addressed."

[39] See Richardson, 14: "'you' is particularly devious, since it can refer to the protagonist, the narrator, the narratee, or the reader; authors using this form regularly play on this ambiguity as well as on its multiple possible meanings."

[40] Borshuk remarks on this aspect of Scooter's narration as a kind of call and response with the reader that serves to establish a community based on shared experiences (174).

[41] This paragraph has been adapted from Petermann, "Unheard Jazz," 230–31.

[42] Ondaatje does not distinguish in the novel between those interviews that are taken from his archival research, those that are his own inventions, and those that are based on real interviews but modified in various ways. In this case, the clarinetist Frank Lewis could not be interviewed by the jazz archive, as he had died in the 1920s. His comments here on "electronic history" are clearly anachronisms, part of Ondaatje's conscious fictionalization of history throughout this "historiographic metafiction," to use Linda Hutcheon's term (see e.g. "Historiographic Metafiction"). On Lewis's death, see Marquis, 137. On the relation between Ondaatje's fictionalized history and textualized jazz, see Petermann, "Unheard Jazz."

[43] Her sudden appearance out of the crowd—"But where the bitch came from I don't know" (129)—echoes Bolden's own arrival on the jazz scene in a parade,

as related by Frank Lewis: "Where did he come from? He was found before we knew where he had come from. Born at the age of twenty-two. Walked into a parade one day with white shoes and red shirt. Never spoke of the past. Simply about which way to go for the next 10 minutes. // God I was at that first parade, I was playing, it was a very famous entrance you know. He walks out of the crowd, struggles through onto the street and begins playing, too loud but real and strong you couldn't deny him, and then he went back into the crowd. Then fifteen minutes later, 300 yards down the street, he jumps through the crowd onto the street again, plays, and then goes off. After two or three times we were waiting for him and he came" (37–38). The reading of this dancer as Bolden's doppelgänger is further supported by her "testing me, taunting me to make it past her, old hero, old ego tested against one as cold and pure as himself" (130), as in a cutting contest, in which new players can challenge those who have established themselves. Similarly, the author figure inscribed in the text sees Bolden as his own doppelgänger, which is reinforced by the abundance of mirror images throughout the novel. Just as Bolden measures himself against those musicians who have gone before, Ondaatje as the implied author measures his own creative achievement against this early jazz innovator.

[44] The narrator of *Jazz* also explicitly acknowledges that she changes the events and characters of which she speaks: "Not hating him is not enough; liking, loving him is not useful. I have to alter things" (161).

[45] The protagonist-narrator, while clearly sharing many biographical features with the implied author Albert Murray, remains unnamed (with the exception of nicknames like "Scooter," "my mister," and "Schoolboy") throughout the series. This is reminiscent of the first-person narrator of Ralph Ellison's *Invisible Man*, who likewise refers to his changed name without ever revealing it to the reader. See also the following statement by Murray in an interview with Charles Rowell: "Scooter is a fictional representation of my consciousness. *He is not, of course, a documentary image of me; rather he is a literary device for dealing with my consciousness*" (Rowell and Murray, 399; italics original).

[46] See also the frequent use of "always" in the novel, as an adverb that indicates "anyhow, anywhere, anytime," suggesting the timelessness or allegorical nature of Scooter's memories, which are not individual but universalized.

[47] See Murray's interview with Tony Scherman: "the United States is a mulatto culture. First, let's put things in a world context. Go back to what [the French poet] Paul Valery called Homo europaeus, a composite of Greek logic, Roman administration, and Judeo-Christian morality. That's what makes a European different from somebody in India, Japan, or Africa. Now send him across the Atlantic. You get . . . a new composite: of the ingenious Yankee, the frontiersman, who's part Indian, and the Negro. All Americans, I don't care if it's a neo-Nazi, are part Yankee, part backwoodsman, part Negro" (Scherman, n.p.).

[48] In particular, these phrases are reminiscent of Fats Waller's "(What Did I Do to Be So) Black and Blue," originally composed for the 1929 Broadway show *Hot Chocolates*. The best-known interpretation of this tune, by Louis Armstrong, is also prominently referenced in Ellison's *Invisible Man*.

[49] My translation from the jacket notes of the German edition.

Part II. The Novel Based on a Particular Piece of Music: J. S. Bach's *Goldberg Variations*

This second analysis section focuses on the structure of novels that take J. S. Bach's *Goldberg Variations* as a model, which bear the official title *Aria mit verschiedenen Veränderungen für Cembalo mit 2 Manualen* (Aria with various modifications for the 2-manual harpsichord) and were first published in 1741. These novels employ both the macrostructure of the theme-and-variations form for the novel as a whole and various microstructural elements, such as when individual chapters exhibit parallels to individual variations. I also consider the question of what it means for a novel to imitate a specific piece of music rather than a whole genre, as is the case with the jazz novels analyzed in chapters 2–4. This leads to a discussion of the function this piece of music has for the texts and why this particular piece has inspired so many writers. Though other pieces of classical music have also served as a model for novels—as, for instance, most famously in Anthony Burgess's *Napoleon Symphony*, structured around Beethoven's third symphony (*Eroica*)—none has had the same resonance as Bach's *Goldberg Variations*.[1]

In addition to the five novels analyzed in the following chapters, numerous other works in a variety of genres reflect the influence of Bach's piece. Dieter Kühn's radio play *Goldberg-Variationen*, written in 1972–73 and first broadcast in 1974, is a dialogue between language and music that plays with the concept of the theme and variations as a means of questioning the role of art in a world in which people are being "abused, beaten, tortured, killed" (Kühn, "Nachwort," 149). Anna Enquist's novel *Contrapunt* adapts the idea that the variations had been composed as a tribute to Bach's deceased son, who had loved the aria. Her novel relates the story of a pianist who deals with the loss of her daughter by playing these variations. More minor references pervade literature, where the piece may stand in for classical art in general, for a rational ideal of music, or for any number of other associations. There is a reference to the piece in E. T. A. Hoffmann's *Kreisleriana* (1814/1815), where the musician Kreisler improvises on the thirtieth variation; in Pascal Mercier's 2004 novel

Nachtzug nach Lissabon (Night Train to Lisbon) the *Goldberg Variations* represent an unachieved dream of artistic beauty that the apothecary and former revolutionary O'Kelly remains nostalgic for decades later; George Tabori's play *Goldberg-Variationen* (Goldberg Variations), which premiered in Vienna in 1991, uses the character Goldberg as the assistant to the godlike director Mr. Jay; and many other examples could be listed.[2] In fact, there was even an episode of the television series *The X Files* entitled "The Goldberg Variation," which aired on December 12, 1999 (season 7, episode 6). The variety exhibited by these examples demonstrates the salience of this particular piece of music for a wide range of cultural production. These texts will not form part of the following analyses, however, in part because of a pragmatic restriction to the genre of the novel. Others, such as Enquist's and Mercier's novels, are excluded for the relatively minor role Bach's variations play in their overarching structure.

One theme that recurs frequently in texts dealing with the *Goldberg Variations* is that of its systematic, even mathematical structure. Yet it is not this rationalistic conception of music alone that fascinates authors such as Richard Powers, but the way its deceptively simple rules can breed infinite complexity. The ability of the piece to transcend its structure is likewise thematized in other works. Though its form can be explained, the content or meaning of the piece remains mysterious. This can be said of music in general, perhaps, but it is precisely the symmetry and regularity of Bach's composition that lends itself so well to such a discussion of the nature of art as a craft or technique that must yet strive to surpass the easily comprehensible rules on which it is constructed.

For experimental postmodern writers, the symmetry of the *Goldbergs'* structure itself poses a challenge. Can a novel be constricted into such a rigid form as to correspond to the way Bach's monumental keyboard exercises are systematically grouped into threes, forming canons on every note of the scale up to the ninth, with one variation for each bar of the original sarabande bass theme? And more important, can such a mathematical construction in literature yield a comparable aesthetic beauty to Bach's composition? The degree to which the novels attempt to maintain this structure varies, as the following discussions will show, but this tension between freedom and constraint—or chaos and order—proves to be a central theme in several of the novels.[3] Thus the challenge of the form is necessary because of the possibilities it opens up on the level of content, such that a reflection on the intermedial imitation of music provides a metafictional reflection on how the form and content of the novel mirror each other.

Text Selection

In selecting the texts for the analyses in the following two chapters, the primary consideration was the centrality of J. S. Bach's *Goldberg*

Variations for the overall structure of each novel. Though this musical work plays a role in several other narrative texts, that role is either more marginal or restricted to content rather than form. In the interest of genre fidelity, Dieter Kühn's radio play *Die Goldberg-Variationen* and Francois Girard's 1993 film *Thirty-Two Short Films about Glenn Gould* have not been included. Instead, the following chapters focus on five novels published between 1981 and 2009: Nancy Huston's *Les Variations Goldberg* (1981; *The Goldberg Variations*, 1996), Thomas Bernhard's *Der Untergeher* (1983), Richard Powers's *The Gold Bug Variations* (1991), Gabriel Josipovici's *Goldberg: Variations* (2002), and Rachel Cusk's *The Bradshaw Variations* (2009). Though this study emphasizes literature in English, these texts are in fact drawn from several national literatures, demonstrating the pervasive influence of Bach's composition on literature from around the world. Huston and Cusk were born in English-speaking Canada, though Huston relocated to Paris and wrote her novel first in French before translating it into English herself, whereas Cusk spent much of her youth in the United States before settling in England. Powers is an American writer, Bernhard an Austrian, and Josipovici was born in Nice, France, and lived in Egypt as a child before moving to Britain at age sixteen.

While this is the first extended study to link together the group of texts I am calling the "*Goldberg*-novels," a few theorists in the field of word and music studies have examined the theme and variations as a musical form used in literature. Calvin S. Brown paved the way with his work on the subject, beginning with his groundbreaking monograph *Music and Literature: A Comparison of the Arts* (1948) and continuing in articles such as "Theme and Variations as a Literary Form" (1978) and his interpretation of a particular example of such an adaptation of the form in "Josef Weinheber's Hölderlin Variations: A Comment and Translation" (1968). Horst Petri is another theorist to systematically consider the literary use of musical forms in his monograph *Literatur und Musik* (1964), which includes chapters on the "variation" and the "contrapuntal variation."

Though there is a small but significant body of research on the musical novels *The Goldberg Variations* (Nancy Huston), *Goldberg: Variations* (Gabriel Josipovici), and especially *Der Untergeher* (Thomas Bernhard), until recently no studies had compared these novels with one another or treated them as members of a group. Theodore Ziolkowski has considered them (with the exception of Cusk's *The Bradshaw Variations*) as "Literary Variations on Bach's Goldberg," but the compressed space of a single article does not allow him to go into great detail on the structural parallels between the novels and their musical model. His focus is thus primarily on the fact of the *Goldberg Variations*' strong influence on novels, the frequency of which within a relatively short period he explains as "a striking symptom of the late twentieth-century Bach renaissance" surrounding the tricentennial of J. S. Bach's birth in 1985 (640). Werner Wolf is unique thus far in having produced excellent interpretations of the musical forms involved in both Huston's and Josipovici's novels in the articles "Intermedial Iconicity in Fiction: Tema con variazioni" and "The Role of Music in Gabriel Josipovici's *Goldberg: Variations*." In the conclusion of the latter article, he briefly alludes to the differing themes evoked in connection with music in the two novels, while a footnote acknowledges Powers's *The Gold Bug Variations* as yet another text "that refers to the same composition of Bach's and would merit a comparison in a more extended frame" (315n25), though this detailed comparison has had to wait for the present study. Another article dealing with Huston's text is Frédérique Arroyas's "Literary Mediations of Baroque Music: Biber, Bach, and Nancy Huston," which provides interpretations of two musical novels by Huston, but does not compare *Les variations Goldberg* with other texts based on the same musical model.[4] There is a considerable body of work on Thomas Bernhard's *Der Untergeher*, largely restricted to a German-speaking context and not yet incorporated into work on other *Goldberg*-related texts. Few of the studies on the musicality of Bernhard's prose explicitly relate the text to the *Goldberg Variations* as a model. Among those few are Gregor Hens's excellent 1999 monograph *Thomas Bernhards Trilogie der Künste* and Liesbeth M. Voerknecht's article "Thomas Bernhard und die Musik: *Der Untergeher*." To date, Jay Labinger's meticulous analysis in "Encoding an Infinite Message: Richard Powers's *The Gold Bug Variations*" is the only study to consider the musical structures in that novel in detail, while Rachel Cusk's *The Bradshaw Variations* has yet to receive any scholarly attention at all.

The present study thus goes beyond existing research on novels based on the *Goldberg Variations*, treating them as a group of texts that share a common musical model. This approach allows for the first in-depth consideration of individual elements of the musical work that are imitated in these texts and a comparison of the different means employed by the texts to achieve their aims. Furthermore, the striking differences in these novels stimulate a discussion of the reasons for using such a piece of music as a model for a literary text at all. Because the texts (and their authors) perceive the music differently, they focus on different aspects of the music and create very different literary adaptations.

Notes

[1] There have been very few other imitations of specific pieces of music, but examples can be found. The best-known case, apart from the *Goldberg* novels, concerns Anthony Burgess's *Napoleon Symphony*, which adapts the form of Beethoven's Fifth Symphony (*Eroica*) and builds on the story of its composition, in which

Beethoven initially dedicated the symphony to Napoleon Bonaparte but then tore up the dedication, calling him a tyrant, and proposing instead Prometheus as the hero of the piece. For a detailed analysis of musical structures in this novel, see Shockley, *Music in the Words*, 75–116. He also analyzes Burgess's "K. 550 (1788)" (from Burgess, *On Mozart: A Paean for Wolfgang* [1991]) as a further example of a text imitating a specific piece, in this case Mozart's Symphony no. 40 (Shockley, 33–44). Another example of a prose text imitating a specific piece of music is Gert Jonke's *Schule der Geläufigkeit* (1977; published in English translation as *Homage to Czerny: Studies in Virtuoso Technique*, 2008), but there are also cases of drama adapting a musical form, as in Jonke's play *Chorphantasie* (2003) and Moisés Kaufman's play *33 Variations* (2007; Broadway production, 2009), based on Beethoven's *Diabelli Variations*. Even if the group of *Goldberg* novels is taken as a special case of the musical novel, the techniques and forms imitated by these novels can be applied to other types of musicalized fiction, whether involving the imitation of other specific pieces, of sonata form, or of a genre of music such as jazz.

[2] Ziolkowski includes as additional examples Ian McEwan's *Saturday* (2005) and Thomas Fahy's *Night Visions* (2004) as novels in which the *Goldberg Variations* provide the sound track to key scenes of the plot (627).

[3] This tension between freedom and constraint, between chaos and order, is one that also plays a significant role in jazz novels such as Ondaatje's *Coming Through Slaughter* and Fuller's *The Best of Jackson Payne*. I return to this shared theme of jazz and *Goldberg* novels in the conclusion.

[4] Arroyas does make a brief reference to Bernhard's *Der Untergeher*, but not explicitly as a novel based on the *Goldberg Variations*.

5: Structural Patterns in Novels Based on the *Goldberg Variations*

Themes and Variations in Music and Literature

IN ITS BROAD SENSE, the term *variation* applies to both music and literature and refers to the modification of something given (*Das Bach-Lexikon*, entry for "Variation," 531). As such, it is a fundamental principle of design. Literary definitions of variation tend to focus on this aspect, including reference to lexical, syntactical, and phonological variation as a means of maintaining interest amidst repetitive structures (i.e., in poetry) or of upsetting readers' expectations (Leech, 256–57). In music, however, there is also a more specific definition of *variation* that is exemplified by not only Bach's *Goldberg Variations*, but also by Beethoven's *Diabelli Variations* and numerous others both before and since. "Im engeren Sinne sind Variationen, wie man sie vor allem in der europäischen Musik der letzten Jahrhunderte findet, längere oder kürzere Folgen von Veränderungen über ein gewöhnlich vorangestelltes Thema" (In a narrower sense, variations as they primarily are found in European music of the last centuries are longer or shorter series of modifications on a theme that is usually presented at the outset; *Das Bach-Lexikon*, "Variation," 531). In music—in contrast to literature[1]—variation is thus not only a principle of composition but also an established form.

The term *theme* also has different connotations in literature and music, and thus needs to be clarified here before I turn to the analysis of novels based on this form. *Grove's Dictionary of Music and Musicians* defines a "theme" as follows:

> THEME ... A piece of musical material in a complete, self-contained form, but used in composition for the purpose of development, elaboration or variation. It is not, strictly speaking, identical with either (*a*) a melody or tune, (*b*) a subject or (*c*) a motive, for the following reasons:
> (*a*) It need not be purely melodic, but may include harmony and texture.
> (*b*) It is longer and more complete in itself than a subject, which may be of no significance until it begins to be worked out by the composer.

(*c*) It is even more extended than a motive, which is too brief to have a formally developed shape of its own.

Variations, being musical discourses on a given piece of material, are thus properly described as being on such and such a "theme," whereas fugues are based on subjects. (409)

Very frequently, the theme to be varied is itself a complete piece, such as a well-known song, as with Schubert's Trout Variations (the fourth movement of the Piano Quintet in A major, also known as the Trout Quintet), which take his own *Lied* "Die Forelle" as their theme. Conventionally, the theme will be clearly presented at the beginning of the piece, after which the variations will distance themselves ever further from that starting point, though retaining elements of the theme in each variation. *Grove's Dictionary* lists several possible types of themes as the "matter to be varied" ("Variation," 670–71), including not only "tune[s]," or "polyphonic texture[s]," but also less obvious elements such as "bass" lines and "harmonic progression[s]" (670). As will be discussed in the following, the theme of Bach's *Goldberg Variations* is a harmonic progression that can be found in the bass line. As such, this theme is actually never stated in isolation. The "Aria" that begins the piece is not in fact the theme itself, but its first variation. As with the different types of material that can constitute the theme, there are also several different strategies by which this initial material can be varied. All require that "in some shape or another the original matter must remain essentially present in the new. . . . The matter to be varied must not merely proliferate; it must itself persist" (671). The theme of a set of variations, then, is not merely a subject that can be expressed in terms of content (such as the "program" of so-called program music), but is a form that must persist in its variations, though it be embellished, drawn out, condensed, moved into a minor key, or otherwise modified.

Literary themes, on the other hand, are rarely defined in terms of form, but almost exclusively in terms of content.[2] In common usage, a theme is often equated with the subject of a text, that is, what the text is about. In literary criticism, it is sometimes related to a *motif*, as a recurring element, or to a *thesis* as the "doctrinal content" (Gudas, 311) of the text. A motif, however, being repeated in very similar form, does not experience the high degree of variation used for a theme, which is more abstract than a concrete phrase. A thesis, too, can often be paraphrased in quite specific terms, an approach that is less successful in identifying a theme, as the latter is less something that can be postulated than an issue or topic for discussion. A theme, then, is something intricately connected to the subject matter of a text, but which also serves to link the parts in the manner of a thread running through the entire work.

In this chapter, I explore the way four novels based on J. S. Bach's *Goldberg Variations* adopt the musical form of the theme and variations.

This involves, as the definitions given here clearly illustrate, a transition from one kind of theme and variation to another. Though both texts and music are capable of varying themes, they traditionally do so in different ways. Indeed, this reflects a primary distinction between the dominant emphasis in verbal arts on signification and the reduced capacity for representation in music. Clearly the themes that breed the variations in these novels do not become musical themes, but use the music as an analogy. At the same time, they do move significantly closer to their musical model in terms of structure than simply restricting themselves to the types of themes and variation native to the novel.

Adapting the Musical Theme and Variations to the Novel

The most immediately recognizable structural parallel in most of the novels based on Bach's *Goldberg Variations* is of course the form of the theme and variations itself. Several of the novels considered here assign chapter divisions and numbers to match the number of variations in Bach's piece. In Richard Powers's *The Gold Bug Variations* and Nancy Huston's *The Goldberg Variations*, the chapters are not only thirty-two in number (corresponding to the thirty variations plus the initial aria[3] and its repetition at the end of the piece), but the first and last are not assigned a number and are instead labeled "Aria," making the correspondence explicit. In Huston's case, the chapters are further labeled "Variatio I," "Variatio II," and so forth, matching the Italian terminology used in Bach's score.

Rachel Cusk's novel *The Bradshaw Variations* does not set apart the first and last chapters paratextually, but the total number is again thirty-two, suggesting that chapters 1 and 32 correspond to the aria, chapter 2 to the first variation, and so on. Though the *Goldberg Variations* are in fact never explicitly mentioned in the novel, the two epigraphs referring to Bach, the word "variations" in the title of the novel, and the fact that Bach is one of the three composers mentioned by the protagonist Thomas Bradshaw (and one of only two that he explicitly learns to play on the piano)[4] together suggest that the structural parallel can only be the *Goldbergs*, as the only major set of variations Bach composed.[5] The number of chapters thus is not coincidental, but gestures toward other parallels in structure between the novel and Bach's work, as will be demonstrated in the following analyses.

In the case of Gabriel Josipovici's novel *Goldberg: Variations*, only thirty chapters are present, suggesting that the "Aria" and its repetition have been omitted. Bach's original title of the piece—*Aria mit verschiedenen Veränderungen*—deceptively suggests that the aria is what is to be varied in the following variations, so that its omission could be taken as concealing the theme on which the variations are based. This would encourage the reader to posit a theme that is implied by the variations but never stated directly. Werner Wolf makes a similar point, suggesting that

> by omitting the narrative analogy to the opening (and concluding) "Aria" in Bach's work and by thus creating a conspicuous absence or *Leerstelle sensu* Iser, (esp. 235), [Josipovici] renders it difficult for the reader to recognize such a theme. Yet one of the well-known functions of marked absences in literature is indeed to activate the reader. In this Josipovici arguably again follows Bach, since in *Die Goldberg Variationen* the theme is not easy to detect either. ("Role of Music," 302; italics original)

In emphasizing the role of the aria for the listener's perception of the theme, Wolf comes close to equating the aria with that theme, as have other literary critics.[6] Yet Wolf's comment that Bach's theme, too, is more subtle than the more frequent "soprano melodies that abound in musical history" (302) shows that he recognizes that the aria is not in fact the theme, but an ornamentation of it, like the other variations.

The actual theme is in fact not, as might be expected, the aria itself, but rather the "harmonic progression" (Schulenberg, 320) in the bass line that underlies not only the aria but each of the successive variations as well. The aria is thus an embellishment of or variation on the actual theme—which Bach called the *Fundamental-Noten* (cited in Schulenberg, 326) and which is sometimes referred to as the "Base" (*The Gold Bug Variations*, 191 and passim), "ground-bass" (Peter Williams, 37), or "fundamental bass" (Peter Williams, 36). The theme is a hypothetical or reconstructed line that never appears in its purest form in any of the variations, including the aria itself.[7] This bass line consists of one note per measure, or thirty-two notes in total. Of course, in each variation these notes are expanded on, as in the triads that begin the aria or the more elaborate figures in the bass lines of several of the other variations. Still, in some form, this theme can be discerned in each variation as the foundation that holds the whole structure together.

Presumably, it is precisely the flexibility of the *Goldberg* theme that lends itself so well to adaptation as textual themes and variations. Instead of working with a melody that is highly recognizable in each of its variations, these novels can choose a theme that is more implied than revealed in each successive incarnation. Just as Bach's theme is subtly present but overshadowed in many variations by virtuoso ornamentation, the themes of these novels may be discreetly lurking behind or beneath other more superficial concerns. Thus, the textualization of the *Goldberg Variations* contradicts assumptions that a theme must be a particular sentence or other statement of an idea that can be recognized in a comparable form throughout its variations.[8] An untrained listener would not, without considerable concentration, be able to detect the bass line permeating all thirty-two movements of the piece, yet it is consistently present, albeit masked by the diverse melodic lines in the right hand. Likewise, a theme in the novels based on the *Goldberg Variations* may be more abstract and less explicitly stated, particularly considering "that literary themes always tend to be much less original and much less specific than musical ones" (Wolf, "Role of Music," 302).

Richard Powers's *The Gold Bug Variations*: Out of Simple Rules, Complexity

An analysis of a novel as a theme-and-variations form presumes an identification of the theme that will be subsequently varied, regardless of whether that theme is clearly stated or more subtly implied, as in Bach's *Goldberg Variations*. Richard Powers's *The Gold Bug Variations*, a highly complex novel, adopts a theme that in its simplicity is a metacommentary on the text itself, which can be summarized as "out of simple rules, complexity." This theme—an idea rather than a specific phrase and thus not dependent on the precise wording used—receives one of its clearest presentations in the novel's version of the aria, the initial poem entitled "The Perpetual Calendar." In four sections that each consist of four four-line stanzas,[9] Powers outlines the omnipresence of patterns that form the basis of all variation, whether in music:

> What could be simpler? Not even music
> yet, but only counting: Do, ti, la, sol.
> Believing their own pulse, four tones
> break into combinations, uncountable. (7)

or in biology, evolution, and genetics:

> From language to life is just four letters.
> How can that awful fecundity come
> from four semaphores, shorthand and dumb,
> nothing in themselves but everything? (8)

The poem, like the variations that will make up the rest of the novel, insists that the source of all life is a simple code,[10] a code that paradoxically contains as potential all the complexity that it breeds—"the complex can be contained in the simple" (364)—and yet in itself cannot predict the myriad forms its progeny will take. The motif introduced in the "Aria's" first line quoted above—"What could be simpler?"—will recur ten times[11] throughout the remainder of the novel, most prominently as an abbreviated restatement of the aria at the novel's close (639).

The novel's premise is thus that every realm of experience can be derived from or traced back to deceptively simple codes such as the notes of a G major scale, the four bases in the genetic code, or—though less obviously stated—the letters of the alphabet or sounds in a language. Powers's novel is constructed on the same premise postulated for music and biology and encourages the reader to search for the underlying code that provides its structural framework. The mathematical and musical principles that structure the three plot strands of this novel will be discussed below in the section "Numerical Structure: Twos and Threes."

Nancy Huston's *The Goldberg Variations*: The Concert Situation

In Nancy Huston's novel *The Goldberg Variations*, thirty audience members give themselves over to their thoughts during a concert performed by their mutual acquaintance Liliane Kulainn. Each audience member's interior monologue forms one of the thirty chapter variations, while Liliane's own thoughts are presented as the "Aria" and its return at the close of the novel, rounding off the cycle. A comparison of all the chapters, despite the wide variety of perspectives and interests associated with the thirty-one characters, reveals numerous overlapping topics. Werner Wolf has identified the following topics as possible themes of the novel's variations: psychological disturbances and different forms of love; political, feminist, meta-aesthetic, metamusical, and metatextual issues; body-related motives; and time ("Intermedial Iconicity," 350–51). Of these, Wolf correctly points out that none is so pervasive as to correspond to Bach's theme except the theme of "time," which is present not only as a topic of each chapter, but is also prominently introduced in the novel's epigraphs, "You have exactly ninety-six minutes" (9) and "You have all the time in the world" (11) ("Intermedial Iconicity," 351).

The critic Frédérique Arroyas, in searching for a theme dealt with by all the variations of Huston's novel, objects to what she sees as a lack of accuracy in Huston's variation of the theme of the initial aria (a theme that she defines as "the performer's reticence and discomfort toward musical performance," 104n13) in the following chapters. Because this specific theme is not present in all the variations, she argues instead for "the overarching concept of musical performance that is present throughout the variations and, in the true spirit of the variation form, each guest's intervention brings about the transformation of the performer's attitude toward musical performance" (104n13).[12] But really, what is taken up by each variation is the concert situation in which Liliane Kulainn performs the *Goldberg Variations* in a private performance for thirty friends from her past and present. The theme that is varied, then, is the situation itself, much as in Browning's *The Ring and the Book*, discussed by Calvin S. Brown as a paradigmatic example of the theme and variations as a literary form (*Music and Literature*, 132–34; "Theme and Variations as a Literary Form," 41–42). The consistent change to this basic theme, which produces the thirty variations, is the change in perspective, as each chapter is narrated by a different member of the audience. Accordingly, the topics on which each narrator reflects during the performance vary with his or her personality, relationship to Liliane and to the other members of the audience, as well as interest in and knowledge—or lack thereof—of classical music.

Of course, Wolf and Arroyas are both correct to point out certain topics that recur throughout the novel, most strikingly thoughts on musical performance as such (Arroyas, 104n13) and on the broader topic of time (Wolf, "Intermedial Iconicity," 351). These can be seen as motifs derived from the broader theme, however, as they are intricately related to the concert situation in which they arise. While listening to Liliane play, the characters' thoughts turn to reflections on the value and status of Baroque music (i.e., Variations 18, 28); to questions of technique (2, 13, 15, 26); and to the role of performer and/or audience (esp. the aria, Variation 1, and the return of the aria). Likewise, they are concerned with time in relation to the duration of the concert (aria, Variations 3, 4, 24, 28, 30, *aria da capo*); to the tempo with which the variations are being performed (Variations 2, 13); to rhythm (Variations 18, 22, 29); to the *Goldberg Variations* and harpsichord music in general as the product of an earlier age (Variations 2, 5); in relation to time as wasted (Variations 10, 14, 18, 28); to music as timeless or a performance as the temporary suspension of time (Variations 3, 12, 20, *aria da capo*); and to the passing of time as evidenced in changes in people present at the concert, especially Liliane and her partner Bernald Thorer, as perceived by family, lovers, and friends from earlier stages of their lives (Variations 6, 7, 8, 9, 10, 11, 16, 21, 22, 25). Yet as pointed out above, these can all be seen as connected to the concert situation in which characters muse on topics that arise as they watch Liliane, think about her performance, or about what they would rather be doing instead.

As Calvin Brown observed in his first study of literary themes and variations (all based on the musical form), the individual variation "departs from the original theme in some specific and consistent way, so that it forms an intelligible unit in itself" (*Music and Literature*, 128). The use of related principles of variation throughout the set allows the work to retain a sense of unity, while each variation is a unique presentation of the unifying theme. For example, Bach's variations can be grouped into threes, with the third of each group (except the last) a canon. Because the second voice of each canon begins at a different interval from the one before (canon at the unison, canon at the second, canon at the third, and so on), each is a distinct piece, though the principle of variation is applied consistently.[13] One of the most successful approaches to the problem of consistent variation in literary imitations of the form is what could be called a character variation, in which the principle of variation is the changing viewpoint, and because each viewpoint is distinct from all the others, the variations are both clearly linked with one another and each is simultaneously "an intelligible unit in itself." This straightforward model is the one adopted by Huston. All the variations in the form of the characters' individual thoughts are linked by the theme of the shared concert situation. These character variations are further linked retrospectively by Liliane's revelation in the final chapter that she has in fact "composed" all the variations, that the thoughts of the thirty other characters have all been imagined by her.[14] This theme thus differs in kind from the theme of Powers's novel, as it is a formal situation or even setting in both place and time that serves to frame the events of the novel, while Powers's theme is closer to the literary sense of the term. It too, however, by virtue of its metacommentary on structures of all kinds, is programmatic for the construction of the novel and thus goes well beyond a mere subject in terms of content.

Gabriel Josipovici's *Goldberg: Variations*: "The Creative Capacity"[15]

Gabriel Josipovici's highly experimental novel *Goldberg: Variations* resists the reader's search for a unifying plot or framing situation for the bulk of the text. The first few chapters initially convey the impression that this novel, like Huston's, is also based on a particular situation as a theme. The writer Samuel Goldberg, in an echo of the legend of Bach's composition of the *Goldberg Variations*, arrives at the estate of Mr. Tobias Westfield around the year 1800, with the task of reading to his patron at night to help him overcome his chronic insomnia. The first chapter, written in the form of a letter to Goldberg's wife, describes Goldberg's arrival and first meeting with Westfield, concluding with the revelation that this letter is in fact the first such text Goldberg has composed to read to Westfield. In this light, the successive chapters appear to be additional pieces written by Goldberg, such that they can be seen as variations on the theme of his commission for Westfield. The first thirteen chapters revolve for the most part around characters related either to Westfield or to Goldberg, while two are dialogues between Goldberg and the man who drives the carriage that brings him to Westfield's estate, and two are short pieces of nonfiction (chapter 5, "The Sand," deals with archaeological excavations on the Orkney Islands; chapter 11, "Containers," is a still-life description of jars and bottles on a shelf).[16]

The postulated linking theme of Goldberg as author of all these variations collapses, however, when chapter 14 introduces a present-day first-person narrator, Gerald. Since this much later figure can hardly have been conceived and invented by Goldberg at the turn of the nineteenth century, the introduction of this figure is a metalepsis that breaks out of the narrative frame that the reader had been led to construct thus far. Nevertheless, chapters 15–18 return to the initial setting; a letter by Goldberg's wife and other chapters deal with the characters previously encountered. Chapter 19, "Back in London," returns to the present day and Gerald, who continues to struggle both with the dissolution of his marriage and with his writer's block. The book project that so absorbs him, however, will not be identified until chapter 25. In this chapter, the narrator Gerald expresses his frustration with his book, despairing, "What have I to do with Goldberg, Westfield, Ballantyne and the rest? What do I know about England or Scotland in the year 1800, or about the Jews of that time or the landed gentry? Why should I want to tell these stories and to tell them in this way?" (171). This chapter provides a new framework for the reader's understanding of the novel so far. Goldberg is not simply the fictional author, but is himself also a character within the book written by Gerald, an intradiegetic author at a higher level.

It is thus not Goldberg's, but Gerald's struggle that unites the various chapters, however loosely, using Goldberg to mirror the narrator's function at another diegetic level. Gerald attempts to justify his inclusion of himself in his book as follows: "I had thought that talking about myself would validate the rest, would give it grounding, authority. But the figure mocks me, telling me that this is a mistake. Perhaps, though, it is a mistake I have to make" (173). Though he seems to require this "confession of failure" (173) to overcome his writer's block, it is not, however, in itself enough to proceed with the book. Instead, it is a reflection on Klee's painting *Wander-Artist* and on the etymology of its title that allows him to proceed. Gerald's definition of the *wander-artist* as "an itinerant public performer" (174) provides him with an image around which to construct the novel. In the following section Gerald is seen from outside, described in the third person, but it quickly becomes clear that the "he" so described is not Gerald, but rather exists on yet another diegetic level, that of the implied author of the novel:[17] "He has tried to enliven things by inventing a present-day figure through which to filter the rest, but far from this giving authenticity to the work, it has only made it seem contrived and false.... He has tried to ground the whole by finally speaking in the first person, but that first person seems as false and hollow as the rest and he has quickly discarded it" (176). The problem of how to finish the book is only resolved after a dialogue with an unnamed "other" (176–78) who is associated with the figure depicted in Klee's *Wander-Artist*. Indeed, the first-person address that emerges at the end of the "other's" dialogue with the implied author figure is continued in the following chapter, "Wander-Artist." This "other" twice refers to the position of his arm in terms like those used for the figure in the painting: "my upraised arm," "arm raised in greeting" (180). He speaks in riddles and encourages the reader to seek to identify him or to interpret his allegorical function. Statements such as "If I was not here, passing through, there would be either the dead weight of history or the dead weightlessness of pure invention" (180) suggest that "the other" embodies the idea of inspiration, or rather the ability to make connections, to "see the importance of between" (177).

Werner Wolf identifies this figure as "the creative capacity," as Goldberg terms it in a discussion with Westfield (157): "as both the embodiment and the reality of the creative capacity, he is ultimately responsible for the entire text as a fiction" (Wolf, "Role of Music," 305). In his search for a unifying theme of the novel's variations, Wolf suggests that "one can identify the following theme or rather themes which give a certain unity to the novel: (a.) most conspicuously the 'creative capacity' (157) explicitly mentioned in chapter 22, and (b.)—somewhat less conspicuously—relations between two human beings, in particular emotional ones and relations that manifest themselves in dialogue" ("The Role of Music," 302). As Wolf observes (303), the theme of the "creative capacity" is broad enough to provide a template for such diverse chapters as those dealing with the process of writing and writer's block, whether Goldberg's (1, 16, 24), Gerald's (14, 19, 23, 25), or the implied author's (26), as well as chapters discussing literature, art, and music (8, 11, 13, 15, 18). The link between writer's block and insomnia is clearly established at various points, as when Gerald writes: "I had no doubt that if I could have slept as she did I would long since have solved the problems posed by the book. But to have slept like that I would not have had to have any problems in the first place" (96).[18] As a result, all the chapters dealing with Westfield's (as well as Gerald's) insomnia can also be seen as variations on the theme of the "creative capacity," in this case in its inversion as the inability to sleep because of a blockage in the writing process. Finally, the remaining chapters, as texts written by one or the other of the intradiegetic narrators (Goldberg, Gerald, or the implied author above him who is introduced in chapter 26), also draw attention to themselves as the result of processes of creation, so that this theme can be seen running throughout the entire series of variations, both in terms of content and as a structural principle.

Rachel Cusk's *The Bradshaw Variations*: Structuring Chaos

Rachel Cusk's *The Bradshaw Variations* consists of a series of thirty-two vignettes from the lives of members of the Bradshaw family: Thomas, his wife Tonie, their daughter Alexa, their Polish lodger Olga, Thomas's older brother Howard and his wife Claudia, his younger brother Leo, his parents, and Tonie's parents, the Swanns. These episodes cover a period of one year from the time that Thomas begins to stay home with Alexa while Tonie goes back to work full time as the head of the English department at her university. Each chapter, narrated in the third person, is focalized through the consciousness of one of these characters, the changing perspectives providing the primary principle for variation. The theme that is varied is less a single idea or specific topic than a complex of related topics, ranging from interpersonal relations and the impossibility of truly understanding another person, to questions of life choices, to the rigidity of familial relationships over time, as well as to meditations on art. Thomas in particular—the focalizer for ten of the thirty-two chapters, including the first and last—is devoting his "sabbatical" (59) to learning to play the piano and frequently reflects on the nature and value of music and art in general. This motif, however, is not broad enough to be the overarching theme of the novel, as it appears only peripherally in the chapters revolving around other characters.

What unites their different stories and situations is a persistent focus on structure. This theme is first announced in the second of the two epigraphs to the novel, attributed to Jean-Paul Sartre: "[Bach] taught us how to find originality within an established discipline; actually—how to live" (bracketed word original; n.p.). Originality within an established discipline, structure and order as providing a necessary framework for creativity: these are ideas that are explored throughout the novel in various permutations. They can be seen in an attention to the detail of the characters' daily schedules—the "established discipline" of their lives—and the role it plays in giving shape to their thoughts. In some cases, the order of routine is seen as stifling creativity, as when Claudia repeatedly complains that the responsibilities of motherhood prevent her from finding time to paint in her studio.

Thomas, who lacks such a rigid order to his days, alternates between embracing his flexibility and struggling to hold onto the rhythm of days and months. For example, before he quit his job he "used to decide various things," such as keeping a diary or sketching other passengers on the train in order to "reclaim" that time "from the wastage of every day," "to sink an anchor down into that narrow channel of time" (71). Later, the arbitrary date of the year is something that he needs to grasp onto, to orient himself in the unfamiliar position of an outside observer of life:

> He tries to remember what month it is. . . . He laughs aloud—it is funny, that he doesn't know what month it is. He says the names of the months to himself. No one name means more to him than any other. . . . He remembers that it is Thursday, that it is January. He feels better. He has accomplished a small but necessary task, something to make himself more comfortable. The year is an event he is observing, not participating in, like an audience watching a play. (116)

Little daily rituals—such as the time when tea is served, exemplified by the discord between Thomas's parents when Mr. Bradshaw is kept waiting for his tea (chapter 4)—are portrayed as necessary supports in the constant struggle to keep a grasp on reality.

Reality and the problematic nature of such a concept is a motif related to the theme that also occurs in many of the novel's variations. The words "reality," "real," and "unreal" are used with striking frequency. For example, Thomas's brother Leo reflects that he had to "break some contract with reality . . . to advance himself" (56); young Alexa stares at a vivid river scene in a museum, "ach[ing] to enter its reality. She feels it, the ecstasy of the imaginary becoming real" (196); other guests at a party "don't seem to belong to the same reality as Tonie. Either they are unreal or she herself is" (211); and the concrete supplants the hypothetical in the form of actual dog food in a business meeting about restructuring a dog food company: "He remembers the way reality itself was made unreal. . . . After all that artificiality the actual had been uncovered. Thomas realized it had been there all along" (70–71).

Similarly, recurring words such as "form," "shape," and "structure" point to the importance of this idea of order in life. For example:

> Everyone here is so *formless* and anonymous. Their bodies look lumpy in the dusk, their faces featureless and indifferent as stones. (211; italics added)

> He wonders whether love is a *form*, like music, that takes what has no name or being of its own and *shapes* it. (86; italics added)

> [Howard's] enduring reality provides what Thomas thinks of as *structure*. (31; italics added)

The importance of order is also emphasized in several scenes involving cleaning up the Bradshaw house (i.e., chapters 8, 13, 14, 16); Thomas helping his mother clear out boxes in her attic (chapter 20); and in the lodger Olga's musings on how the Bradshaws can live in such an untidy environment (chapter 9). The implication is that form is considered more important than content, though the Sartre quotation at the novel's outset reveals that it is precisely the interaction between the two that is essential.

Finally, one other motif gains prominence that is related to the main theme of structure, one that grows out of the tension between content and form. This is the problem of interpersonal relationships, particularly between family members, which suffer from an unbridgeable "chasm" (133) between people, since one can only know another person's outer form and not their inner self. Outer form is not merely the physical, but also the impression of someone gained from outside that becomes a pattern against which every subsequent action is measured. Several characters reflect on this topic, both as general realizations "that it is impossible to fully understand another human being" (30) and as specific instances of bafflement at another person's seemingly uncharacteristic behavior that forces a reassessment of that person, for example after a party when "Tonie feels, suddenly, that she does not know Claudia at all. She is aware of Claudia's body, her hands with their rings on the steering wheel, her atmosphere coming at her across the dark. But her knowledge of this entity—Claudia—has been marginalized" (95).

The development of these motifs across numerous permutations allows a consideration of the theme of form in its many facets. The importance of form for content is also expressed in its opposite, in the seemingly unbridgeable gulf between form and content, which leads to the recognition of the inaccuracy of surface appearances and the resulting misunderstandings as individuals seek to reconstruct a hidden meaning beneath. Art, particularly music, is postulated as one way of giving form to nebulous material, of organizing it and thus making it possible for meaning to be produced. As a result, art can be seen as a kind of parallel to everyday struggles to organize the material of one's perceptions, as both aim to order chaotic and often unwieldy raw material into a manageable and aesthetically pleasing structure. As with the other novels, this theme has not only implications for the content of the text, but also relates to the structural decision to use an art form—a piece of music—as an aesthetic and structural model for ordering the story of the Bradshaws' everyday lives.

Numerical Structure: Twos and Threes

Bach's masterpiece of the theme-and-variations form is a model of numerical symmetry.[19] The thirty-two movements of the *Goldberg Variations* correspond precisely to the thirty-two bars of the original theme (or the thirty-two bars in all but the few variations that demonstrate the technique of diminution, in which two bars of the theme are condensed into one bar of the variation). Additionally, the number thirty-two can be broken down into other numbers that are integral to the structure of the whole piece: twos and fours. Specifically, each movement consists of two halves, each containing sixteen measures[20] and further reducible to four groups of four measures. This structure is explicitly discussed in the first lines of *The Gold Bug Variations*:

> What could be simpler? Four
> scale-steps descend from Do.
> Four such measures carry over
> the course of four phrases, then home. (7)

The square established in these first four blocks of four is embellished to a cube in that not only are the first sixteen bars mirrored in a second half, but each half is also repeated to yield a perfect cube of sixty-four measures.[21] Such mathematical structures were described by Bach's contemporary Johann Matheson as "an aid in establishing the 'Grundriss,' or outer architecture, of a given work, as well as in arranging and ordering its inner parts" (Franklin, 232).[22]

Merely through the adoption of the number of chapters to match the numbers of variations in Bach's piece, these novels infuse their own works with the numerical symmetry of the original. The lack of repetitions at the end of each section, however, somewhat weakens the impression of perfect symmetry. In fact, though, performances of the *Goldberg Variations* do not always preserve the repetitions (see, most famously, Glenn Gould's 1955 recording) and it is questionable whether all the repetitions would have been performed in Bach's time.[23] What is more, the symmetry and mathematical regularity of the piece is not necessarily immediately apparent to a listener. Though the overall number of movements can easily be discerned, the patterns of twos and fours are less obvious, such that Peter Williams points out: "That the repeat of the *Aria* was not written out is a reminder that any symmetry or number-play pointed out in this account of the *Goldberg* is not obtrusive or made distractingly obvious" (92).

The internal division into two equal halves of sixteen bars each corresponds precisely to a division of the entire piece into the first sixteen and the last sixteen movements. Indeed, the sixteenth variation marks the beginning of the second half by means of its character as an overture in the French style (and labeled "Ouverture" in the score). Beginning "with a tonic chord on the downbeat, like many orchestral overtures" (Schulenberg, 331), this movement signals a new beginning at the set's midpoint. To further underscore the symmetries that characterize the *Goldberg Variations*, this variation that opens the second half draws greater attention than the other variations to its own binary structure. Though all the variations—including the aria—are divided into two halves, this is the only variation to include a change of time signature for the second half. The piece thus takes on an entirely new character halfway through, as it moves from a stately cut time (noted as ¢) to a fugue in $\frac{3}{8}$ time.[24]

Although it would be an exaggeration to claim that the novels imitate the form of the overture in the sixteenth variation, several of them do highlight this section as somehow different from what went before or otherwise marking a break that can be seen as initiating a new beginning of the series at the midpoint. The internal division of the movement that mirrors the larger division into halves is taken up by Josipovici in a chapter that provides a microcosm of the larger novel. Specifically, the problem of composing variations on a theme that occupies the novel (and its various intradiegetic writers) is dramatized in a scene based on Bach's

Musikalisches Opfer (*Musical Offering*) in a *mise en abyme* of the novel's structure (Wolf, "Role of Music," 298, 300).

This chapter has a majestic character, with its focus on Goldberg's meeting with the King, which corresponds to the majestic beginning section of the sixteenth variation. Goldberg, like Bach before him, is summoned before the King of Prussia and asked to extemporize on a given theme. The first portion of the chapter is related in third-person narration, describing Goldberg's performance at court and including the first variation on the royal theme. In the second half of the chapter, a switch in narrative form takes place as the third-person narration is replaced by a letter from Goldberg to the King. This, too, is an echo of the story of Bach's *Musikalisches Opfer*, in which the composer, upon returning home to Leipzig, composed additional and more complex fugues than those he had performed at court. Goldberg, similarly, writes to the King expressing his dissatisfaction with his performance and offering sketches for several additional texts on the King's theme, "A man who had enough wanted everything, . . . As a result he was left with nothing" (112). Indeed, the texts Goldberg provides can be seen as forming a parallel to the movements of Bach's piece, with a first, somewhat longer tale of Judas corresponding to the initial solo movement, "seven tiny tales" (121) as an equivalent to the seven canons, and finally "a longer narrative, divided into three parts" (122), which could be compared to the trio sonata or chamber music sections. The precise form of this collection of "variations" that Goldberg sends to the King demonstrates of course only a loose correspondence to that of Bach's *Musikalisches Opfer*, but it is clear enough to underscore the parallels between the character Goldberg in the novel and the composer Bach, such that the writing that makes up the novel is interpreted with relation to a musical model in one of Bach's compositions. Thus the sixteenth chapter, beginning the second half of the novel, emphasizes the strategies at work in the entire text and mirrors the binary divisions in the musical parallel of the sixteenth variation.

In the other three novels, the sixteenth variation is also somehow set apart, though less dramatically than in Josipovici's text. In *The Gold Bug Variations*, for example, chapter 16 consists entirely of a letter from Franklin Todd to Jan, who has not heard anything from him in approximately half a year. In that respect, it marks a turning point in her year where she attempts to pinpoint his location both in space and in time. Slow international postal delivery and ambiguity in the format of the date—12/6/85 can either be interpreted as the 12th of June or December 6—lead her to believe he has only just sent the letter a few weeks before, when in fact he had written it over half a year earlier, before Ressler's death and his own return from the Netherlands to the United States. Because the chapter consists only of this letter, it is unique in its lack of internal subdivisions.[25] It is striking, however, that this chapter is set apart not by an obvious binary division, as in the musical model, but in the lack thereof, whereas all other chapters contain much more prominent divisions.

In addition to twos, fours, and multiples thereof, the number three is also essential to the structure of the piece.[26] If the initial aria and its repetition *da capo* at the end are bracketed, the remaining thirty variations can be divided into ten groups of three. This structure is emphasized by the order of the different types of variations Bach employs. Each third variation from the third to twenty-seventh is in the form of a canon on an ascending interval. The third variation is thus a canon at the unison, the sixth is a canon at the second, the ninth is a canon at the third, and so on up to the twenty-seventh, which is a canon at the ninth. The conclusion to this grouping of threes is the thirtieth variation, which instead of a canon at the tenth takes a quite different form as a *quodlibet*. The other two variations in each group of three can be loosely classified as duets and free variations, following Schulenberg's terminology (320), or alternatively as dances and arabesques (Peter Williams, 40). Regardless of the precise classification, the majority of the variations in these two groups can be less rigidly categorized than the canons, which clearly form a kind of skeleton or framework for the piece's larger structure.

The question then arises as to what role this "group-of-three" structure plays in the novels based on the *Goldberg Variations*. It would be possible to group at least some of the variations in Huston's novel into groups of three, each group presenting the thoughts of either two men and a woman or two women and a man, but various other groupings would be equally possible (for example, with regard to which characters know or refer to one another in their monologues). As a result, the tripartite grouping mechanism does not seem to be a very strong structural principle, if indeed it can be said to be operating here at all. The same is true of Josipovici's and Cusk's novels. In each case, such potential groups of three are varied within themselves: Josipovici's novel makes use of different points of view and text genres, whether third-person or first-person narration, dialogue or letters, each group of three chapters partaking of at least two of these types; Cusk's novel varies the focalizing character so that each group contains chapters focalized by different characters, though in some cases Tonie or Thomas have two chapters in succession. Compared with narrative themes and variations such as Josef Weinheber's poem "Variationen auf eine hölderlinsche Ode," with its much more rigid groupings based on types of meters and similar features,[27] any threefold pattern discernable in these novels seems accidental at best. Overall, the principle seems more to be local contrast than a rigid structure based on triplet groups.[28]

In contrast, Powers's novel in particular is fascinated by this mathematical regularity. Its protagonist Stuart Ressler waxes lyrical on the coincidence of shared numerology between this piece and the genetic code he and his colleagues at the University of Illinois were struggling to crack in 1954. In addition to the role of binaries mentioned above, *The Gold Bug Variations* employs a tripartite structural pattern in a somewhat unexpected manner. Rather than constructing every third variation or chapter as a canon, as does Bach, Powers adopts the structure of the canons themselves as a way of ordering the plot lines of the novel. As Jay Labinger astutely observes, the three plot lines—relating events from 1957–58, 1983–84, and 1985–86—relate to one another in the same manner as the three voices in the canons (Labinger, 86–88).[29] The canonic structure goes beyond the mere number of voices, however, assigning two plot lines to the imitative roles they have in Bach, while the third line provides a kind of unifying accompaniment. In the *Goldberg Variations*, the third line of each canon serves to tie the two imitative lines together harmonically, also taking up the primary function of preserving the bass theme of the piece.[30] In Powers's novel, the love story between Jan O'Deigh and Franklin Todd runs roughly parallel to that between Stuart Ressler and Jeannette Koss twenty-six years earlier. The two lines are also slightly shifted in terms of the calendar, the primary events—meeting, first date, first kiss, etc.—in the two relationships occurring approximately two months earlier for Jan and Frank than for Stuart and Jeannette. This temporal displacement between the plot lines corresponds to the (usually one-measure) delay before the second voice enters in Bach's canons. Powers's novel thus does not apply the canonic structure to those variations that in the original piece are canons, but turns the entire novel's structure into a canon of this type.[31] Nonetheless, the individual chapters do contain some parallels to the corresponding variations, as discussed below.

The canons, despite being so apparent in the structure of the musical variations,[32] do not play a noticeable role in the other novels considered here.[33] Despite a wide variety of textual forms used in Josipovici's *Goldberg: Variations*, their distribution does not conform to the tripartite structure of the musical model.[34] Likewise, the chapters that would correspond to the canons are neither consistently dialogic nor do they contain three voices or any that strike the reader as imitative. In Cusk's and Huston's novels, too, the character that serves as focalizer or narrator encounters or refers to other characters, but again, there is no discernable pattern to correspond to the three voices in the canons used regularly in the "canonic" chapters.

The only example that relates directly to the structure of the canons is one that points up the exception in Bach's piece. The general pattern, as mentioned above, is that the canons have three voices, though only two mirror each other while the third weaves in and out of their pattern, doing something different and linking them together (usually in the left hand, while the two canon voices are primarily in the right hand). The "canone alla nona" (Variatio XXVII) diverges from this pattern by omitting the accompanying bass line. Rachel Cusk alludes to this anomaly in her twenty-eighth chapter, which is unique in lacking a narrative voice. This is the only chapter presented solely as dialogue, as if it were the script of a play. The third-person narrator present throughout the rest of the novel—omniscient, though focalized through the consciousness of various characters—is missing in this chapter, as is the "ambient noise," so to speak, provided by description, commentary, linking phrases, etc.

The reader is thus confronted with the dilemma of why this and only this chapter is presented in this way. No text-internal justification for such a switch in format is present, so that the missing narrative voice can only be explained by means of the parallel to the missing accompaniment voice in the last of the canons. To be sure, more than two voices can be heard in this dialogue between Claudia on the phone with her sister Juliet and her husband and children carrying on a conversation with her at the same time. Still, the presentation of this exchange divested of the usual third-person narration provides a parallel to the use of the two voices of the ninth canon without the third voice that accompanies them in the other eight. The impersonal narrator's voice is thus cast as the one that unites all the chapters but the twenty-eighth, just as the bass line follows the contours of the theme in all but the twenty-seventh of Bach's variations.

Microstructural Elements

The exposed nature of the twenty-seventh variation as the only chapter in Cusk's novel to consist solely of dialogue is one of many examples in which not only the overarching structure of the *Goldberg Variations* but also microstructural elements of individual variations play a role in shaping the texts. This section considers several such examples of structural imitation at the level of individual variations, concentrating on elements such as tempo and time signature markings (especially the *alla breve* marking in the twenty-second variation and the *adagio* of the twenty-fifth) and the use of minor mode (in only the fifteenth, twenty-first, and twenty-fifth variations). There are, of course, numerous other elements of the *Goldberg Variations* that could be expected to lend themselves to imitation by the texts, though only relatively few such elements are in fact taken up by the novels. In contrast to the macrostructure of the form as a whole, which is reproduced in similar forms in the four novels, the choice of microstructural elements to further intensify the parallels between musical work and novel is much more idiosyncratic. Though Powers's *The Gold Bug Variations*, for example, includes numerous intradiegetic discussions of the structures at work in Bach's piece, including nearly all the individual variations, only relatively few of the elements mentioned are recognizably imitated by the text. Similarly, while Huston's chapters frequently begin *in medias res* or end abruptly, the presence or absence of these features rarely coincide with Bach's use of *attacca* entrances or fermatas at the end of the corresponding variations.

Another element that would seem to lend itself to imitation in the texts would be the voicing of the individual variations. Bach's variations vary in the number of voices employed from two (nine variations are duets) to four, with approximately half the total number containing three voices (as in the majority of the canons).[35] Though Powers modifies the three-voiced structure of the canons to construct his three-stranded plot, this voicing characterizes the novel as a whole, rather than mirroring the piece's structure at the level of the individual variations. Early in the novel, the narrator Jan draws attention to this three-voiced structure in Bach:

> Tonight, at the old sticking point, I hear another voice in the bass, below the love duet. However entwined the upper lines, another figure informs them, insists on singing along. All two-part voice separation harbors a secret trio in dense fretwork. Three in nature is always a crowd. A chord. A code. If science was that man's perpetual third party, the scientist himself was mine. (41)

This commentary occurs in chapter 2. The corresponding second variation indeed contains two imitative voices—the "love duet" that Jan initially hears—and a third in the bass, yielding a trio. Despite this parallel, it is quite apparently not the case that the chapters corresponding to two-voice variations consistently contain only two of the three plot strands or that the number of subdivisions in Powers's chapters matches the number of voices in Bach's variations, though this would have been conceivable. Jan's reflections on the voicing of the variations, like the other comments on the *Goldberg Variations*, occur on the level of thematization rather than imitation. The placement of these musical ekphraseis, however, allows the discussion of each variation to line up with the chapter that corresponds with that variation, such that the *fughetta* of variation ten is discussed in the tenth chapter, and so forth. Similarly, Huston's characters reflect on the variations that are being played as they produce the interior monologues that form the structural parallel to those variations. The parallel is between the content of the chapters and the musical structure rather than being an imitation of that structure. Indeed, the *only* direct imitation of the voicing used in Bach's variations in any of the novels can be found in Cusk's omission of the narrator in chapter 28 as a reflection of the missing third voice in the corresponding canon, as discussed in the previous section.

Other possible elements for imitation not used by these novels include the number of manuals indicated in the score (composed for the harpsichord, nearly all the variations are labeled as to whether one or two manuals or keyboards should be used for performance)[36] and the need for hand crossing in performance, which occurs in eleven of the thirty-two variations.[37] Likewise, the genre of the individual variations—such as a gigue (variation 7, labeled *al tempo di Giga* in the score), *fughetta* (variation 10), or an overture (variation 16)—is surprisingly underexploited in the imitation of the piece by the novels. The reader would certainly not be amiss in searching for dance-like elements in chapters based on variations that are gigues, polonaises, passepieds, or other dances, but these novels do not emphasize such elements, if indeed they are present at all. As with the discussion of trio voicing mentioned above, the intradiegetic explanations of the *fughetta*'s construction (207–10) and the *quodlibet* (629–30) in *The Gold Bug Variations* remain on the level of thematization, describing but not recognizably imitating the form of those musical variations.

The thirtieth variation is a *quodlibet* (a Latin term meaning "as you like" or "what pleases"), or an improvised combination of diverse segments of songs. It can also be defined as the technique of simultaneously presenting multiple texts or melodies. The thirtieth variation is a rare example of an instrumental *quodlibet*, in which various popular folk songs of the time were aesthetically combined (*Das Bach-Lexikon*, 435). The thirtieth chapter of *The Gold Bug Variations* also incorporates an "imaginary content analogy," to use Wolf's term,[38] as the standard interpretation of Bach's thirtieth variation identifies two of what might be several excerpts of folk songs woven together. One of these, "ich bin so lang nicht bei dir gewest [sic]," can be translated as "I have been away from you so long," which may refer to the aria that finally returns after thirty intervening variations immediately after this movement. In Powers's novel, an automatic teller machine is rigged to play the *quodlibet* when Jan attempts to make a cash withdrawal, an action that Todd has set up in order to announce his return to her after a year's absence of working on his dissertation. Thus the association of the thirtieth variation with an impending return (that is, of the aria) is paralleled with a reunion of the main characters in the novel. This is, of course, a parallel in terms of plot development and does not involve strictly formal parallels of the kind considered elsewhere in this study.

There are, however, a few microstructural elements that do play a role in the structure of the texts and are examined more closely in the following sections. The first considers features of time notation: though tempo markings, fermatas, and time signatures are largely ignored by the novels, the marking *alla breve*, indicating a reduction of note values by one half, does play a role in two of the novels. The following section then turns to evidence for a minor key in the chapters based on variations 15, 21, and 25 in contrast to the G major of the remaining variations.

Time Notation

A possible parallel to the structure of individual variations could be the use of more or less abrupt beginnings and endings in the chapters to correspond with the presence of fermatas, cadences, or *attacca* beginnings to the variations. In Huston's *The Goldberg Variations* twelve variations end abruptly with dashes or three dots[39] while five conclude with an open question.[40] Eleven variations begin *in medias res*, in the middle of sentences.[41] There is no discernable pattern, however, linking the ellipses used in Huston's chapters with the beginnings and endings of the individual variations. The fifteenth chapter does indeed make a direct reference to a comparable figure in the Bach variation: "Now I remember why it is you love this fifteenth variation more than all the rest: instead of resolving on the tonic, it prolongs its questioning with three notes from the right hand—three notes still rising up to the unknown?" (92). Similar questioning endings, however, cannot be detected in the variations that correspond to the other four chapters of the novel that end with questions (Aria, 19, 24, and 25). Though Bach's nineteenth variation does offer very little sense of closure, the other three (the initial Aria and variations 24 and 25) all end quite decisively with fermatas, so that the parallel of the question in the fifteenth and nineteenth chapters should not be emphasized too strongly, as it only corresponds to the musical form in two of the five cases.

Though the harpsichordist Liliane and her page-turner Adrienne in Huston's novel both mention the repeats in Bach's score and the flexibility the performer has in whether or not to take the repeat, this temporal element, too, seems to be missing from the novel.[42] Presumably this is easily explained by the different role repetition plays in music and in text. A reader—particularly of a prose text such as a novel—has much less patience with repetitions of entire passages and would be likely to skip them. In classical music, however, the repetition serves to anchor what has been heard in the listener's mind, keeping it present as a contrasting section appears afterward. The different approaches to repetition can be seen clearly in the return of the aria at the close of the novels. Though the notes of the musical aria are the same—despite a change in perceived character after the thirty intervening variations—the words used by Liliane are certainly not identical. The reader recognizes the return of the initial voice, but the content of her monologue has changed, such that it is not a repetition of what she said in the first chapter, but an extension or further variation of it. It is a matter for debate to what extent this process is paralleled by the return of the *aria da capo* in the *Goldberg Variations*; a listener—or indeed, the performer—might endow the same notes with different meaning, but despite changes in interpretation, the form remains much more closely linked to the first appearance.[43]

Alla breve, the marking in the score that indicates that the twenty-second variation should be played with note values of half their usual length,[44] is used by Powers as the section heading for his twenty-second chapter. Unlike all other chapters except the aria, chapter 16 (as discussed above, the section on twos and threes), and *aria da capo e fine*, chapter 22 does not contain multiple sections with their own headings. Each chapter has an average of 4.1 section headings, ranging from one to eight, with the majority at three, four, or five.[45] Chapter 22 thus stands out from the others with its single section heading. It still contains all three plot strands, but they have been compressed into a single section rather than the usual three or more sections. The alternation between plot strands is thus more abrupt and jarring for the reader, without the typographical division that the reader has come to expect as an indication that he or she should anticipate a switch to one of the other plot strands. This alternation is not only more abrupt, but also much more rapid. Whereas typical sections in other chapters frequently cover ten or more pages (though shorter segments also occur), the segments in chapter 22 are three, seven, and six pages long. What is even more unusual is that the sections Jan narrates about herself in 1983 and 1985 are interwoven in a way that these two lines had not been previously. Clearly beginning around Christmas 1985, after receiving Frank's letter, she soon immerses herself in memories of the year they spent together in 1983–84. The section dealing with Ressler in 1957 remains distinct from the other plot lines, but the concluding section of the chapter begins in late 1983 and switches within the section to 1985, again with memories and dialogue from 1983 to 1984.

Jay Labinger explains this structure not by reference to the time marking *alla breve*, but by comparing it to the fugal technique of the *stretto*, "where the musical voices follow one another at shorter temporal intervals than the previously established pattern" (87–88). Though considering this chapter a *stretto* would seem to adequately describe its structure, there is no logical reason for a fugal parallel here, and his contrast between a perceived *stretto* in chapter 22 (rather than the expected *diminution*) and the *augmentation* of chapters 13 and 14 suggests that he is mixing his musical metaphors (see 88). Though certain other variations are fugues (especially Variatio X, labeled *fughetta*) and are discussed in Powers's novel as such, the twenty-second variation is not fugal in construction. It thus seems much more appropriate to explain the unusual construction of chapter 22 in relation to the musical model at hand, which is the *alla breve* movement in the *Goldberg Variations*. Indeed, the *alla breve* marking calls for note values to be cut in half, which causes each line to take half the time it would have in the previous movements. The more rapid entrances of the three plot lines in this chapter can thus appropriately be explained as an imitation of cut time in this section.[46]

In the other novels, other strategies are used to make reference to the time marking in the twenty-second variation. In Huston, this occurs only on the level of thematization, when Reynaud, the narrator of Variatio XXII, begins his monologue with rumination on "how time flies!" (124), specifically on the perceived acceleration of life's pace with increasing age: "time goes by faster and faster as you get older" (124). This chapter is not, however, shorter than the others or otherwise compacted in a temporal sense, so that the subtle reference to reduced note values is not an instance of imitation but merely an indirect thematization.

Josipovici's novel chooses an interesting means of cutting the duration of the chapter to correspond to the *alla breve* marking in the corresponding variation. The twenty-second chapter consists of a dialogue between Goldberg and his employer Westfield, but only Westfield's text is printed. Goldberg's intervening questions and answers are left inaudible, though they may often be inferred:

> It is a pleasure to have you here, Mr Goldberg.
> No no. Please do not try to be polite. You are here because I am paying you.
> That is true.
> That is true as well.
> Civilised conversation does a man good.
> *Particularly* civilised conversation in the dark. (156; emphasis original)

The dialogue has thus been cut in half, though in a different manner from the cut time of the musical model. Still, it provides an analogy to the twenty-second variation, and the contrast with Powers's text demonstrates how varied the approaches a text may take to imitating or alluding to musical structures.

Variations in a Minor Key

Another element of the individual variations that may be imitated in the texts is whether a given variation is composed in a major or minor key. Like the initial aria, nearly all the variations are in G major. There are only three exceptions, all in the parallel key of G minor: Variations 15, 21, and 25. Minor keys are traditionally associated with a more melancholy atmosphere than are major keys, something that a text is quite able to evoke by other means. The three chapters in question in Huston's novel, particularly the twenty-first and twenty-fifth variations, could all be considered minor in a musical sense, as they deal with a strong sense of loss. There is also an explicit marking of the minor key in chapters 15 and 25, where the narrators reflect on this aspect (88, 139). Wolf points out the parallel between the twenty-fifth chapter and the twenty-fifth variation in G minor, referring to the "pervading loneliness and dejection of the correspondent voice in Huston's text" (350). On the other hand, several other chapters share this melancholy, regretful mood; Christine in chapter 11 provides a strong parallel to Viviane in 25, though Bach's eleventh variation is in the major key. In Cusk's novel, too, the most tragic or melancholy events are not restricted to those chapters that correspond to minor variations. Instead, the most dramatic catastrophe—when Alexa falls ill with meningitis, bringing her parents' reversal of domestic roles to an abrupt end—takes place in chapters 28–30, though variations 28–30 are not at all tragic in mood. The events related in chapters 15, 21, and 25 are all to some extent regretful and could thus be considered a minor key, but not significantly more so than other chapters in a similar vein.

The Gold Bug Variations echoes the minor variations 15 and 25, though there is nothing particularly melancholy about the twenty-first chapter. In the fifteenth, a discourse divided into four sections on "*Classification,*" "*Ecology,*" "*Evolution,*" and "*Heredity,*" Jan's study of natural science leads her to question the purpose of life and to lose hope in the idea of progress: "Left with a diminished, far more miraculous place ... what hope is there that heart can evolve, beat to it, keep it beating?" (336). As in Huston's novel, this fifteenth chapter ends with a question, in an echo of the rising conclusion of the fifteenth variation. The events of the twenty-fifth chapter are much more closely geared toward a minor variation, especially one described as "the most profound resignation to existence ever written" (554) and "most chromatic catastrophe ever composed" (557). The section headings serve as warnings of the events about to unfold: "Disaster," "Uncle Jimmy" (Todd's and Ressler's coworker who suffers a severe stroke just after their computer hacking has accidentally caused his health insurance coverage to be dropped), "Disaster (continued)," "Losing the Signal" (after Ressler's colleague commits suicide, a speaker at his funeral explains that "Joey lost the signal. Read the message wrong" 551), and "Disaster (conclusion)." All these sections not only depict tragic events, but are also expressed in a pervasive tone of despair.

The fact that Powers's novel focuses on only one of the three minor variations as the locus of tragedy and despair is related to the specific musical model the novel is based on. *The Gold Bug Variations* focuses on Glenn Gould's famous 1955 recording of the piece. His is the record Jeannette Koss gives to Stuart Ressler at the beginning of their brief relationship, and which he proceeds to study obsessively, and in this performance, Gould sets the twenty-fifth variation strikingly apart. His tempi are generally very fast and are characterized by a "frenzied charge" (Huston, 78); the twenty-fifth variation is a notable exception. While the other variations range from 29 seconds to 2 minutes and 16 seconds, the twenty-fifth variation is 6 minutes and 28 seconds long. A comparison with recordings by other musicians reveals that the contrast between Gould's tempo for this variation and for the other variations is much more extreme.[47] Gould himself refers to the "strategic position" of the third G-minor variation, coming as it does after "twenty-four vignettes depicting . . . the irrepressible elasticity of what was termed 'the Goldberg-Ego,'" providing a contrast in the form of a "master stroke of psychology" (Gould, 27). Powers's treatment of the twenty-fifth variation as distinct from the minor variations that went before is thus an imitation of the particular interpretation of the piece presented by Glenn Gould.

The Concept of Time Implied by the Theme-and-Variations Form

The principle of variation, whether in music or literature, contains elements of both repetition and change. A given theme recurs in numerous successive variations, but never in the identical guise. Though the variations are dealing with the same material, they do so in different ways, such that there is a tension between stasis (repetition) and dynamism (development) inherent to the form. Some definitions of the theme-and-variations form emphasize only the dynamic elements, as when Arroyas speaks of the "movement, exploration and change" (103) conveyed by the form and Petri quite firmly assigns the form to the dynamic side of the dualistic system of dynamic and static musical forms (24). Still, the static element produced by repetition of similar material should not be overlooked. This tension has interesting consequences for the plot of a variation-based novel and for the concept of time thus implied by the form.

Such a novel does not depict a traditional linear plot progression, with each event building on what has gone before, but rather returns again and again to the same material. Each variation, after all, builds not on the previous variation, but on the theme itself, so that the development of the thematic material is one of accretion rather than progress. Likewise, these novels overwhelmingly choose to emphasize individual vignettes, discrete units,[48] rather than a conventional plot. In the novels considered here, this feature is most apparent in Huston's *The Goldberg Variations*, in which each chapter is a self-contained unit with a unique narrator, none reacting directly to any of the others, but only to the concert situation as their shared theme. Josipovici's *Goldberg: Variations* likewise succeeds in keeping the individual variations quite distinct, so that a plot progression is only very loosely implied by the presence of overlapping characters or isolated motifs rather than by a direct influence of one chapter on the successive chapters. Powers's *The Gold Bug Variations* and Cusk's *The Bradshaw Variations*, on the other hand, more strongly suggest a plot development that proceeds across all the variations. While

Powers's chapters maintain a sense of distinctness by virtue of the juxtaposition of the three plot lines, each progresses linearly through time—with a strong link to the calendar as a structuring principle—and is clearly a case of development rather than accretion. Cusk's chapters, though also following one another sequentially over the course of a year, are yet somewhat more self-contained than Powers's chapters. They seem rather to be vignettes taken from the lives of the Bradshaws, depicting individual scenes that in many—though not all—cases could occur in a different order than the one given and are thus less dependent on a chronological progression than Powers's resolutely sequential plot episodes.

The variations in Bach's work, as in other sets of variations, are not only individual treatments of a theme that can stand alone, but are also united to form a larger work. The unity within which this variety[49] is allowed to unfold is of course predominantly underscored by the presence of the theme in some form in each variation. Beyond this, however, other devices serve to hold the disparate parts together to form a unified whole. Gould's second recording of the piece in 1981, for example, employs precisely calculated tempi to make the transitions between variations more continuous and organic.[50] In Bach's case, the numerical structure and systematic symmetry of the piece discussed above is a strong linking principle. Though the order of some of the variations could perhaps be changed, the canons that make up every third variation, the division of the whole into equal halves, and the total number of movements that corresponds to the number of bars of the theme create an impression of an overarching logic that unites the disparate parts into a whole. Finally, the means by which the piece is concluded are significant for *The Goldberg Variations*' overall structure. As Brown observed, finding a conclusion to a set of variations poses a unique problem for the composer. How is the listener to know, having become accustomed to hearing one variation after another, when the last variation has been reached and there will not be any further variations? There is a risk of open-endedness and a sense of incompletion inherent in the form, and the composer must find a way of clearly marking the conclusion of the piece. Brown outlines two possible approaches to this problem:

> In general, there are two ways of doing this. The first is to have the last variation return to a form far closer to the original theme than those immediately preceding it. . . .
> The second way of concluding is to have a final section (often a formal coda) which the listener immediately senses to be something so unlike what has preceded, that it cannot be another beginning, and hence must be a conclusion. . . . To put all this into a couple of simple metaphors, the composer can end a set of variations either by closing the circle or by flying off at a tangent. ("Theme and Variations as a Literary Form," 36)

In the case of Bach's *Goldberg Variations*, the first method is clearly in evidence. The thirty-second and last movement of the piece is not merely similar to the theme, it is an actual repetition of the theme's first appearance in the aria. After the increasing virtuosity of the preceding variations (especially 28 and 29), the return of the lyrical and subdued aria is clearly a conclusion to the work as a whole, providing closure to the set by returning to the journey's beginning. It is not, however, exactly the same as the beginning, but represents the possibility of a new beginning. When the aria is repeated at the end of the piece—indicated in the original score by the marking *aria da capo e fine* (= aria from the beginning and end)—it does not produce the same impression as at the outset. Upon its return the aria sounds different—perhaps wistful, more self-aware—by virtue of all the intervening variations, after being away so long.[51] Repetition with a difference is thus the dominant musical principle of the variations.

Such a repeat of the aria not only provides closure, but by linking the end with the beginning, also confirms the work's shape as circular and theoretically infinitely repeatable. That this set of variations can be seen as a cycle is evident in numerous musicological studies.[52] The term "cycle" in musical usage is well established with relation to the song cycle, particularly those by Schubert and Schumann, which operate on a similar principle. Though the songs are not variations on a given musical theme, they are similarly linked by the same lyrical speaker or a common "poetic subject" (*Grove's Dictionary of Music*, entry for "Song Cycle," 962). Examples such as Beethoven's *An die ferne Geliebte* also involve a return to the same melodies used at the beginning in order to form a conclusion (ibid). In the case of *The Goldberg Variations*, the work as a "true cycle, with a perceptible large structure" (Schulenberg, 321) is evident in its numerical groupings, though it is debatable to what extent this structure is "perceptible" to a noninitiated audience.[53]

The novels based on *The Goldberg Variations* show a keen interest in the cyclical nature of the piece. Of the four novels discussed here, Josipovici's *Goldberg: Variations* is the least cyclical. Yet because both the first and last chapters depict Goldberg's arrival at Westfield's estate, the last chapter can be interpreted as a new beginning of the same events. On the other hand, there is also a sense of closure to Goldberg's stay there: he has completed his task and put Westfield to sleep (see chapter 28). Likewise, Gerald has been able to complete the novel he had been struggling with, so that the end of the novel represents the end of a process, though there will presumably be another book, another commission, etc. Significantly, there is ambiguity between these two possibilities: in chapter 28 Goldberg writes that "it is all over" (183), that "it is as though I sense that I will not start again, that all is over for good" (183), but the following chapters 29 and 30 both depict his arrival at Westfield's estate, so somehow he is indeed beginning again. This is an appropriate parallel to the role of the aria in Bach's piece as constituting both a return to the beginning and a sense of an ending.

Cycles, as indicated above, are particularly evident in recourse to the calendar and the natural cycle of the year. Rachel Cusk's *The Bradshaw Variations*, for example, covers a period of one year from the time Tonie starts her new job as head of the English department in September and Thomas stays home with their daughter Alexa to the time they revert to their previous roles the following September after Alexa falls ill with meningitis. Likewise, other things that had been changed during the year have also been negated: the dog the Howard Bradshaws adopt in chapter 5 is killed in chapter 31, Thomas's piano playing has come to an end; even Tonie's long dormant interest in sex that was revived over the course of the year has dissipated. The novel thus represents a period of experimentation that concludes at the end of one calendar cycle. After one year of unconventional domestic roles—Thomas as a *"househusband"* (113; italics original) in charge of childcare and the home, Tonie as a working woman attending to her career and going on business trips—they return to the beginning, so to speak, by resuming the traditional roles they had occupied before the year began. Whereas Tonie's first chapter showed her on the train to work, pondering the other passengers, Thomas's last chapter shows him in an equivalent position. The situation is the same as at the beginning, though the roles have been reversed, which shows that the end of the cycle is similar to its beginning, but not identical with it.

With regard to the seasons of the year as a model of cyclical time, *The Gold Bug Variations* is the most explicit, with several sections entitled "The Perpetual Calendar" (in the aria and chapters 8, 12, and 29) and dates, seasons, or other references to the month or time of year present in nearly every section of the book. The calendar, as Jay Labinger has observed, also provides a means of linking the three plot strands temporally:

> Powers frames the narrative lines within the calendar, which is another key structural element of the text. All three lines start around the same date, just after the beginning of summer. In fact, O'Deigh's meeting with Todd, which initiates line 2; her learning of Ressler's death, which starts line 3; and her reuniting with Todd, which terminates the narrative, all take place on *exactly* the same date, June 23. All three lines run for approximately one year. (87)

Not only does time progress over the course of the year but the seasons and dates are repeated as well, creating parallels between the present and the past. This yields a sense of overlapping of different points in time, a sense that all events of the past are somehow still occurring in the present. This is further evidenced by the "today in history" motif, taken from one of the reference librarian Jan O'Deigh's bulletin boards in which she posts events from history that correspond to each day's date. The phrase is used as the title of eight sections throughout the novel, found in chapters 1, 2, 3, 4, 5, 7, 13, and 24. This overlapping of disparate points in time can also be related to overlapping lines in music. Listening to the fugal entrances of the tenth variation, Jan is reminded of anatomical transparencies that can be layered one on top of another: "With Dr. Ressler pointing them out, I heard the successive reentrant voices, layering one on top of another, musical analogs of those plastic anatomical overlays in biology books. Each transparent sheet contains its own, separate hierarchies—circulatory, skeletal, nervous. But each overlay, flipped on the stack adds its system, compacts its parts into a surprising, indivisible composite" (208). To a lesser extent, the same simultaneity is suggested for the variations themselves. Glenn Gould's notorious humming during his performance, which can just barely be detected in his 1955 recording of the twenty-first variation, is described as "a variation beyond the variation," "the thirty-third *Goldberg*" (462), which is performed simultaneously with the twenty-first. This desire to compress the variations and superimpose them is still present in Gould's later recording of the piece in 1981, which Franklin describes to Jan as having many variations begin *attacca*, as if the pianist were "anxious to hear how they might sound all at once, on top of one another" (636). The element of "sameness," the theme that provides the harmonic framework shared by all the variations, allows them to be conceived of as simultaneous, though they are performed sequentially. This is comparable to the way the novel teases out the three strands of the canons and alternates between them, so that what conceptually should overlap but the text can only present sequentially can still imply music's capacity for simultaneity.

The element of simultaneity is even clearer in Huston's *The Goldberg Variations*. Though each character's interior monologue is presented sequentially, consisting only of the time it would take for the corresponding variation to be played, the thoughts of each character can be presumed to continue beyond this temporal framework to cover the entire performance. This continuity is emphasized in a number of the variations by beginning *in medias res*—or *attacca*, to use the musical term—and ending with ellipses. Thus all thirty audience members can be assumed to follow their own trains of thought at the same time, despite the fact that the reader can only eavesdrop on those thoughts individually, one after the other. Actually, Liliane's final section at the end of the novel makes it clear that she herself has imagined the thoughts of all thirty audience members. This suggests that she focuses on each guest in turn, so that even within the framework of the novel as Liliane's creation, the characters' thoughts do not in fact extend beyond those presented here, as Liliane cannot concentrate on all thirty simultaneously.

The Goldberg Variations also contains some of the most explicit comments on the form as a cycle, as well as on music and time in general. When Liliane's voice returns in the last chapter as the "Aria," she describes her performance as a "wheel [that] has gone through a complete revolution" (171) and considers the possibility of beginning again at the first variation:

> In fact, I don't know if I *will* stop. . . . Perhaps I'll start over again immediately, with the Variatio I. Just when they think we've got nothing more to say, we could pull a stunt like that on them, eh, my little harpsichord? What do you say? Shall we give the wheel another spin? Go all the way around again? Maybe the stories we'd tell would be completely different. In fact I'm sure they would. But no—it's wonderful to stop, too. (172; italics and ellipsis original)

This is the most explicit treatment of the *Goldbergs* as a cycle, metaphorically seen as a wheel that could be turned again after the completion of one revolution, with the aria in the ambiguous position of comprising both beginning and end. Liliane's comments form a close parallel to the role of the aria in the piece itself, as it also signals both a return to the beginning and a sense of closure to the set of variations as a whole.

Huston's novel reveals its interest in time not only in connection with the cyclical nature of the composition, but also throughout many of the other variations. As observed above, time is closely connected with each of the variations and with the theme of the performance. Several of the comments on time relate specifically to a musical conception of time, as when Liliane opens the performance by reflecting on the "space of time [that] has opened" (13). Though she seeks to ignore the constraints of time—by taking off her watch—she recognizes that she is "at the mercy of this time" (13). The music she performs is conceived as a fragile object that she "carr[ies] through time, not through space" and she is very much aware of time passing as she performs (17, 170–71). Yet time is not so straightforward; it is not merely present as a measure of the length of the piece, as something objective that stubbornly marches on irrespective of this musical performance. Liliane also conceives of the performance as a dream—specifically "a midsummer night's dream" (89, 171)—from which people will awaken. Out of a kind of frozen timelessness they will return to the usual passage of time in the world outside of the concert. The musical performance, as also suggested by an unnamed writer in Variatio X, represents a break from the ordinary understanding of time, which is bound up with language:

> For [love and music], and only for them, can I bear wasting time—because they occur outside of language . . . the reason they bestow on me the exceptional privilege of living in the present is that, in

spite of everything, they're circumscribed in time. You can't go on fucking indefinitely; every piece of music has a beginning and an end. I'm safe because I know in advance that the disappearance of language is only temporary.
This is not a waste of precious time, but rather a precious waste of time. (66)

Other characters, on the other hand, are still very much aware of the passage of time even as they listen to the music, such as when some of them do indeed consider the concert to be a waste of time that could be better spent otherwise.

This opposition between the duration and timelessness of music is very well captured by the two epigraphs to the novel: "You have exactly ninety-six minutes" and "You have all the time in the world" (9, 11). The first epigraph points to the way music is circumscribed by time, the way it unfolds sequentially over a particular duration. The second epigraph focuses not on this practical aspect of the performance but on the perceived timelessness of music, the way music is only accessible in a kind of perpetual now. Though music can quote something from the past, a motif that occurred before (such as the theme that is repeated in the variations), it cannot talk about the past; music can only speak in the present tense. When the theme recurs, it is not described as something that existed previously, as in the linguistic use of the past tense, but is made present anew. Appropriately, all the interior monologues are presented as thoughts that arise as they are related, in a kind of dramatized present rather than a narrative past tense.

Perhaps the most accurate summary of the contradictory position(s) on time taken in this book is Liliane's statement at the end of the book: "Time does not exist; . . . there are any number of times; and . . . each of them has an end" (172).[54] Time is multiple, nebulous, and it is complicated by the various functions it has for music and for narrative. Time is immovable, an infinite progression that can be measured in minutes, days, or years, and yet it is perceived subjectively by each individual at any given moment. Time unfolds in a linear sequence, yet music allows simultaneity and recursivity, undermining the idea of a singular temporal strand.

The concept of time implied by narrative is linear and progressive. Any given moment in the text can refer back to what went before and what will happen later through the use of tenses. The text thus has a conception of past, present, and future. The musical concept of time, on the other hand, allows for an expansion of the present moment. Any reference to the past actually brings that past into the present through repetition; whereas the text's reference to the past event is not the same as the present-tense event itself, music's use of repetition conflates the two.

There is thus a kind of timelessness to the eternal present of the musical work, which is evident in the observation that "the Standing Now of the piece is more being than becoming" (Powers, 284).

Time as a linear progression is only evident when compared to events outside of the music. For example, saying that the piece takes 96 minutes (as in the epigraph to Huston's novel) relates it to the concept of time outside of the concert, in which 96 minutes can also be the time it takes to watch a movie, to clean the kitchen, to drive a certain distance, etc. Within the framework of the musical event, however, 96 minutes has no meaning whatsoever. This can probably be said of time in general—it can only be measured in relation to events. The perception of the time of any single event cannot be quantified except as a comparison, since time is a relative concept. Music in general and a cyclical work such as the *Goldberg Variations* in particular provide an opportunity to discuss the perceived timelessness of the aesthetic experience and to point out the paradox[55] inherent in concepts of temporality.

Notes

[1] Sets of literary variations as a form can seemingly without exception be traced to musical models. See e.g. Brown, "Theme and Variations as a Literary Form."

[2] The following discussion is based on the definitions given by Fabian Gudas in *The New Princeton Handbook of Poetic Terms*, 311–12; Jeremy Hawthorn in *A Glossary of Contemporary Literary Theory*, 258–59; and Roger Fowler in *A Dictionary of Modern Critical Terms*, 248–49. Only this last definition makes explicit reference to the "structural implications" of a theme in linking the parts of a text (249).

[3] An aria was initially a loosely defined form, until the term was used after 1600 primarily for a particular type of self-contained vocal piece in an opera. Definitions from the eighteenth century retain a broader understanding of the term, as when Johann Gottfried Walther (*Musikalisches Lexikon*) defines the term as any melody, whether sung or played instrumentally. He emphasizes a binary division within the aria, in contrast to earlier strophic song forms. As a genre of instrumental music, the term "aria" began to be used in the early seventeenth century and referred to movements with a lyrical melody that were not oriented toward dance forms, but which serve as melodic and harmonic-rhythmic starting points for sets of variations (*Das Bach-Lexikon*, entry for "Arie," 47–48).

[4] The only other composers mentioned by name in *The Bradshaw Variations* are Schubert and Beethoven. Of the pieces that Thomas learns to play on the piano, only an *adagio* by Beethoven (which one is not clearly indicated, but Thomas's mention of the other movements—"the *allegro molto e con brio* and the *grave*" [85]—suggest that this must be the *Adagio cantabile* from the Piano Sonata no. 8 in C Minor, op. 13, called the *Pathétique*) and Bach's C-major prelude and fugue from the *Well Tempered Clavier* (117) are explicitly identified. At the start of the novel, Thomas listens to a recording of Schubert's *Fantasiestücke* (5).

⁵ The only other variations by J. S. Bach are BWV 989, Aria variata in A Minor (composed 1707–13) and BWV 991 *Air mit Variationen in c-Moll* (composed in 1722). Neither work is nearly as large a set of variations as the *Goldbergs*, as the earlier work consists of a clearly stated theme and ten variations, while the C-minor variations are a fragment. See Peter Bach, http://www.bach.de/werk/cembalowerke.html. See also *Das Bach-Lexikon*, entry for "Variation," 531–32, which does not mention BWV 991, but does mention a few other of Bach's works that could be considered sets of variations if a looser definition is used.

⁶ See also Arroyas, 104n13.

⁷ Compare the "Ursatz" or fundamental line in Schenkerian analysis.

⁸ Such a rigid concept of the theme is of course also possible, though it is far more likely in poetry than in longer prose works. See for example poems such as Josef Weinheber's "Variationen auf eine hölderlinsche Ode" and others discussed by Brown in "Theme and Variations as a Literary Form."

⁹ This structure of sixty-four lines corresponds to the measures in the aria (and the majority of the variations), if all repeats are taken: two halves of 16 bars each, each half played twice = 64 measures.

¹⁰ Jay Labinger discusses the two different types of codes explored in the novel, those based on "substitution" and on "generation," demonstrating that the setbacks experienced by the characters are invariably due to underestimating the power of generative code, taking it for a simple substitution. He correctly points out that the patterns underlying the *Goldberg Variations* are taken as a model of generative code and thus linked with DNA (80–85).

¹¹ The question "what could be simpler" occurs in the aria (7, 7, 9); Variations 1 (11, 13, 23, 25), 8 (157), 21 (459), and 27 (588), along with numerous additional uses of the words "simple," "simpler," and "simplest." Variation 12 introduces a related motif, "How different can you get?," which is repeated four times (249, 250, 253, 253), while other variants occur in chapters 12 ("How smart can you get?" 259) and 15 ("How much more complicated can the card deck get?" 321).

¹² Ziolkowski claims that a statement in Mme Fournier's monologue (Variatio IX) "sums up the apparent theme of the novel . . . 'That's the true meaning of concerts nowadays, Nathalie. Classical music has been totally perverted; it only reflects the neuroses of our society' (p. 61)." Like Arroyas's other too-specific theme, the idea of concerts of classical music as a demonstration of society's neuroses strikes me as rather too subjective an interpretation to be applied to the novel as a whole. Instead, I argue for the concert situation as the theme, and Ziolkowski's (and Mme Fournier's) suggestion is a possible implication that arises from that theme.

¹³ The melodies of the canons are also all distinct from one another, so that it is not only the increasing interval between the voices that differentiates them. The structure of the canons is discussed below.

¹⁴ Liliane's position as both the performer of Bach's piece and as the composer of the characters' monologues will be discussed more fully in the section of chapter six on the interaction between the performer and the composer.

[15] The "creative capacity" has been identified by Werner Wolf in "The Role of Music" as a possible theme of the novel, as will be discussed in the following. The phrase occurs in the novel itself in chapter 22 (157).

[16] In chapter 14, "Unterlinden," the first-person narrator Gerald describes seeing a still-life painting at a museum that corresponds to the description provided in chapter 11, "Containers." Retrospectively, then, chapter 11 can be read as an ekphrasis of a painting rather than merely an imitation of ekphrastic techniques.

[17] Ziolkowski cites Josipovici as stating "in an interview that it was Klee's painting that 'suddenly took on a pivotal role in the book' and enabled him finally to finish it" (636). This parallel between the author's own writing process and that of this unnamed speaker in the novel strengthens the identification of the speaker with the implied author, though this is complicated by the associations of this speaker with the figure in Klee's painting.

[18] The topics of insomnia and writer's block are also clearly linked on pages 5 and 17.

[19] For the "anomalies" in the *Goldberg Variations*' symmetrical structure, however, see Schulenberg, 321.

[20] Again, with the exception of variations 3, 21, and 30, which all condense two bars of the theme into one in the variation and thus only have 16 measures each.

[21] Peter Williams provides a (partial) list of the various binaries at work in the *Goldberg Variations*, ranging from those discussed above to the two manuals required for its performance, the two keys of G major and minor, and even to note values of halves, quarters, eighths, etc. (43–45).

[22] Franklin discusses the debate between Matheson and Lorenz Mizler, in which the former argued that mathematics was a part of music, a tool to be used in composition, while Mizler claimed that music could be seen as a part of mathematics, calling mathematics the "Heart and Soul" (235) of music. Franklin argues that Bach, in composing the *Goldberg Variations*, was well aware of this debate and sees the piece as exemplifying the first position, in which mathematics plays a "facilitating" role in composition (235).

[23] See e.g. Schulenberg, 322: "Few purchasers of the original print . . . would have regarded it primarily as something to be used for playing through from cover to cover."

[24] Furthermore, one measure in the theme is extended to two measures in this second half in a process called augmentation, though the beat remains approximately the same, so that the bass line would seem to progress at the same speed.

[25] The only other chapter to contain only a single section heading is chapter 22, labeled "Alla Breve" (as in the *Goldberg Variations*), in which there are indeed separate sections, but which succeed one another more rapidly because of the cut time *alla breve* indicates.

[26] Indeed, the number thirty-two is not only divisible by multiples of twos and fours, but itself is made up of a "3" as well as a "2."

[27] See Brown's analyses of this poem in "Josef Weinheber's Hölderlin Variations" (1968) and "Theme and Variations as a Literary Form" (1978).

[28] On the principle of "local contrast" in the *Goldberg Variations*, see Schulenberg, 322. See also Schulenberg's comment on the "threefold pattern" as "a purely constructive device, intellectually satisfying but largely irrelevant to the way in which one plays or hears the work" (321).

[29] My discussion of Powers's tripartite plot structure is largely based on Labinger's observations.

[30] The one exception is the canon at the ninth (variation 27), which dispenses with the third voice and contains only the two imitative lines, which themselves incorporate the bass theme into their melodic line.

[31] Labinger observes additional parallels to Bach's canons in Powers's novel in the use of inversions: "Some of the parallels between the lines are inverted, just as in two of the canons. Koss desperately wants children but is sterile; O'Deigh is afraid to have children and has had herself sterilized. Koss leaves Ressler to return to her husband, and never sees Ressler again; O'Deigh does not return to her former lover, and eventually gets back together with Todd" (Labinger, 87). Other examples could also be listed, such as the contrast in chapter 25 between Uncle Jimmy's stroke and Joe Lovering's suicide or the way the theme of simplicity yielding complexity is turned around: "waiting for this impossible complication to become the first of simplicities" (258).

[32] Though the imitative quality of some of the canons is not always obvious to a listener, whereas some other variations sound imitative that are not (Peter Williams, 40), the labels "canone all'unisono," "canone alla seconda," and so forth are among the relatively few explicit paratextual markings in the score, emphasizing this structural element over many others that are not so visibly marked.

[33] A notable exception is Thomas Bernhard's 1983 novel *Der Untergeher*, which Gregor Hens has convincingly argued is structured like a piece of three-voice counterpoint, with the characters Glenn Gould, Wertheimer, and the narrator taking up the three interwoven lines of the composition. It would be a stretch, however, to claim that this represents a three-part canon as found in Powers's novel, as the characters' biographies reflect a much higher degree of contrast. While there are only few inversions between Powers's plot lines of 1957 and 1983, Bernhard's characters Gould and Wertheimer are consistently portrayed as taking opposite trajectories. See Hens, 33, 53.

[34] Ziolkowski claims—without providing any evidence for this claim—that "in every third chapter (Bach's canon) the progression of the narrative is interrupted by letters or thoughts of people related to Westfield and Goldberg" (636), yet such interruptions are not restricted to the chapters that would correspond to Bach's canons. In addition to presenting the thoughts of Westfield's first wife (chapter 3), his son (chapter 6), Goldberg's daughter (chapter 9), Westfield's second wife (chapter 12), and Goldberg's wife (chapter 15), chapters 7 (Westfield's friend and physician, Ballantyne) and 13 (Goldberg's friend Sinclair) also function very similarly by focusing on "people related to Westfield and Goldberg." The pattern is disrupted after this point, as chapters 18, 21, 24, and 27 are not focalized on people related to Westfield and Goldberg in this manner (chapters 18, 21, and 24 involve Westfield and/or Goldberg directly, while chapter 27 is narrated in the first-person voice of the figure in Klee's painting *The Wander-Artist*).

35 Fifteen of the thirty-two movements have three voices, notably eight of the nine canons (Aria, 2, 3, 6, 9, 12, 13, 15, 18, 19, 21, 24, 25, 26, Aria da capo); nine are duets (1, 5, 7, 8, 11, 14, 17, 20, 27), four are four-part movements (4, 10, 22, 30), and four are mixed (16, 23, 28, 29).

36 Fourteen of the variations contain the marking "a 1 Clav," indicating the use of just one manual (1, 2, 3, 4, 6, 9, 10, 15, 16, 18, 19, 22, 24, 30); eleven variations are labeled "a 2 Clav" (8, 11, 13, 14, 17, 20, 23, 25, 26, 27, 28); three are labeled "a 1 ovvero 2 Clav" (for either one or two manuals, 5, 7, 29); and for the remaining four variations there is no indication of the number of manuals, though one manual would be appropriate (Aria, 12, 21, Aria da capo).

37 Hand crossing is required in variations 1, 5, 8, 11, 14, 17, 20, 23, 26, 28, and 29 (though 29 is really more a case of overlapping chords).

38 See Wolf, *Musicalization of Fiction*, 63: "imaginary content analogies only make use of the literary signifieds, usually in the form of 'poetic' imagery but also in the choice of other, narrative correlatives of music (such as a poet overhearing a singing girl). In contrast to word music and structural analogies, imaginary content analogies supply what is tendentially absent in music: a referential content."

39 Chapters 3 and 10 each end with an ellipsis indicated by three dots, while chapters 1, 2, 4, 5, 7, 9, 18, 22, and 23 end with a dash. Chapter 17 is alone in ending on an incomplete sentence terminated only by a comma.

40 The aria and chapters 15, 19, 24, and 25 all end with question marks.

41 Chapters 2, 4, 6, 8, 10, 11, 18, 21, 28, 29, and 30 each begin with three dots.

42 Repeats are even less evident in the other novels, where they are not so much as mentioned. In Powers's case, they would also be unexpected, as the particular interpretation of the *Goldberg Variations* that the novel takes as a model—Glenn Gould's famous 1955 recording—does not repeat any sections at all.

43 An example of how the second instance of the aria at the end of the piece is different from its first appearance not only in interpretation but also in form is the slightly slower tempo taken by Glenn Gould in his 1955 recording for the second version of the aria, or the fact that Murray Perahia, in his 2000 recording of the piece, does not take the repeats in the Aria da capo that he had carried out in the aria (and indeed in all of the variations). Gould's 1955 recording does not take any repeats at all, though his 1981 version repeats the first section of all the canons and a few of the other variations.

44 "ALLA BREVE (Ital. = lit. 'in shortness'). The expression *alla breve*, placed at the beginning of a composition, [indicates] a time of either two or four beats in a bar, but at a double rate of movement . . . the signature of *alla breve* time is the semicircle crossed by a vertical stroke, ¢ . . . where the stroke through the signature was used to indicate that each note was to be halved in time value, *i.e.* the rate of the movement doubled" (*Grove's Dictionary of Music and Musicians*, vol. 1, entry for "Alla Breve," 113).

[45] Seven chapters have three section headings (1, 13, 19, 24, 27, 28, 29); seven chapters have four (4, 6, 8, 11, 12, 18, 23); nine have five (3, 5, 7, 9, 15, 17, 25, 26, 30); two have six (2, 14); two have seven (20, 21); and only the tenth chapter has eight section headings.

[46] This is an example of the potential ambiguity in assigning literary techniques to a specific musical model. If a given textual form may represent either a *stretto* or cut time as indicated by *alla breve*, other markers are needed to make a definitive identification, which points to the importance of explicit thematization in connecting intermedial imitation with a particular musical form.

[47] Murray Perahia, for example, plays the majority of the variations slightly more slowly than Gould (the only exceptions are 7, 21, and 28, all of which are only slightly faster). His twenty-fifth variation is also the longest, but is only 2 minutes and 20 seconds longer than the next longest (including both repeats), whereas Gould's twenty-fifth is four-and-a-quarter minutes longer than the next longest variation.

[48] This feature is in fact similar to an effect discussed in jazz novels (see chapter 3), in which an episodic structure is also used. In that case, however, it is not based on the classical form of theme and a set of variations, but on the structure of jazz choruses. The principle, however, is a similar one, as a series of discrete units are strung together, united by reference to common thematic material.

[49] See *Grove's Dictionary of Music and Musicians*, entry for "Variations," 670: "The principle [of variation] is that of variety within unity, secured by the reproduction of limited musical material in changing aspects, and is fundamental to composition."

[50] Gould discusses his revised interpretation of the piece in detail, focusing on the changed temporal relationships between variations, in his interview with Tim Page on disc 3 of *A State of Wonder: The Complete Goldberg Variations (1955 & 1981)*.

[51] The folk songs quoted in the *quodlibet* of the thirtieth variation seem to hint at the return of the aria; "ich bin so lang nicht bei dir gewest [*sic*]," the German for "I have been away from you for so long," can be taken to be the voice of the aria itself, returning after an absence of thirty variations. See e.g. the discussion of the folk songs in the *quodlibet* in *The Gold Bug Variations*: "The complainer is the sarabande Base, back at last, in unmistakable outline underneath the flurry of simultaneous quotes. I've been a great distance, a long time gone. Sometimes unrecognizable. But it's not my fault; had my mother served up more than thin fare, all this circumlocution would never have been necessary" (Powers, 630).

[52] The term *Zyklus* is more prominent in German studies of *The Goldberg Variations* than its English counterpart "cycle," though both have been applied to this piece. See *Grove's Dictionary of Music and Musicians*, entry for "Cyclic Form," 569: "The form of a musical work in several movements, usually a symphony or a chamber work in sonata form, in which one or more themes appear in more than one movement, often only in the first and the last. . . . The German equivalent of the term is often used much more loosely for any sonata-type work in several movements."

⁵³ Schulenberg questions, however, whether Bach would have considered the work a cycle, speculating that the variations were probably not intended for performance as a whole but instead could be taken out of their context in the set and performed in an abbreviated form. He implies that the work is less a "true cycle" than an "ideal cycle" (322).

⁵⁴ The sentence "Time does not exist" occurs once earlier in the novel, in the monologue by an anonymous admirer or secret lover of Liliane in "Variatio XII: Peace" (76).

⁵⁵ See Powell, 50: "Il éxiste toutefois une dialectique entre le passage du temps 'réel' et l'apparente atemporalité de la musique" (There is always a dialectic between the passage of "real" time and the apparent atemporality of music).

6: Composition, Performance, and Reception in Novels Based on the *Goldberg Variations*

IN ADDITION TO the structural elements of Bach's *Goldberg Variations* discussed in chapter 5 as a model for literary texts, the piece can also be examined with respect to its composition and performance history. In particular, the story about the circumstances of the piece's composition reported by Bach's first biographer Johann Nikolaus Forkel in 1802— already nearly sixty years after the work's publication—has seized the imagination of a number of writers.

The first section focuses on the legend according to which Bach composed the piece for performance by the young harpsichordist Goldberg to give comfort to an insomniac in his sleepless nights. The name by which the piece is commonly known can be traced to this story, amply demonstrating the power of persuasion it has had throughout history, both on the reception of the piece in general and on writers such as Gabriel Josipovici.[1] Next, I look beyond the composition itself to question the relationship between composition and performance. As with any performance art, music exists not in the form of a single work that reflects the composer's intentions, but is re-created anew with each performance. Though the ideal for many performers of classical music is that of fidelity to the work itself, each performance yet remains distinct, such that the performer plays a key role in the production of musical meaning. In this section, I examine the way this relationship between composer and performer is negotiated in Nancy Huston's *The Goldberg Variations* from the perspective of the performer. By the end of the novel, the harpsichordist Liliane sees performance as a kind of composition, one that is emphasized in the novel's construction when this narrator figure establishes herself as the intradiegetic author of all the monologues that precede her own.

The second section of this chapter then completes the transition to the performance side of the musical work. It first examines one example of the exceptional performer, the Canadian pianist Glenn Gould, whose unconventional 1955 interpretation of *The Goldberg Variations* was a sensation and highly influential not only in the realm of music but also on works of literature. This most famous recording of the piece is explicitly thematized at great length in Richard Powers's *The Gold Bug Variations* and is even mentioned as a source of contrast in Huston's novel as well. Furthermore, Gould himself appears as a central character in Thomas Bernhard's novel *Der Untergeher* (*The Loser*), in which he takes on the traits of the romantic genius. Next, the section goes on to consider the amateur performer, particularly in Rachel Cusk's *The Bradshaw Variations*. This novel does not discuss the *Goldberg Variations* explicitly, but the most prominent character, Thomas, spends a year learning to play the piano. His struggles with the instrument as a late but diligent learner form a complement to those of the professional performer in the previous section.

In the following section, the focus is on the third side of the communicative triangle; after composition and performance, I then consider the role of the audience's reception of the work. The audience's perspective is dramatized most vividly in Huston's novel, in which thirty audience members reflect on the piece, the performance situation as such, and anything else that goes through their minds while Liliane plays the harpsichord. After the live performance, the focus shifts to a recording. Here again, Glenn Gould plays a role, as it is his 1955 recording that features so prominently in Powers's *The Gold Bug Variations*. In this novel, the record is not merely the medium by which the performance is made available to the listening character Stuart Ressler, but is significant in its materiality. This will complete the circle, since Ressler as a self-taught listener becomes an amateur composer by the end of the novel, composing pieces that ironically are not intended for performance.

The three aspects of composition, performance, and reception—which provide a contextual complement to the work-immanent structural analyses of chapter 5—will thus be considered in their separate facets but remain very much interconnected. This interconnectedness is further exemplified in the novels' shared focus on questioning the roles of the communicative triangle, eliding first the composer, then the performer, and even the work as such. This postmodern destabilization of the artwork is the subject of the final part of this chapter.

Composition

The Legend of Composition: *Goldberg: Variations*

Though Bach's set of variations bears the official title *Aria mit verschiedenen Veränderungen*, it is commonly referred to as the *Goldberg Variations*. This popular title has its origins in the legend that grew up around the piece's composition. Supposedly the piece was commissioned by the Russian ambassador to Dresden, Hermann Carl, Reichsgraf von Keyserlingk, for the harpsichordist in his employ, Johann Gottlieb Goldberg, to perform for him to help alleviate his insomnia. According to the biographer Johann Nikolaus Forkel, Count Keyserlingk kränkelte viel und hatte dann schlaflose Nächte. Goldberg ... musste in solchen Zeiten in einem Nebenzimmer die Nacht zubringen, um ihm während der Schlaflosigkeit etwas vorzuspielen. Einst äusserte der Graf gegen Bach, dass er gern einige Clavierstücke für seinen Goldberg haben möchte, die so sanften und etwas muntern Charakters wären, dass er dadurch in seinen schlaflosen Nächten ein wenig aufgeheitert werden könnte. Bach glaubte, diesen Wunsch am besten durch Variationen erfüllen zu können, die er bisher, der stets gleichen Grundharmonie wegen, für eine undankbare Arbeit gehalten hatte. (Forkel cited in Peter Williams, 4–5)

[was often unwell and then had sleepless nights. On these occasions, Goldberg had to spend the night in an adjoining room so that he could play something to him during this sleeplessness. The Count once remarked in Bach's presence that he would very much like to have some keyboard pieces for his Goldberg, of a character so gentle and somewhat merry that he could be a little cheered up by them in his sleepless nights. Bach believed that he could best fulfil this wish with some variations, which until then he had held to be a thankless task because of the harmony always being the same.][2]

Music historians, however, doubt this version of events on a number of counts. First, there is no dedication to the Count in the printed score, such as one would expect if he had in fact commissioned the piece. Also, although Bach visited the Count in Dresden in November 1741, the piece would presumably have been composed a few years earlier, when Goldberg (1727–56) would almost certainly have been too young to have been the intended performer (see e.g. Peter Williams, 5; Rampe, 931–32). Likewise, the description "gentle and somewhat merry" hardly seems to do justice to the complexity and diverse character of the variations. The idea that the pieces were intended to put someone to sleep is hardly a flattering one for the composer. Heinz Hermann Niemöller observes, furthermore, that Forkel's story is characterized by a romantic conception of music and composition that is anachronistically projected onto the earlier baroque period (4–5, 23–24).

Be that as it may, it is not the historical record that fascinates the novels based on the *Goldberg Variations*, but precisely this romantic legend. It is thrice alluded to in Huston's *The Goldberg Variations*, though the characters confuse the performer Goldberg with the patron Keyserlingk, taking Goldberg to be the insomniac for whom the piece was written:[3]

Apparently old Mr. Goldberg was one hell of an insomniac. He's the one who asked big-shot Johnny Sebastian for a bit of melodic and harmonic sleepin' draught. [spoken by the French-Canadian Dominique in Variatio V] (38)

... not only Bach but a whole series of composers; not only Goldberg but a whole crowd of insomniacs; not only the eighteenth century but all the ages past and yet to come. [spoken by the harpsichordist Liliane in the return of the Aria] (169–70)

In the lengthy description of the variations in chapter 27, Powers includes a version of Forkel's composition legend:

> Bach's first biographer tells the story, already thirdhand, of how Count Kaiserling [*sic*], former Russian ambassador to Saxony, employed a young harpsichordist named Goldberg, one of Bach's star pupils. Goldberg's duties included making soft music in an adjoining room on those frequent nights when the Count had trouble sleeping. The Count commissioned Bach to compose for Goldberg something "of a soft and somewhat lively character," to assist against this periodic insomnia. A musical calmative, a treatment that now consists of two tablets and the low drone of talk radio. . . . (*The Gold Bug Variations*, 577)

Though this version of events is not explicitly challenged, an awareness of Forkel's possible unreliability is demonstrated by the phrase "already thirdhand." Powers's novel is not, however, particularly concerned with the circumstances surrounding the piece's composition and focuses instead on its structure and to a lesser extent on its reception by listeners. The comments on composition quoted here, like those in Huston's novel, do not go beyond the level of thematization.

The novel that makes the most use of the legend of how the *Goldberg Variations* were composed is undoubtedly Josipovici's *Goldberg: Variations*. In addition to thematic parallels to this composition story in frequent references to sleep and insomnia, as well as to challenges of composing on commission, the novel imitates or re-creates the composition legend of the *Goldberg Variations* by translating it into another time period and medium. The novel's opening depicts the arrival of the writer Samuel Goldberg at the country estate of Tobias Westfield. Several differences between Forkel's story and the novel are immediately discernable: The setting has been changed from 1741 Germany to 1800 England and the Russian count has been replaced by an English gentleman. What is more, the character Goldberg in the novel is not a thirteen-year-old prodigy who plays the harpsichord, but an older Jewish writer with a family of his own. The shift from musician to writer will prove to be particularly significant, as it has consequences for the type of performance Goldberg is expected to give.

Initially, Goldberg expects to read from some of the many books he has brought with him to Westfield's house, comforting his patron while he lies awake nights and trying to lull him to sleep. In the first chapter, it becomes clear that Westfield expects something more. He had previously hired a harpsichordist, but instead of being relaxed into sleep, the music irritated him. Simply being read to will also be insufficiently soothing, as he claims to have "read all the books that have been written, . . . and it makes [him] melancholy" (3), so he instead asks Goldberg to compose new texts specifically for the occasion. Goldberg, then, is not merely the performer, but is placed in the role of the improviser, or the spontaneous composer. This is also reflected in the novel's title, *Goldberg: Variations*. Whereas the title of the musical piece is ambiguous as to the precise role of Goldberg—he could be the patron who commissioned the piece and to whom it is dedicated, the performer who made it famous, or even somehow the subject of the piece—the colon in Josipovici's title suggests that Goldberg is the speaker and the variations are what he has to say. Goldberg thus takes on the role of the author from the first paratextual information that confronts the reader, going beyond the model of his namesake the harpsichordist to incorporate facets of both Goldberg and Bach. The equation of Goldberg (in the novel) with Bach is strengthened by the episode in chapter 16 (111–25), in which he reenacts Bach's improvisation and composition of the *Musikalisches Opfer*. The collapsing of the figures of performer and composer will also be the focus of the following section.

Performance as Composition: *The Goldberg Variations*

With its thirty-two vignettes told from thirty-one different first-person perspectives (the first and last are both narrated by Liliane, the harpsichord player), Nancy Huston's *The Goldberg Variations* is an example of the collaboration between performer and audience in the musical performance, as will be discussed later in this chapter. The novel also negotiates the relationship between the composer and performer, however, particularly in the sections narrated by Liliane. She reflects on her role at the center of the performance, but she is not alone in doing so. Other characters also make comments questioning the distinction between composer and performer, such as "Madame Kulainn is one hell of an artist. Or maybe it's Bach" (148), which point to an ambiguity in the source of musical meaning. Though the classical music aesthetic and conventions of its performance practice assign pride of place to the composer, with the performer generally expected to reproduce the ideal work as faithfully as possible, there is a postmodern recognition in this novel that the composer—or author—is dead (see Roland Barthes's "Death of the Author"), that his or her intentions are inaccessible or even irrelevant, and that the performer is free to create the piece anew in each performance. This can be seen in a small way in the freedom Liliane has over decisions such as whether or not to take some or all of the repetitions (see the page-turner

Adrienne's comments, 18) and her "slow choices of *tempi*" (as observed by the music critic Jacques, 23; see also a similar comment by another audience member, 78).

Liliane's role not only as performer but also as composer is not established, however, until the last chapter of the novel. She begins her last monologue with a description of herself as a kind of vessel, the medium of musical performance that comes from somewhere else and passes through her: "The notes came. I drew them from the instrument, one after the other, I allowed them to come, trying not to do them too much violence. And when they came, they carried with them an entire universe. . . . I was afraid, at times, as I juggled with all of this, that I wouldn't be able to control it—perhaps it was stronger than I was?" (169–70). Soon after, however, she explicitly identifies herself as not only the performer of a work that can be traced back to Bach, but also a composer in her own right:

> It's true that all of this was imagined by me. But there's no such thing as a me that's *only* me. I'm the one who composed every single variation. Using the notes of Bach. Using the people in this room. All in my head. I'm sure I got a few things wrong. In fact, my ideas were pretty vague when I set out. I wasn't even sure who knew whom, what had happened first and what came later, how the different events would intertwine. . . . I *pretended* to be speaking for thirty people. Not in the French sense of the word, as pretention, but in the English sense, as make-believe. (170; ellipsis original)

There is ambiguity as to what precisely "all of this" refers to: Is it the musical performance? Or is she referring to the novel that the reader holds in his or her hand? As it turns out, Liliane connects the two. It is by inventing the monologues from the perspectives of her thirty audience members that she is able to really hear the music she plays for the first time:

> Towards the middle of the performance, imperceptibly, the meaning of the concert itself began to change. Here and there—just fleeting moments, but nonetheless—I got the impression I was actually hearing the music. *The music I was playing.* That's something that had never happened to me before. . . . This is something I could never admit to the others—that up until now, I'd never heard the music. How beautiful it is! How come everyone else knew about it before I did? (171; italics original)

The music only achieves meaning for Liliane when she as a performer accomplishes an act of creation—in this case, one transposed into another medium, when she "composes" the variations as a series of verbal monologues. The meaning is clearly not permanently resident in the musical work as such, but must be at least partly invested by the performer. She uses the "notes of Bach" to compose the variations anew, imitating this musical model in a textual form.

Performance

The Genius Performer: Glenn Gould in Thomas Bernhard's *Der Untergeher*

The role of the performer in connection with the *Goldberg Variations* is of course most prominent in texts such as Huston's that foreground the performance situation. The frequent association of this particular piece with a famous pianist, however, means that a particular performer from music history also plays a strong role in the way the piece is viewed by literature. The recordings of Bach's *Goldberg Variations* that are most famous today were not performed on a harpsichord, as in Huston's novel, but on a Steinway piano, by the Canadian virtuoso Glenn Gould. His 1955 recording was an instant sensation and continues to be the best-known interpretation of the work, despite the fact that Gould actually re-recorded the piece in 1981, shortly before his death in 1982. Gould's landmark recording of the *Goldberg Variations* takes up a central role in Richard Powers's *The Gold Bug Variations*, as will be discussed below. Gould himself, on the other hand, is not only alluded to in several of the novels dealing with the *Goldberg* set, whether as a model or a source of contrast,[4] but also figures as a major character in Thomas Bernhard's 1983 novel *Der Untergeher* (translated into English as *The Loser*).[5]

Der Untergeher, narrated by an unnamed former pianist, tells the story of three music students who had met and shared a house while studying piano in Salzburg nearly thirty years before the time of the narration. In addition to the narrator, the other two pianists are Wertheimer and (a fictionalized version of) Glenn Gould. Unlike Gould, who went on to become an international success, Wertheimer and the narrator eventually give up the piano in resignation at never being able to achieve the level of proficiency they immediately recognized in their friend Glenn. The occasion for the narrator's reminiscences on their shared studies and their divergent paths afterward is the recent suicide of Wertheimer, whom Gould had nicknamed "der Untergeher" (the failure) from the beginning.

Though the novel is postmodern in its idiosyncratic syntax, use of repetitions, and stream-of-consciousness style—the entire novel consists of a single paragraph—the conception of Gould as a genius is highly indebted to romantic concepts. Both Wertheimer and the narrator are extremely talented pianists and could have become successful piano virtuosi, yet they see at once that Gould is in a class apart, as "der beste, wenn wir auch noch nicht zu sagen gewagt haben, daß er *der beste des*

Jahrhunderts sei" (the best, though we didn't yet dare to say that he was *the best of the century*, 8, italics original).

The character Gould is only loosely based on the historical figure, but does resemble him in certain idiosyncratic respects. One striking passage on Gould's performance ideal is particularly relevant here, and does reflect the historical Gould's attempt to mould his physiognomy to that of his instrument (see Hens, 29):

> Glenn hatte zeitlebens Steinway selbst sein wollen, er hatte die Vorstellung, *zwischen* Bach und dem Steinway zu sein nur als Musikvermittler und eines Tages zwischen Bach und dem Steinway zerrieben zu werden, eines Tages, so er, werde ich zwischen Bach einerseits und dem Steinway andererseits zerrieben, sagte er, dachte ich. Lebenslänglich habe ich Angst, zwischen Bach und Steinway zerrieben zu werden und es kostet mich die größte Anstrengung, dieser Fürchterlichkeit zu entgehen, sagte er. Das Ideale wäre, *ich wäre der Steinway, ich hätte Glenn Gould nicht notwendig*, sagte er, ich könnte, indem ich der Steinway bin, Glenn Gould vollkommen überflüssig machen. Aber es ist noch keinem einzigen Klavierspieler gelungen, sich selbst überflüssig zu machen, indem er Steinway *ist*, so Glenn. Eines Tages aufwachen *und Steinway und Glenn in einem sein*, sagte er, dachte ich, *Glenn Steinway, Steinway Glenn nur für Bach*. (118–19; italics original)

> [All his life Glenn had wanted to be the Steinway itself, he imagined himself *between* Bach and the Steinway as just the mediator of the music and that one day he would be crushed to death between Bach and the Steinway, one day, he said, I will be crushed to death between Bach on the one side and the Steinway on the other side, I thought. For my whole life I'll be afraid of being crushed to death between Bach and Steinway and it's the greatest effort for me to escape this horror, he said. The ideal would be, *if I were the Steinway, I didn't need Glenn Gould*, he said, I could, by being the Steinway, make Glenn Gould completely superfluous. But not a single pianist has ever succeeded in making himself superfluous by *being* Steinway, Glenn said. To wake up one day *and be Steinway and Glenn at once*, he said, I thought, *Glenn Steinway, Steinway Glenn just for Bach*.]

As Gould expresses it to the narrator, he sees the performer (himself) in an intermediate position between the instrument (Steinway) and the composer (Bach). To escape this tension, he longs to merge with the instrument to become "Glenn Steinway" or even just "Steinway," making Glenn Gould invisible and eliding him from the act of musical communication.[6]

All of this is still firmly on the thematization side of the thematization-imitation divide. The discussions of Gould as a performer of the *Goldberg Variations* and other pieces become important for the imitation of music, however, when the narrator's own performance is considered. Though he has renounced the piano—having given his valuable Steinway grand piano to the mediocre daughter of a local schoolteacher—he remains fascinated by Gould and indeed with the phenomenon of artistic creation. Having turned from music to writing, he reveals that he has been working on a book project on Gould—*Über Glenn Gould* (About Glenn Gould) (see 51, 81, 106–10)—for several years. Interestingly, Wertheimer is also said to have written a book, though only the title remains: *Der Untergeher* (78–79). Bernhard's novel incorporates aspects of both books, neither reproducing the narrator's writing project on Gould nor Wertheimer's philosophical collection of anecdotes. Instead, the focus has shifted somewhat to tell the story both of the genius Gould and of the loser Wertheimer, as filtered through the narrator's perspective, such that it is really the story of all three figures. In discussing his writings on Gould, the narrator in fact states:

> Wenn ich meine Beschreibung von Glenn Gould wirklich nocheinmal versuche, dachte ich, dann werde ich in dieser auch *seine* Beschreibung Wertheimers vorzunehmen haben und es ist fraglich, wer der Mittelpunkt dieser Beschreibung sein wird, Glenn Gould oder Wertheimer, dachte ich. Von Glenn Gould werde ich ausgehen, von den *Goldbergvariationen* und vom *Wohltemperierten Klavier*, aber Wertheimer wird in dieser Beschreibung eine entscheidende Rolle spielen, was mich betrifft, denn für mich war Glenn Gould immer mit Wertheimer verbunden gewesen, gleich in was für einer Beziehung und umgekehrt Wertheimer mit Glenn Gould und vielleicht alles in allem spielt doch Glenn Gould in Beziehung auf Wertheimer die größere Rolle, als umgekehrt. Tatsächlicher Ausgangspunkt muß der Horowitzkurs sein, dachte ich, das Bildhauerhaus in Leopoldskron, die Tatsache, daß wir völlig unabhängig voneinander aufeinander auf uns zugegangen sind vor achtundzwanzig Jahren lebensentscheidend, dachte ich. Wertheimers Bösendorfer gegen Glenn Goulds Steinway, dachte ich, *Glenn Goulds Goldbergvariationen gegen Wertheimers Kunst der Fuge*, dachte ich. (220–21; italics original)

> [If I really take up my description of Glenn Gould again, I thought, then I will have to deal with *his* description of Wertheimer and it is questionable who will be the center of this description, Glenn Gould or Wertheimer, I thought. I'll start with Glenn Gould, with the *Goldberg Variations* and the *Well-Tempered Clavier*, but

Wertheimer will play a decisive role in this description, as far as I'm concerned, since for me Glenn Gould was always connected with Wertheimer, regardless of which relationship, and on the other hand Wertheimer with Glenn Gould and maybe all in all Glenn Gould plays a greater part with respect to Wertheimer than the other way around. The actual starting point must be the Horowitz course, I thought, the sculptor's house in Leopoldskron, the fact that we approached each other completely independently of each other with life-changing results twenty-eight years ago, I thought. Wertheimer's Bösendorfer versus Glenn Gould's Steinway, I thought, *Glenn Gould's Goldberg Variations versus Wertheimer's Art of the Fugue*, I thought.]

This passage explicitly links the narrator's writing on Gould with that on Wertheimer, linking his "*Glennschrift*" (106) with the novel of which Wertheimer is the title figure, *Der Untergeher*. Additional comments along these lines further confirm the links between the characters,[7] as when the narrator muses that writing about Gould will allow him to understand Wertheimer better (224–25). More generally, the three are constantly compared and contrasted with one another in explicit terms, such that they appear alternately as reflections or as foils of one another. The narrator sometimes equates his situation with Wertheimer's in opposition to Gould's and then later distances himself from Wertheimer, linking himself instead with Gould. As a result, the three appear as legs of a triangle—distinct but interconnected. The discussions of Gould's performances can thus be read as a reflection on the narrator's performance in telling the story of the novel, though he never claims for himself the genius he ascribes to Gould.

The narrator also seems to ascribe to a different ideal of the performer than does his more famous friend, or perhaps is simply less successful in achieving it. Though the narrator might seem to elide himself from the picture by never revealing his name or much of his own story, the narrative is completely saturated with his own voice. In addition to narrating in the first person, the narrator also inserts himself into the narrative through the use of phrases such as "dachte ich im Gasthaus stehend," or simply "dachte ich" with extreme frequency. These phrases, which Hens calls the narrator's "ostinato" (33), not only contribute to an idiosyncratic individual voice, but also continually draw the narrative back to the narrator by emphasizing that the entire plot is filtered through his own memory and opinions. This is a performer who—merely by speaking in the first person, but especially through his very distinctive narrative style—makes his presence felt quite strongly throughout the text. Still, the focus on an interpreter of Bach's music— for it is precisely Gould's performance of the *Goldbergvariationen* that is repeatedly said to have "destroyed" ("vernichtet") Wertheimer—is paralleled by the narrator's performance as an interpreter of the three pianists and their interconnected lives.

The Amateur Performer: *The Bradshaw Variations*

In contrast to extraordinary performers such as Gould who are (naïvely) associated with innate genius, the amateur performer must struggle to attain even modest technical proficiency. An example of such a learner can be seen in Rachel Cusk's *The Bradshaw Variations*, in which Thomas Bradshaw spends his year at home learning to play the piano. Though his family is skeptical about his attempts at the piano—and indeed about his "sabbatical" (59) in general—Thomas is unconcerned about the time he is perceived to be wasting: "'You can't spend a whole year playing the piano,' [his brother] says. . . . Thomas looks surprised. 'Why not?' 'It's—it's a waste, isn't it?' '*I* don't think so,' Thomas says" (60; italics original). Chapter 11 focuses on a piano lesson at the apartment that his teacher, Benjamin, shares with his boyfriend Ignatius. On the occasion of this lesson, Thomas reflects on his methods in learning this new skill, ones that seem to him less natural and "honest" than he feels they should be:

> The truth is that for the past week Thomas has worked on the *adagio* like a solitary prisoner tunneling under the fortress walls. He is slightly ashamed of it, his secret determination, the rigidity of his methods, the insistent, repetitive labour he has put into it, for this is how he has always got the things he wanted in life, ... It has always seemed that work occupied the place where something more natural ought to have been, something instinctive and innate, something he associates with honesty, though he doesn't know exactly why. (83)

Thomas's "repetitive labour" emphasizes the importance of practice and determination in musical skill, something that must be worked at diligently in order to see progress. And indeed, Thomas's performance of the Beethoven *adagio* in this scene impresses not only his teacher, but also Ignatius, a "real pianist, not a teacher but a performer" (85), who comes out of the next room "applauding and exclaiming loudly" (84). Hard work clearly does lead to results and is portrayed as a necessary component of the learning process and as preparation for the performance. Still, Thomas's sense that his diligence masks a lack of innate talent, "something more natural" (83), reflects a romantic ideal of the genius performer who can channel the music without investing all that repetitive effort.[8] The contrast here to the romanticized depiction of Gould in Bernhard's novel is quite striking. Though *Der Untergeher* does not deny that Gould invests considerable practice time in achieving his success, his portrayal as being in a class apart from even other talented piano students continually emphasizes the innateness of his prodigious gifts.[9] Thomas clearly does not begin his experiment with the piano with such an advantage, but must work diligently for each new improvement in his playing.

For the amateur pianist, the piano remains a foreign object. In contrast to Gould's desire to fuse with his instrument in *Der Untergeher*, Thomas sees the keyboard of the piano as "a far-off frozen landscape, a place as beautiful as it is inhuman, whose silence is occasionally interrupted by the sounds of struggle before swallowing them up again" (82). This passage captures his anxiety about performance before he plays the *adagio* for his teacher, but also more generally his feeling of distance from the instrument and the art form as such. His approach to learning a piece by determinedly practicing it again and again requires "play[ing] each bar until its sanity has been broken down and become a rattling box of madness" (83). This focus on the mechanical side of musical performance is reminiscent of Liliane's too-cold style in Huston's *The Goldberg Variations*, which prevents her from actually hearing the music as she plays it. Neither Thomas nor Liliane can see the forest for the trees—they can't hear the music as music because of their intense concentration on the minute techniques of fingering.

But like Liliane, Thomas also experiences a moment of release, in which he stops thinking about what he is doing and simply does it:

> For an instant his mind is filled with the white light of performance, the strange featureless lucidity left behind by the knowledge that he mustn't think, that his brain must be vacated, that instead he must act; and the next time he checks, he sees that he is already halfway down the first page, and the thinking makes him falter so he quickly vacates his brain again and returns to his hands. There is an awful passage that is like inching along a narrow ledge, and then a period when he seems to be safe in miles of firm level ground; then suddenly it is a cataract, a rushing to the edge, to disaster, and over he goes, swept down through the complexity and out the other side, where there is stillness and daylight and the untidy room with Benjamin sitting in his chair. (84)

A too-close focus on the mechanics of playing the piano causes him to stumble, and he must "vacate his brain" in order to perform with fluidity. It is clear that thinking, perhaps implicitly contrasted with a process more akin to feeling the music, is a hindrance in the desired performance style. This successful manner of playing is here called the "white light of performance" and allows him to transcend the notes on the page to create an overall performance of the piece that is capable of moving his listeners—quite in contrast with the practice exercise of "tick-tocking along with the music" (89) to emphasize the piece's tempo and rhythm, which his daughter finds incomprehensible.

Reception

Chronologically located after the accomplishment of the composer and often simultaneous with that of the performer is the esthesic experience of reception by the listener. This may involve a live performance, in which the audience's experience overlaps temporally with that of the performer, though the performer has prepared for the situation in advance and the audience may continue to reflect on it afterward. It may also, however, involve a recording, in which the experiences of performer and listener are both temporally and spatially separated from one another. The interaction that is possible in a live performance is thus lacking,[10] though the recorded performance gains the opportunity for repeated listening, as the transient musical event is made permanently accessible. The following sections explore these two types of classical performances, one as the harpsichord concert in Nancy Huston's *The Goldberg Variations* and the other as the Glenn Gould record that figures in Richard Powers's *The Gold Bug Variations*.

Variations in Audience Reception: *The Goldberg Variations*

The role of Liliane Kulainn, as the performer of the concert that is the theme of Huston's novel *The Goldberg Variations*, has been discussed above. Here, I focus instead on the other end of the communicative chain involved in this performance, on the audience members who listen to her play. As Liliane's partner Bernald observes in the fifteenth variation, their "simultaneous presence in this room is as much a part of the performance as the music itself" (91). The concert situation and the multiperspectival structure of the novel offer an ideal opportunity to compare the reactions of different listeners, as each chapter is narrated by a different member of the audience and reflects different attitudes and preconceptions, different levels of familiarity with and interest in the music.

While some characters focus primarily—or at least initially—on the music currently being played, others seem to be sitting in the concert more or less against their will, more interested in what happened the day before or is scheduled for later, than in the music. Most experience a wandering of attention during the performance, regardless of whether they are actually interested in the music or not. Something about the situation sets them off on a chain of free associations, so that their attention turns to plans, memories, philosophical or political ruminations, obsession over perceived personality defects, etc.

Among those particularly interested in the performance as music is Franz Blau, who is apparently a friend of Liliane's partner Bernald and is knowledgeable about classical music. In his monologue (Variatio XIII), he begins with reflections on the relatively slow *tempi* Liliane uses, comparing her performance (favorably!) with that of Glenn Gould. Other reflections directly related to the music include thoughts on the piece's composition for Count Keyserlingk, Bach's use of different time signatures and a rhythmic pulse that pervades the entire set, and Liliane's playing as "slightly flat and monotonous" (78) and "a bit too systematic, too conscientious" (79). This triggers a digression to her preferences in music and disdain of the romantics, her inconsistencies, and from there to his mother as the only woman he has ever felt comfortable with. At this point, he seems to have stopped listening to the thirteenth variation altogether, considering instead the empty space his mother has continued to leave behind since her death twenty years before and his attempts to fill the silence when he can't sleep at night by listening to music.[11] Only the last sentence of the chapter—"Oh! A drop of *ritardando* wouldn't have done any harm" (82)—brings his attention back to the concert situation as such.

Other characters who profess less interest in baroque music allow their thoughts to wander from the outset.[12] Several are present in the audience not to hear the concert, but because of their personal connection to Liliane, Bernald, or even to another audience member who has more or less dragged them along, such as the French-Canadian Dominique in Variatio V, who professes he "wouldn't even be here if it weren't for Christine; she used to play the flute with this Liliane" (40). Instead of focusing on the music, he makes disparaging comments about French society in general and about Liliane in particular, as well as about classical music. Presented in joual (a variety of French spoken in Montreal, often associated with the working class) in the original French version of the novel ("Joual" is also the title of the chapter), the English translation relates his thoughts in slang that emphasizes the class differences he discusses.[13] Dominique's only direct thoughts on the music being performed relate to the legend of the piece's composition for an insomniac, which he finds quite appropriate, since the music seems to bore him to the point of falling asleep: "That's why the chairs are so goddamn uncomfortable—make sure we won't go driftin' off to dreamland. It ain't fair, given that this music was written specially for the very purpose" (38). He concludes his interior monologue by asserting that he would rather listen to folk songs than the music of the "Intelligentsia," as he puts it: "I prefer that 'Alouette' to all the Count Goldbergs in the world served up roasted on a golden platter" (42).

Other characters focus on their relationships with either Liliane or Bernald and the ways in which they are perceived to have changed. Examples include former lovers of Liliane such as Pierre (6), Hélène (7), Writer (10), Christine (11), Viviane (15), and the "Anonymous" speaker of Variatio XII, who fantasizes about making love to her. Similarly, Carpenter (8), a "Student of Bernald's" (23), and Simon Freeson (14) all lament changes in their old friend or teacher Bernald Thorer, often giving Liliane the blame for those changes,[14] while Liliane's father Kenneth Kulainn (21) reflects on what a stranger his daughter has become.

In addition to these thirty perspectives on the performance from members of the audience, the novel also provides us with two monologues by Liliane herself, which serve to frame the novel. Liliane is of course the performer of the piece, but when she begins to listen to the music as she plays it, she also becomes engaged in the reception side of the communicative triangle. A performer may play for herself as well as for others. At the beginning of the concert Liliane seems to regard not herself but the music as possessing agency. She asserts in her first interior monologue that she has "no access to the music itself. I'm here to bring it forth and they are here to absorb it, but the music blossoms in an intermediary space that touches neither them nor me. In fact I'm executing, not interpreting" (14). In Variatio XI the character Christine remembers Liliane saying that if she listened to the music she would be so caught up in its beauty that she'd stop playing or risk "slowing down, fascinated by [her] own fingers, in the middle of a *prestissimo*" (72), such that the roles of performer and listener seemed for her to be incompatible. By the end of the performance, however, something has changed: "Here and there—just fleeting moments, but nonetheless—I got the impression I was actually hearing the music. *The music I was playing.* That's something that had never happened to me before. . . . This is something I could never admit to the others—that up until now, I'd never heard the music. How beautiful it is! How come everyone else knew about it before I did?" (171; italics original). The act of composition—"tickl[ing] all the strings of [the audience's] souls, one after another" (144) by inventing their thirty monologues—is what allows Liliane to achieve the necessary distance from her playing to actually perceive the music as music, rather than merely as notes on a page and as a matter of technical mastery. While she was initially only "executing" the music, now she is indeed "interpreting" it (14). Her revelation at the end of the novel, however, forces a change in reception for the reader as well, as the question of point of view becomes extremely ambiguous. If Liliane has in fact imagined the thirty intervening monologues, then they do not represent thirty different perspectives on the concert situation after all. The reader must reevaluate the novel in light of this new information, considering the thirty other narrators to be imagined by the one main narrator, their perspectives perhaps slanted or exaggerated or indeed entirely fictive. The concert situation as a whole is even drawn into question—do these thirty characters exist in Liliane's world at all?

What becomes clear is that these audience members—on whichever level of diegesis they may be located—are necessary for Liliane as a performer. Focusing only on her playing, she had been unable to hear how the music sounded to a listener. By imagining the points of view of an audience, however, she gains an outside perspective on her performance. She requires this change of perspective in order to be able to "hear the music" for the first time. Described as cold and mechanical (in chapters 5, 8, 12, 13), she had been too fixated on the technical side of her playing, and the creative act of putting herself in the position of her listeners allows her to gain the agency she initially lacked and achieve the needed distance to perceive the work as a whole and enjoy it as an aesthetic object.

Listening to the Recorded Performance: *The Gold Bug Variations*

Performance—or rather, one particular performance—also plays a role in Richard Powers's *The Gold Bug Variations*. In this novel, Glenn Gould's 1955 recording of Bach's variations is given as a gift to Stuart Ressler just two years after its release and accompanies him throughout the remainder of his life. This is Ressler's first introduction to classical music and it blows him away. While searching for the genetic code that underlies all life, Ressler learns to identify codes in the mathematical matrix[15] of Bach's *Goldberg Variations*. At the same time, this particular record also takes on the status of a sacred object, as a gift from Ressler's lover Jeannette Koss at the very beginning of their secret relationship. While the music is discussed in detail at many points throughout the novel, the physical object of the record and this particular interpretation by Gould in 1955 also receive consideration. The record, which Ressler at one point throws across the room in frustration, acquires scratches that affect the listening experience, as reflected in this exchange between Koss and Ressler:

> "Were they that scratchy when I gave them to you? What do you play them on, a Mixmaster?" . . .
> "Oh, those," he says, "I hardly hear the scratches anymore. Surface mutations." (280)

Though Ressler has learned to ignore the scratches (and characteristically equates them with genetic mutations that do not affect the species as a whole), they draw attention to the materiality of the record as a medium, as a recording of a performance rather than the live performance itself.

The particular interpretation of the *Goldberg Variations* recorded on the disc Koss gives Ressler is not explicitly identified by the name of the pianist, but is clearly revealed by a number of references to the pianist's biography and musical style. For example, on receiving the record, it is referred to as "a two-year-old recording of Bach's *Goldberg Variations* in a debut performance by a pianist who has the bad taste to be both as Canadian as Avery and a shade younger than Ressler" (156). This alone is enough to indicate to Bach enthusiasts that the recording in question must date from 1955 and have been recorded by the Canadian pianist

Glenn Gould, but other evidence is also sprinkled throughout the novel. In the following winter, Ressler

> stumbles across a photo essay of the twenty-odd-year-old-pianist, interpreter of the *Goldberg* recording that Koss gave him. . . . [T]he boy is young, single, romantically eccentric, a crank hypochondriac, never seen without his panoply of pills and jars of spring water. . . . He sings out loud while recording—ghostly, alternate vocalizings the technicians can't muffle. He has a carefully worked-out, outlandish theory about recordings rendering the concert obsolete. Yet the nut is a genius. (421)

This description in the magazine picks up on the idiosyncracies for which Gould was famous, and which connect him in many ways to Ressler, who is nearly the same age and in his own way an isolated and eccentric genius. Much later, in 1982, Ressler hears the piece on the radio but is astonished to realize it is not the same recording. This allows for a comparison of Gould's two interpretations of the same piece:

> "It's the Canadian kid, beyond a doubt. The inimitable playing style, that muffled humming in the background tracks trying for a Platonic, thirty-third variation just beyond the printed score. Playing the piece that woman gave him. . . .
> "But in an instant's listening, he's shocked to hear that it's not the same piece, not the same performance. It's a radical rethinking from beginning to end, worlds slower, more variegated, richer in execution. A lot of the variations enter attacca, without pause, the last notes of one spilling into the first notes of the next, anxious to hear how they might sound all at once, on top of one another." (636)

Like the scratches on the damaged record, this comparison with another version emphasizes the recorded nature of the performance. Though every performance is different, Ressler has spent twenty-five years listening to the exact same performance captured in 1955 in the recording studio. It is only by encountering a second recording by the same pianist—still recognizable by his "inimitable playing style" (636)—that the uniqueness of that first performance becomes apparent. Indeed, its transience is also emphasized, as Gould chose to create a significantly different interpretation in his later recording, including in 1981 many of the repetitions that had been omitted entirely in 1955, changing the tempi to reflect a different ideal of continuity between variations of the set, etc.[16]

Powers's novel makes it abundantly clear that Gould's interpretation of the *Goldberg Variations* is the model used. Among other things, Gould's focus on the recording studio and technology rather than the concert hall, the idiosyncracies mentioned above, and his habit of singing while recording are all thematized in the novel. These aspects also form important parallels with the character Stuart Ressler, as well as relating to the scientific ideals of the novel as a whole. Gould's singing in the background, for example, is clearly audible in his early recording of the canon at the seventh, Variation 21. In the twenty-first chapter, Ressler listens to this variation and wonders at the unusual sound that he only gradually is able to identify as singing:

> He sits wedged in the inseam between wall and floor, listening, thinking that he can hear distant song straining the contour of a variation beyond the variation. . . . Then he figures it: the pianist singing, caught on record, humming his insufficient heart out. Transcribing the notes from printed page to keypress is not enough. Some ineffable ideal is trapped in the sequence, some further Platonic aria trail beyond the literal fingers to express. Sound that can only be approximated, petitioned by this compulsory, angelic, off-key, parallel attempt at running articulation, the thirty-third *Goldberg*. (461–62)

In addition to adding authenticity to the description of this listening experience by focusing on the unusual character of Gould's performance, this passage also gets at the preconditions for performance more generally. Gould's singing in the background of the twenty-first variation is seen as an attempt to reach the "ineffable ideal" of the set of variations, the version of the music that underlies all the individual variations—or all the piece's disparate performances—but is never directly stated. Because the theme is rather implied than revealed, Gould can only "approximate" this music by supplementing the current variation with an addition of his own.

This novel also, in reflecting on Gould's recorded performance from 1955, shifts the focus from the composer's or performer's genius to that of the piece itself: "This fluke, beautiful assortment says they are here alone. Certainly a message: the sentient musical line makes that explicit. A messenger, undeniably, at the piano. But no sender. No sponsor. Only notes, vertically perfect, horizontally inevitable" (157). The record is not perceived as an expression of anyone's intentions, such as those of the composer, who is elided from the picture entirely. Instead, the act of listening to the recorded performance is an instance of communication only between the piece of music itself and the listeners. What is more, the novel argues convincingly that any meaning contained in the piece or the performance is found there by the listener. Ressler hears in Bach's variations the genetic code that underlies all life. Jan O'Deigh, later, hears the embodiment of all that mattered to Ressler and through him, her relationship with Frank Todd. This is why the music of the *quodlibet* (Variation 30) emanating from the cash machine at the end of the novel brings her to tears.

This emphasis on the listener's role in his or her relation to the recorded work of art fits in well with Walter Benjamin's famous statements on the work of art in the age of its technological reproducibility. By weakening the aura of the original work, the mass-produced copy such as a film or a musical recording participates in processes of democratization. The music is, for one thing, made available to a much wider audience than those who have access to exclusive live performances in the concert hall. At the same time, the tension between the record of the performance and the performance itself—not to mention the work as an ineffable and unrealizable ideal—remains, which is significant for the discussions of the *Goldberg Variations*, their performances by Gould, and the material record through which Ressler experiences them.

Yet not only does Ressler spend twenty-five years on the receiving end—the esthesic side, in Nattiez's terms—of the musical communicative act by listening to Gould's record, but he also partakes of other roles in the communicative triangle as well. When Todd finally dares to ask Ressler how he could bear to disappear from the world of science and spend twenty-five years in obscurity, the former geneticist responds with surprise, "But I never quit science" (609). He goes on to explain that his life's work has been the attempt at constructing a system that would be analogous to the language of the brain, yet he has not been pursuing this goal in a laboratory, but in a field he describes as

> "not a particularly popular or accredited line of research these days." . . . He went to his attaché case, brought it back to the table, and unzipped it. It poured forth, like a flushed warren, long, stiff, manila-colored, heavily pencilled-over scores. Musical scores. "This one is a woodwind octet," he announced self-consciously. "Look here. I stole this bit from Berg. But he stole a similar bit from Bach, so I'm safe from lawsuit."
> . . .
> "You're a composer," I said, a thrill coursing at the forbidden word. "Yes, I guess I am." He sounded as startled by the revelation as we were. "I even went back to school awhile, although the pieces have remained hopelessly amateur." (610)

Largely self-taught as a composer just as he had been as a listener, Ressler remains fascinated by the mathematical precision and combinatorial possibilities of music that first struck him upon listening to the record of the *Goldberg Variations* so many years before. The fact that it is this side of the music that speaks to him emphasizes once again the important role that the recipient plays in the construction of musical meaning. This "geneticist-turned-musical-recombiner" (612) is a code solver, someone who seeks patterns and rules that allow bewildering complexity to be traced back to simple origins, whether in genetics, programming languages, or in music. Another listener would hear something different and the piece would have a different meaning altogether.

Death of the Composer, the Performer, and the Original Work

A motif that runs through all the *Goldberg*-based novels considered in this chapter is a profound skepticism toward the primary components of musical communication as generally perceived. The composer is no longer considered the sole source of musical meaning, occupying a position both anterior to and more authoritative than that of the performer. Indeed, in none of these novels does Bach as composer figure prominently at all, and the only treatment of the composer to appear in these novels is when the performer usurps the composer's prerogative in creating the musical event him- or herself. Goldberg in Josipovici's *Goldberg: Variations* is no longer merely the virtuoso executer of the composer's wishes, but composes his own (literary) pieces for performance. Similarly, Liliane in Huston's *The Goldberg Variations* goes beyond her role as performer to engage in an act of creation when she "composes" all thirty of the audience's monologues. She thus transcends her initial perception of her role as performer as a vessel through which the composer pours his music, a mere conduit, turning the performer instead into a source of musical meaning in her own right. Bernhard's *Der Untergeher* and to a lesser extent Cusk's *The Bradshaw Variations* also focus on the act of performing, whether by a genius or an amateur, to the exclusion of any consideration of the composer or even of the work itself.

If the performer thus is moved into the foreground of the musical event, he or she still does not become the sole arbiter of musical meaning. The recipient, too, is important for these novels. In Josipovici's novel, the target audience Tobias Westfield is quite active in the production of Goldberg's work, as he simultaneously occupies the role of the commissioner of that work. At the same time, several of Goldberg's pieces resemble transcripts of dialogues with his employer, which exemplify a more direct type of interaction between performer/composer and listener. Still, while these novels do not generally emphasize audience-performer interactions to such an extent as the jazz novels considered in chapter 4, it is clear that the listener plays a key role in creating musical meaning. In Huston's novel, the principle of variation is that of a change in perspectives among the thirty audience members. This text demonstrates quite clearly the extent to which a given piece of music will have different meanings for each listener—even though these listeners have all been imagined by Liliane herself. There is also an awareness that each individual listening will produce new meaning, as when an audience member remarks in Variatio XXIX "I could listen to it a thousand times, and each time I would notice something new" (159).

Difference in audience perspectives is of course not restricted to the live performance, as Powers's *The Gold Bug Variations* demonstrates.

Here, the musical event is only available as a recording and is thematized in its materiality as such. The record has highly personal meaning for its listeners, meaning that also changes over time, despite the fixity of the medium. This emphasis on the record as a physical object also draws attention to another element of musical communication that is destabilized: the "work" of art is not stable, ideal, or immutable, but is very much in flux. The focus on performance is in part responsible for this questioning of the idea of an "original," since each performance is a new musical event, related in type to some concept of "the work," but constituting different tokens. This can also be compared to Saussure's distinction between *langue* and *parole*; the performances are instances of *parole*, of actual utterances, and the "work" is an abstract concept equivalent to *langue*. These novels focus almost exclusively on *parole*.

At the same time, this destabilization of the original work is also indebted to an interest in mediality per se. If music, like the text, is only accessible in a particular medial form—whether a live performance or a record, a reading or a printed text—then that form is significant for the meaning of the work. The fact that these novels seek to translate music into another medium by textualizing it shows that music is constantly being created anew. In such a context, how can a single individual's conception of that musical work be held to be the only correct one? Postmodern intermedial novels thoroughly undermine such assumptions, extending Barthes's notion of the "death of the author" to the "death of the composer." What is more, while several of the novels voice an aesthetic that could be called the "death of the performer,"[17] they all argue convincingly for the "death of the original,"[18] very much in keeping with Benjamin's claims about the loss of aura in the age of mechanically reproduced art in mass distribution. Time and again, the emphasis on the performer's and audience's roles in constructing musical meaning means that the original work loses its authority. For example, Gould's singing along with the twenty-first variation as thematized in Powers's *The Gold Bug Variations* yields yet another variation of the variation, and the scratches on Ressler's copy of the record create a second version of even the most fixed kind of performance (i.e., recorded rather than live).[19] Arroyas points out that Huston's *The Goldberg Variations* also engages in a "desacralization of the musical work" (103), since the variety of audience perspectives takes the work "off its pedestal and place[s it] within the sociological framework of its users" (101). At the same time, each novel demonstrates that different audience perspectives yield different interpretations of the same live performance, where "the original" is not accessible at all.

In total, this produces a palimpsest-like structure of the work and its performances. This many-layered structure of the musical object is furthermore repeated in the novels, most strikingly in Huston's *The Goldberg*

Variations, where the reader reassesses the thirty variations after learning that Liliane composed them all, rather than thirty different audience members. By imitating this structure, these novels extend the palimpsestuous[20] nature of performance art (or art in general) to the written text, such that performance plays a strong role not only on the level of thematization but also of imitation.

Notes

[1] This legend also provides the starting point for Dieter Kühn's radio play *Goldberg-Variationen* (1976). It is based on the same situation in which a piece is commissioned for the purpose of keeping an insomniac company, and here the names of Keyserlingk and Goldberg are retained, though the setting would appear to have been moved to the twentieth century. The radio play is constructed as a multimedial dialogue between Keyserlingk, played by an actor with spoken lines, and Goldberg, who plays the piano but does not speak. There are not as many variations as in Bach's work or in the novels discussed here, however: only sixteen instead of thirty-two. Also of interest is the fact that the radio play conceives of Goldberg's playing as contemporary improvisation rather than performance of a work by another composer, i.e., Bach.

[2] Johann Nikolaus Forkel, *Über Johann Sebastian Bachs Leben, Kunst und Kunstwerke* (1802), 51–52; cited and translated by Peter Williams, 4–5.

[3] Of the three times the history of the piece is alluded to, twice Goldberg is mistaken for the insomniac patron, as in the quotes given here. Only in the thirteenth variation is Goldberg correctly identified as the performer of the piece: "Of course she's not a virtuoso like the young Goldberg himself" (78).

[4] See e.g. the reference in Huston's *The Goldberg Variations* to "the frenzied charge of a Glenn Gould," to which Liliane's slower, more subdued interpretation is appreciatively compared (78).

[5] The German term "Untergeher" has much stronger and more tragic connotations than this English translation, suggesting concepts such as "Weltuntergang" (the end of the world). Even "failure" would have been a more accurate translation than the relatively weak "loser."

[6] Arroyas briefly refers to this in a footnote as an example of what she calls "disappearing selves" (102n11). This proposed elision of the performer is an interesting reversal of the way the composer is elided in each of these postmodern texts.

[7] Gregor Hens discusses the three characters as the three voices of a piece of counterpoint (33). Gould represents the upper voice, the narrator the ostinato bass line, and Wertheimer the struggling middle voice. See 53: "Die Rolle Wertheimers, dessen Untergang schon im Motto als unausweichlich und folgerichtig dargestellt wird, entspricht der Mittelstimme in der kompositorischen Struktur des *Untergehers* und steht somit in direkter Konkurrenz zur Oberstimme Glenns.... Der Erzähler wiederum repräsentiert das rhythmisch-gleichbleibende Substratum in diesem Arrangement—eine Rolle, die keinerlei Ornamentierung bedarf." (The role of Wertheimer, whose downfall has already been presented in

the motto as inescapable and consequential, corresponds to the middle voice in the compositional structure of the novel and is thus in direct competition with the upper voice of Glenn. The narrator, in turn, represents the rhythmically constant substrate in this arrangement, a role that foregoes any ornamentation.) For a very different and less convincing analysis of the novel as contrapuntal, cf. Olson, who identifies three fugal themes not represented by the three characters, but by "Gould dying at fifty-one, Wertheimer committing suicide, and Gould being obsessed with fugal perfection" (80).

[8] This same ideal can also be seen in Jack Fuller's jazz novel *The Best of Jackson Payne*, in which the title character conceals the effort and theoretical knowledge that goes into his playing, pretending not to be able to read music in a tactic another character refers to as his "jungle genius jive" (19).

[9] *Der Untergeher* does not explicitly discuss the innovations in recording practice for which Gould was also known. Rather than performing in a concert hall, Gould early switched to the recording studio in a search for technical perfection that could only be achieved through the use of multiple takes. The performances that have the largest impact on the plot of the novel, however, are for the most part live and relatively private performances for the narrator and Wertheimer, which ended the careers of both characters.

[10] See e.g. Erika Fischer-Lichte on the "autopoietic feedback loop" (39 and passim), in which a performance relies on the shared "now" of performer and audience. In the case of a recorded performance, this interaction is disrupted: "Mediatized performance invalidates the feeback loop" (68).

[11] This insomnia links the character to the Count Keyserlingk of legend.

[12] The wandering thoughts of the audience members during the performance can be compared to those that keep insomniacs awake at night, forming an appropriate parallel to the legend of the piece's composition as a comfort to Count Keyserlingk in his sleepless nights.

[13] Actually, while Dominique's language in Huston's English translation is certainly informal in register, there are relatively few dialect elements present (such as "ain't" in the passage quoted below). The use of "n'" instead of "ng" at the ends of words and the deletion of "th" in "them" as in "those veins can't have honest-to-goodness red blood flowin' in 'em" (41), for example, reflect a pronunciation typical of standard (North American) English in a spoken context.

[14] A different perspective on Bernald's rupture—his sudden cessation of lecturing, publications, etc.—is given by a "Pupil of Liliane's" (4), who celebrates that new-found silence.

[15] See Don Franklin, "Viewing the *Goldberg Variations* as a Musico-Mathematical Matrix."

[16] See Gould's 1981 interview with Tim Page, as recorded on disc 3 of the CD set *A State of Wonder: The Complete Goldberg Variations 1955 and 1981*.

[17] See, for example, the fictional Gould's desire in Bernhard's *Der Untergeher* to fuse with his instrument and disappear as a performer. Liliane in *The Goldberg Variations* also initially perceives herself as a vessel through which the music passes unchanged rather than as playing an active role in bringing it forth. Ressler's

unperformed and unpublished compositions in Powers's *The Gold Bug Variations* can also be seen as a circumvention of the performer's role.

[18] I am indebted to Jutta Ernst for suggesting this term.

[19] Of course the record itself as a mass-produced copy that lacks on original is also a means of killing the authority or "aura" of the original work of art, as elucidated by Walter Benjamin.

[20] As Sarah Dillon explains in her study of the palimpsest, the usual adjectival form is *palimpsestic*. Gérard Genette's coinage of the term *palimpsestuous* allows for a distinction between the "process of layering that produces a palimpsest" (*palimpsestic*) and "the structure that one is presented with as a result of that process" (*palimpsestuous*) (Dillon, 4).

Conclusion

THE IMAGE OF THE PALIMPSEST introduced at the end of the last chapter is a useful metaphor for the musical novel as a genre. Just as the *Goldberg* novels with their reassessments of the interaction between composition, performance, and audience response envision a piece of music as a number of performances superimposed on an increasingly elusive and unstable "original," the musical novel as a whole adds additional layers to the musical model that it employs. While every text builds on those texts that go before, the palimpsest that is the musical novel consists not only of textual layers, but also of forms associated with another medium. It layers its content on a structural framework taken in part from music, but which is then fleshed out by textual means. In addition to these work-immanent aspects, the musical novel—like any text—is dependent on the active participation of the reader so that its meaning can unfold in a new way with each successive reading.

By employing structures and forms borrowed from music, the musical novel does not actually make that music present to the reader. Instead, it intermedially evokes, adapts, and imitates the music, presenting an alternate and supplementary version of it. Readers, depending on their knowledge of the musical model, are given the opportunity to compare the two medial forms, though the novel can also be read and enjoyed independently. A lack of knowledge about jazz or about Bach's *Goldberg Variations* will strip one layer from the palimpsest, yet will not render the musical novel as a whole incomprehensible or devoid of interest. In the case of novels based on the *Goldberg Variations*, familiarity with the specific musical model of this individual work is perhaps more directly necessary for an appreciation of the novels' accomplishments. Some, such as Powers's *The Gold Bug Variations*, try to circumvent this problem by including extensive descriptions and analyses of the musical work within the novel. A reader unfamiliar with the piece thus receives enough information about the structures being imitated to pick up on some of the patterns and techniques used by the novel. In other cases (e.g., Josipovici's *Goldberg: Variations* and Cusk's *The Bradshaw Variations*), the references to Bach's piece are much less explicit and are liable to be missed by readers not intimately acquainted with the piece. In Cusk's novel, though Bach is mentioned, the *Goldberg Variations* are never actually referred to at all and only structural parallels allow the observant and musically knowledgeable reader to recognize a connection to the piece.

Because jazz novels do not rely on the structures of a single piece of music, a more general familiarity with the genre may be sufficient for the reader to recognize the forms implemented. Yet here, too, some of the novels make an attempt to identify or label the musical parallels through thematization, from Fuller's explicit musico-theoretical discussions of call and response and trading fours in Quinlan's embedded writings in *The Best of Jackson Payne*, and Crouch's discussion of call and response in the sermon depicted in *Don't the Moon Look Lonesome*, to Cartiér's more subtle references to African American rhythms in *Muse-Echo Blues* and *Be-Bop, Re-Bop*.

Interestingly, the techniques used by novels to imitate either jazz or the *Goldberg Variations*—a musical genre or an individual piece of baroque music—are quite similar. Rhythm and timbre play a much stronger role in novels based on jazz than they do in the *Goldberg* novels, a contrast that can be derived from the different rhythms and timbres employed in the two musical genres, but both structural elements and the performance situation are central to all the novels considered here. The musical structures imitated—riffs, call-and-response patterns, a sequence of choruses, and the album structure in jazz; theme and variations, numerical patterns, and changes in voicing or time notation in the *Goldberg Variations*—vary across the two groups, but the narrative means employed often overlap. Riffs and themes both depend on repetition in a varied context for their recognition, though a riff involves the repetition of the precise or very similar wording and a theme tends to be repeated in terms of content rather than form. Both serve to tie together disparate parts of a narrative by linking them to a central idea, whether that be the way Carla has constructed her racial and regional identity as "the Norwegian girl from South Dakota" in *Don't the Moon Look Lonesome* or the overarching theme of complexity bred from simple rules in *The Gold Bug Variations*.

The macrostructure of the two groups of novels also exhibit strong similarities, despite the contrast in musical models. The variations of the Goldberg novels yield an episodic structure that mirrors the skyscraper-like series of discrete units favored by jazz novels in re-creating a chorus structure. Though the reasons for the pattern are different, both musical models focus less on development than on the repetition and variation of a particular structure or theme, which is imitated in a similar way in the jazz novels and the Goldberg novels.

Though classical music is perceived as being much less interactive than jazz music, as exemplified in the latter's call-and-response patterns and live performances that may incorporate a high degree of audience interaction (including dances and parades), the novels based on the *Goldberg Variations* question this view of classical music. They foreground the performance and reception sides of music making, such that the work itself—while certainly still relevant for the text with its mathematical regularity—is by no means the sole focus. Both jazz novels and *Goldberg* novels give the performer/narrator a distinct and prominent voice, not only in Albert Murray's Scooter novels and in Toni Morrison's *Jazz*, but also in Nancy Huston's *The Goldberg Variations* and Thomas Bernhard's *Der Untergeher*. In all these cases, the performer demonstrates his or her ability to change the score, to revise the performance in an improvisatory manner, supplanting a composer or author that would traditionally stand behind the text. Even in the case of a recorded classical performance, as with Glenn Gould's 1955 rendition of *The Goldberg Variations*, the performer is able to modify the composition by singing along with the piano and producing "the thirty-third *Goldberg*" (Powers, 462), and the listener actively participates in the mutability of the performance by contributing his or her own associations, differing levels of comprehension or interest, or even by scratching the record and producing "surface mutations" (Powers, 280).

The important question remains of what the music *means* for these novels. As discussed in chapter 1, there remains a lively debate over what, if anything, music means and how it produces that meaning. The position taken by this study emphasizes the intrinsic references of music within its own closed system, through the establishment of patterns, repetitions, breaches with conventions, etc., which make connections to other parts of the piece or to forms and patterns shared by other pieces of music. In addition to this intramusical level, however, meaning that is essentially extrinsic to the musical work as such can be contributed on the poietic level, through processes of creation by the composer and performer, as well as on the esthesic level, through the interpretations of listeners (see Nattiez).

As interpretations of and responses to music, musical novels are first and foremost acts of esthesis, in which the text develops what may be very individualized associations with a piece of music or genre. Through the creative act of poiesis, these associations are converted into another artwork, this time in the medium of text rather than music. Yet reactions and responses to music by listeners occur not only extratextually but also within the novels themselves. On the level of content, musical novels frequently depict music as a projection space for the listener. This includes not only audience members but also the (intratextual) performer and composer, who also listen to and experience the music they produce, though their involvement with the poietic side of musical meaning means that they also influence to some extent the way that music is perceived by other listeners. Music is valued and enjoyed in part because of its willingness to remain ambiguous in terms of meaning: "But music—what a vacation! No way you can pin down the ideas floatin' around in there" (Huston, 40). If it doesn't mean anything specific, it can mean whatever the listener wishes it to. In some of these novels, music serves as a symbol of a particular culture—for example, of African American culture in jazz novels like Morrison's *Jazz* and Crouch's *Don't the Moon Look Lonesome*—though in others it is a symbol of creativity and release, as in Gailly's *Be-bop*, without any ethnic or cultural restrictions (occurring within the very different social context of jazz in late twentieth-century France). In Ondaatje's *Coming Through Slaughter*, the race of the characters is completely ignored, so that the music can be divorced from this particular ethnic context and instead stand more generally for the tension between freedom and constraint—a meaning jazz music also takes on in Fuller's *The Best of Jackson Payne* and that is also a central theme in Cusk's *Goldberg* novel *The Bradshaw Variations*. For Stuart Ressler in Powers's *The Gold Bug Variations*, Bach's *Goldberg Variations* is a symbol of the numerical patterns and combinatorial rules also found in genetics—"listening with a code-breaker's urge, taking noise and turning it to pattern, thinking to find with ear and voice a surrogate, an emblem for the melody of the self-composing gene" (575)—while at the same time serving as a carrier of memories of a long-past love affair. For some of the listeners at Liliane's concert in Huston's *The Goldberg Variations* Bach's music symbolizes a decadent and elitist capitalist culture. For other characters, it is significant as an interruption from everyday life, a release from conscious thought, while for others it means something different each time.

On a structural level, the novels are fascinated with music in part because of the intrinsic references of music, that is, to the way music creates a coherent system without necessarily referring to anything outside itself. Music is imitated as a system of internal references and patterns, in the case of the *Goldberg Variations* involving mathematical structures, which can be applied to the structure of these novels. In literature's constant quest to find new ways to tell stories, music provides one possible model of how information can be organized and presented. These unexpected forms often disrupt the reader's expectations of a narrative text, thus requiring a more active involvement in the interpretation of the text. Music for the reader thus poses an unfamiliar challenge, drawing on associations with music that cannot be contained within the novel itself, just as any reading experience requires the reader's input in order to create a collaborative meaning. For some readers, the use of music might include them as part of an in-group familiar with the forms, techniques, and jargon of that idiom. For others, it might have an excluding effect, as the text becomes incomprehensible because the patterns cannot easily be explained without recourse to musical background knowledge. This particular experiment with the form of the novel—like many other postmodern experiments—thus restricts the potential audience of the musical novel, though providing a challenging and rewarding experience for those readers who do "crack the code" and revel in the recognition of musical parallels.

I now wish to return to the question of why novelists engage in such intermedial experimentation and what the identification of musical patterns can offer the reader. The reader who recognizes an intermedial parallel between the text and a musical model can better understand, first of all, how the novel works, one of the primary goals in reading a text, particularly a difficult one. Unexpected and complicated forms make more sense and yield a kind of epiphanic satisfaction when the pattern is discovered. Of course, the search for pattern and the decoding of textual puzzles is but one approach to reading. The perhaps more significant question is—what does the addition of music to a novel in this manner add to the novel's meanings or message?

One way of approaching this question is to return to the themes that recur in both groups of texts. Of these, most prominent is the idea of music as a means of giving order to chaos and the musician's struggle to find a balance between freedom and constraint. Too little structure results in chaos, whereas too much inhibits the musician's freedom, as seen vividly in the fictional portraits of jazz musicians such as Buddy Bolden in *Coming Through Slaughter* and Jackson Payne in *The Best of Jackson Payne*. This same theme, however, permeates the Goldberg novels as well, as in the theme of order and chaos that structures *The Bradshaw Variations* or the way simple mathematical or genetic rules breed creative complexity, giving creative order to chaos in *The Gold Bug Variations*. This last example, like the many instances of metareferential writing within these musical novels, points to one of the uses music has for these texts. Music becomes a writer's tool for structuring chaotic material; it is a form that helps to make sense of disparate content.

The main answer to the question of why these novels draw on music as a model thus has to do with metareferentiality: by drawing on the model of another medium, the text calls attention to its own mediality and its own processes of artistic creation. Very often in a musical novel, the production of a piece of music is cast as a parallel to the writing process and the figure of the musician as an alter ego of the author figure in the text.

This is very apparent in novels with an overt focus on writing within the text. For example, Jack Fuller's *The Best of Jackson Payne* revolves around the process of writing a biography of a jazz musician, a biography that is stylistically inspired by Payne's music and that takes on the form of a greatest-hits album. Michael Ondaatje's *Coming Through Slaughter* similarly dramatizes the search for a historical musician and the writer's tendency to see himself in that musician figure.

Another novel in which the characters struggle with their own writing is Thomas Bernhard's *Der Untergeher*, in which the narrator's book on Glenn Gould can be read as a parallel to Gould's musical accomplishments, specifically his recordings of the *Goldberg Variations*. Gabriel

Josipovici's *Goldberg: Variations*, too, draws the two arts together in that the musician of the Goldberg legend who performs in order to soothe his patron through sleepless nights is recast as a writer, who must compose original texts for a similar purpose. In fact, the majority of the musical novels analyzed in this book contain not only characters who are musicians, performers, or composers, but very often also those who literally are writers. There are Jan's and Frank's books on Ressler (who becomes a composer) in Powers's *The Gold Bug Variations*, Scooter's progression from musician to author by the end of Murray's *The Magic Keys*, the musicologist Quinlan tracking down the musician Payne in Fuller's *The Best of Jackson Payne*, the author figure tracking down the musician Bolden in Ondaatje's *Coming Through Slaughter*, and several others.

In other novels, the parallel to writing becomes clear only at the climactic conclusion, as when the narrator of Toni Morrison's *Jazz* seems to become the book itself: "*I like your fingers on and on, lifting, turning. . . . Look where your hands are. Now*" (**229**; italics original). Another such revelation occurs at the end of Nancy Huston's *The Goldberg Variations* when the harpsichordist Liliane reveals that she has written or "composed" the thoughts of the thirty audience members at her concert, such that the performer is not only composing music but composing text as well. In examples such as these, the play with forms borrowed from another medium is a means of metamedially reflecting on the text's own structure. The text uses music to explore new modes of writerly expression, as in the Fuller, Josipovici, Ondaatje, and Bernhard examples, or looks for new ways to reach out to readers, as in the Morrison and Huston examples.

In its attempt to delimit and define the genre of the musical novel, this study has examined the two groups of jazz novels and novels based on the *Goldberg Variations* not as an exhaustive treatment of the genre, but as case studies that reflect some of the many ways prose texts may employ musical structures, techniques, and effects. Of course, many other types of text could be added to further complete the picture. Though the findings of this study suggest that similar textual means are used to imitate music of different genres, further analyses are needed to confirm this for other types of music such as pop, rap, rock, or music of other traditions from around the world. Some work is beginning to be done in this area (see e.g., Viol, Smyth, Tillmann, Hoene), but a wide field remains.

Another productive comparison would involve the expansion of work on the musical novel to that of poetry that imitates music. There is a large body of blues and jazz poetry, though relatively little criticism has focused on the specific musical forms and techniques imitated in those poems. Certainly the elements of rhythm and timbre could be expected to play a more significant role in poetry based on music than in musical prose, but more work would need to be done to analyze the process in detail. In the jazz novels examined here, poetic meter, for example, serves as a bridge between prose and musical rhythms, in a way that would necessarily differ in a poetic context.

Adaptation of musical forms is not restricted to the written text. Plays such as Gert Jonke's *Chorphantasie* and Moisés Kaufman's *33 Variations* demonstrate that musical forms may also be systematically and productively applied to dramatic work as well. Analyses of such imitations would need to deal with the accompanying multimediality that is lacking in musical novels, but the interaction between inter- and multimediality in stage productions and films is a fruitful field for further research.

In considering how to conclude a study of the musical novel, it seems appropriate to examine the endings employed by the musical novels themselves more closely. Depending on its musical model, such a novel might choose to recapitulate its beginnings, like the *aria da capo* of Bach's *Goldberg Variations*, which Huston employs as a return of Liliane's narrative voice in the final chapter of *The Goldberg Variations*: "I don't know if I *will* stop . . . Perhaps I'll start over again immediately, with the Variatio I. . . . But no . . . yes it's the end now" (172; italics original). Similarly, Powers very briefly states this return to the beginning as "Da Capo e Fine / What could be simpler? In rough translation: Once more with feeling" (639). Morrison's *Jazz* ends by transferring the task of meaning production from the narrator to the reader: "Say make me, remake me. You are free to do it and I am free to let you because look, look. Look where your hands are. Now" (229). Fuller's *The Best of Jackson Payne*, with its emphasis on a multiplicity of voices and opinions, ends on a quote that picks up the theme of never actually knowing the truth about Payne, whether from his life or his music: "But you never knew Jackson and never could. 'Cause he's the only one who could have told you. And that sweet never blew the truth once in his whole damn life" (321).

A further model of a conclusion is that of the skyscraper-like chorus structure that can go on and on as long as the band has something to say: "And as if to guard against any Aristotelian misconceptions about an end, it is likely to stop on an unresolved chord, so that harmonically, as well as rhythmically, everything is left up in the air" (Kouwenhoven, 129). Like Murray's series of Scooter novels that each pick up where the hero's adventures left off in the previous volume, the examination of musical fiction will continue with each new group of texts to analyze and new genre to include and compare. I hope to have shown, however, that with these analyses of the various forms that the musical novel may take, everything is not "up in the air" but has gained a systematic classification of types of intermedial imitation, along with new insight into the productive influence musical models have had on contemporary fiction.

Appendix: Diagrams of Intermediality in Selected Novels

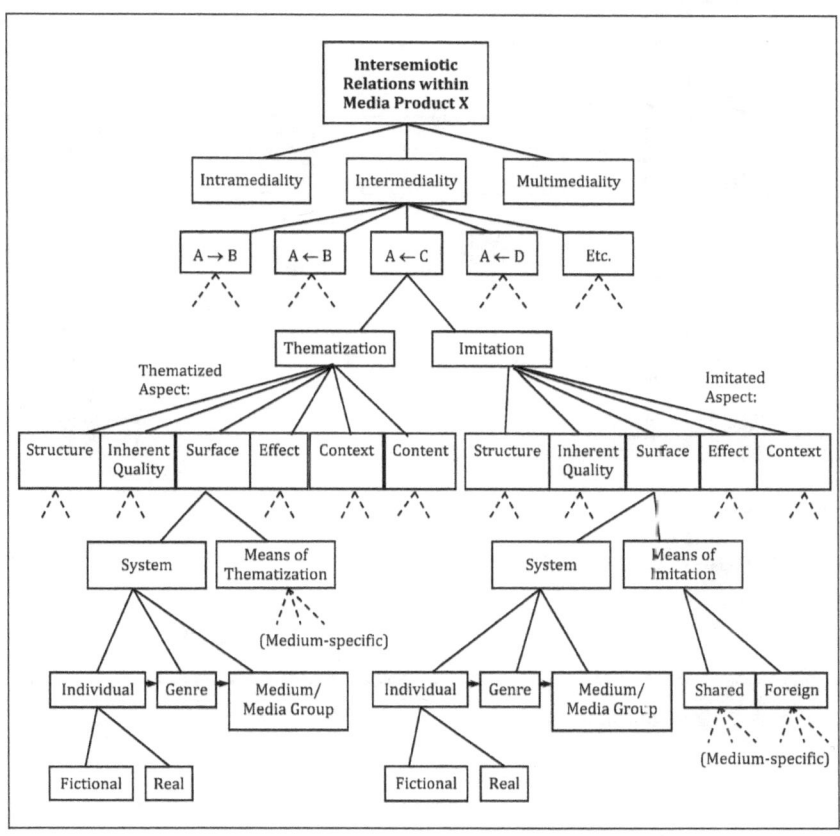

Fig. A.1. A new model of intermediality.

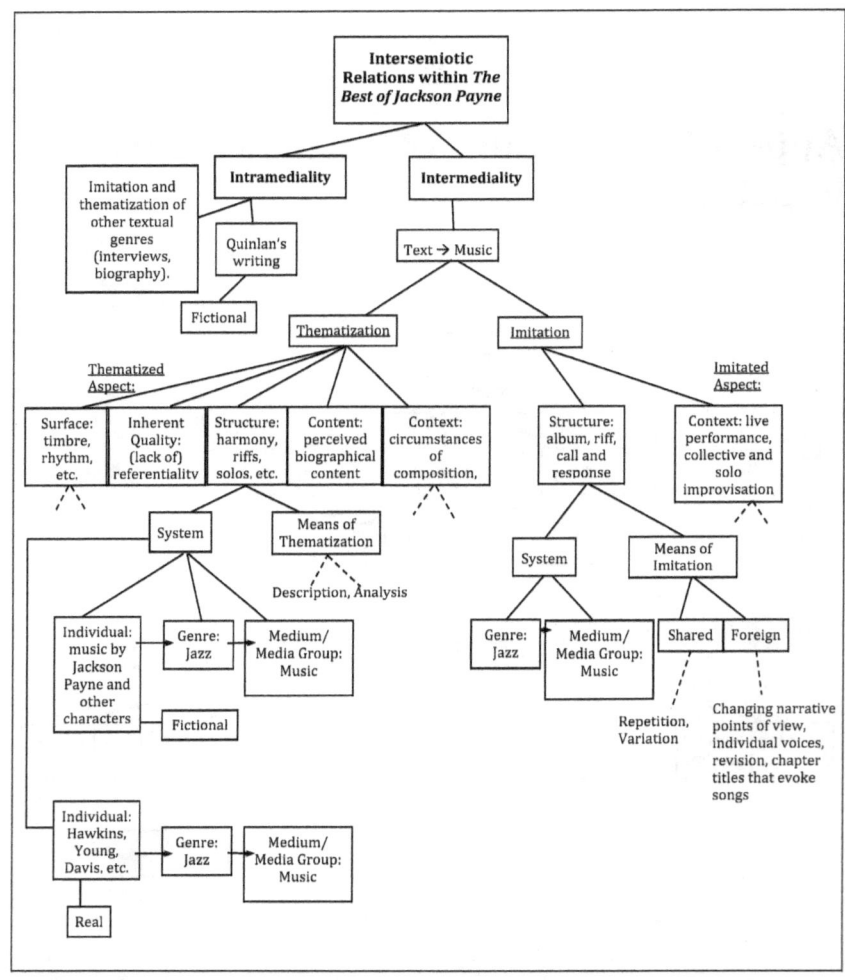

Fig. A.2. Intermediality in Jack Fuller's *The Best of Jackson Payne* (2000).

APPENDIX ♦ 221

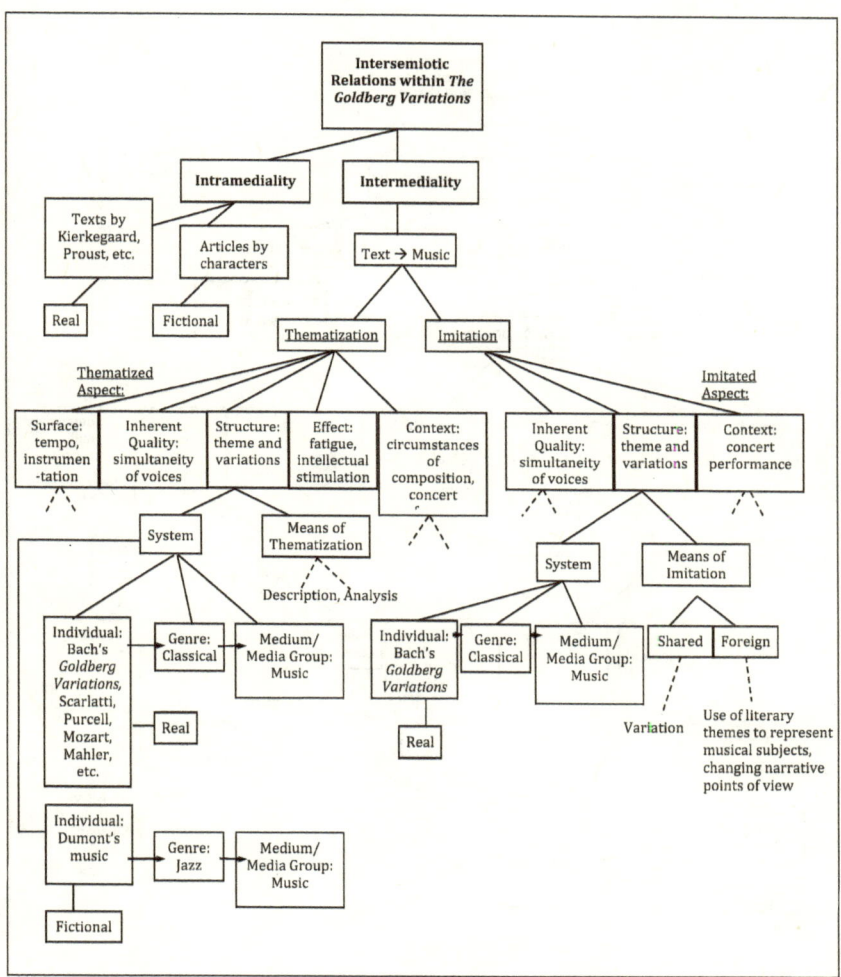

Fig. A.3. Intermediality in Nancy Huston's
The Goldberg Variations (1981/1996).

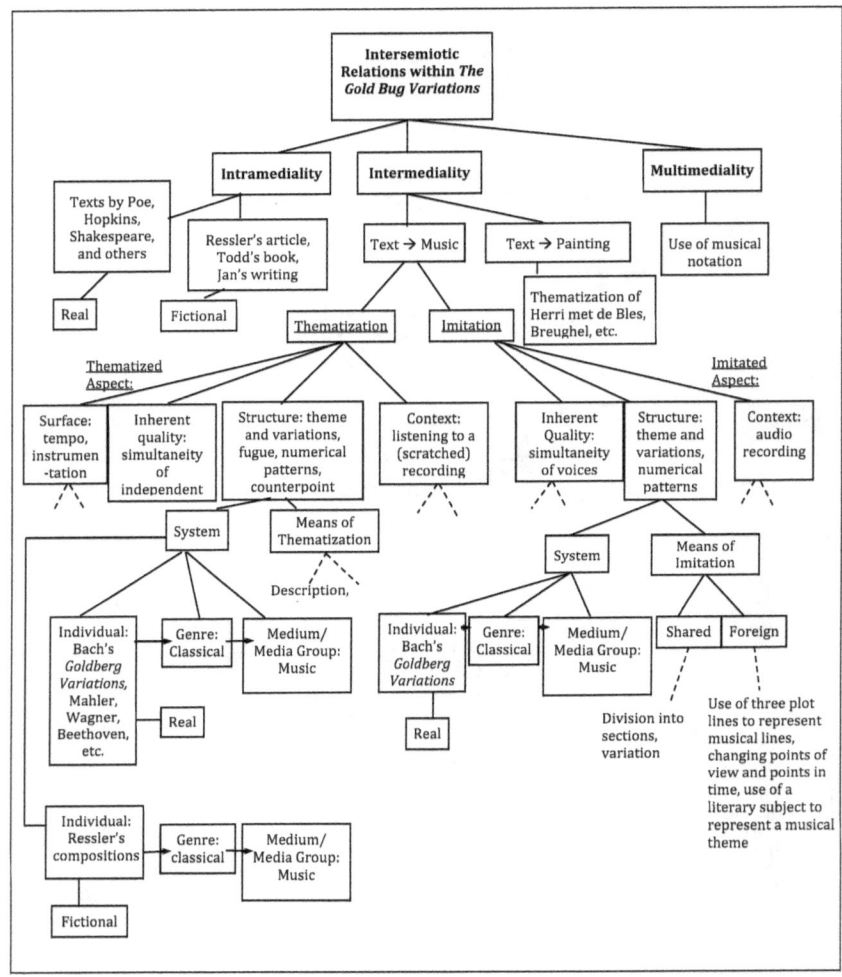

Fig. A.4. Intermediality in Richard Powers's *The Gold Bug Variations* (1991).

Works Cited

Adorno, Theodor W. "Music, Language, and Composition." In *Essays on Music*, edited by Richard Leppert, translated by Susan H. Gillespie, 113–26. Berkeley: University of California Press, 2002.
Albright, Daniel. *Untwisting the Serpent: Modernism in Music, Literature, and Other Arts*. Chicago: University of Chicago Press, 2000.
Alder, Erik, and Dietmar Hauck. *Music and Literature: Music in the Works of Anthony Burgess and E. M. Forster*. Tübingen: Francke, 2005.
Aronson, Alex. *Music and the Novel: A Study in Twentieth-Century Fiction*. Totowa, NJ: Rowman and Littlefield, 1980.
Arroyas, Frédérique. "Literary Mediations of Baroque Music: Biber, Bach, and Nancy Huston." In *Essays on Word/Music Adaptation and on Surveying the Field*, edited by David Francis Urrows, 93–114. Word and Music Studies 9. Amsterdam: Rodopi, 2008.
Auden, Wystan Hugh. "Anthem for St. Cecilia's Day." In *Collected Shorter Poems: 1927–1957*, 173–75. New York: Random House, 1966.
Bach, Johann Sebastian. *Goldberg-Variationen BWV 988*. 1741. Edited by Rudolf Steglich. Munich: G. Henle, 1978.
———. *Ich will den Kreuzstab gerne tragen BWV 56*. 1726.
Bach, Peter. "Bach.de." 2004–2013. http://www.bach.de/werk/cembalowerke.html.
Das Bach-Lexikon. Edited by Michael Heinemann. Laaber: Laaber, 2000.
Baker, Houston A. *Blues, Ideology, and Afro-American Literature: A Vernacular Theory*. Chicago: University of Chicago Press, 1984.
Bakhtin, Mikhail. "Discourse in the Novel." Translated by Caryl Emerson and Michael Holquist. In *The Dialogic Imagination: Four Essays by Mikhail Bakhtin*, edited by Michael Holquist, 259–422. Austin, TX/London: University of Texas Press, 1981.
Barry, Sister M. Martin, O. P. *An Analysis of the Prosodic Structure of Selected Poems of T. S. Eliot*. Washington: Catholic University Press, 1969.
Barthes, Roland. "The Death of the Author." 1967. In *Image-Music-Text*, 142–48. New York: Hill and Wang, 1977.
Benjamin, Walter. "The Work of Art in the Age of Its Technological Reproducibility (Second Version)." Translated by Edmund Jephcott and Harry Zohn. In *Selected Writings, Volume 3 1935–1938*, edited by Howard Eiland and Michael W. Jennings, 101–23. Cambridge, MA: Belknap Press of Harvard University Press, 2002.

Berendt, Joachim-Ernst, and Günther Huesmann. *Das Jazzbuch: Von New Orleans bis ins 21. Jahrhundert*. Frankfurt: Fischer, 2007.
Bernhard, Thomas. *The Loser*. Translated by Jack Dawson. New York: Knopf, 1991.
———. *Der Untergeher*. 1983. Frankfurt: Suhrkamp, 1988.
Blacking, John. "The Problem of 'Ethnic' Perceptions in the Semiotics of Music." In *The Sign in Music and Literature*, edited by Wendy Steiner, 184–94. Austin: University of Texas Press, 1981.
Böhn, Andreas. "Intra- und intermediale Formzitate im Film als Medienreflexion." In *Formzitat und Intermedialität*, edited by Andreas Böhn, 13–44. St. Ingbert: Röhrig, 2003.
Borshuk, Michael. *Swinging the Vernacular: Jazz and African American Modernist Literature*. New York: Routledge, 2006.
Brown, Calvin S. "Josef Weinheber's Hölderlin Variations: A Comment and Translation." 1968. In *Musico-Poetics in Perspective: Calvin S. Brown in Memoriam*, edited by Jean-Louis Cupers and Ulrich Weisstein, 191–200. Word and Music Studies 2. Amsterdam: Rodopi, 2000.
———. *Music and Literature: A Comparison of the Arts*. 1948. Hanover: University Press of New England, 1987.
———. "The Relationships between Music and Literature as a Field of Study." *Comparative Literature* 22 (1970): 97–107.
———. "Theme and Variations as a Literary Form." *Yearbook of Comparative and General Literature* 27, no. 2 (1978): 35–43.
Bucknell, Brad. *Literary Modernism and Musical Aesthetics: Pater, Pound, Joyce, and Stein*. Cambridge: Cambridge University Press, 2001.
Burgess, Anthony. *Napoleon Symphony*. 1974. London: Serpent's Tail, 2012.
———. "K. 550 (1788)." *On Mozart: A Paean for Wolfgang*. New York: Ticknor & Fields, 1991.
Cartiér, Xam Wilson. *Be-Bop, Re-Bop*. New York: Ballantine, 1987.
———. *Muse-Echo Blues*. New York: Harmony, 1991.
Cataliotti, Robert. *The Songs Became the Stories: The Music in African-American Fiction, 1970–2005*. New York: Peter Lang, 2007.
"Charlie Parker Discography." *Jazz Discography Project*. http://www.jazzdisco.org/charlie-parker/discography.
Clüver, Claus. "Inter Textus / Inter Artes / Inter Media." *Komparatistik: Jahrbuch der DGAVL* (2000/2001): 14–50.
———. "Quotation, Enargeia, and the Functions of Ekphrasis." In *Pictures into Words: Theoretical and Descriptive Approaches to Ekphrasis*, edited by Valerie Robillard and Els Jongeneel, 35–52. Amsterdam: VU University Press, 1998.
The Concise Oxford Dictionary of Literary Terms. Edited by Chris Baldick. Oxford: Oxford University Press, 1990.
Cooper, G. Burns. *Mysterious Music: Rhythm and Free Verse*. Stanford: Stanford University Press, 1998.
Cortez, Jayne. "You Know." In *Blues Poems*, edited by Kevin Young, 101–3. New York: Knopf, 2003.

Crouch, Stanley. *Don't the Moon Look Lonesome*. New York: Pantheon, 2000.
Culler, Jonathan. *The Pursuit of Signs: Semiotics, Literature, Deconstruction*. London: Routledge & Kegan Paul, 1981.
Cupers, Jean-Louis, and Ulrich Weisstein, eds. *Musico-Poetics in Perspective: Calvin S. Brown in Memoriam*. Word and Music Studies 2. Amsterdam: Rodopi, 2000.
Cusk, Rachel. *The Bradshaw Variations*. London: Faber and Faber, 2009.
Daly, P. M. "Intertextuality of Word and Image." In Hoesterey and Weisstein, *Intertextuality*, 30–46.
Dillon, Sarah. *The Palimpsest: Literature, Criticism, Theory*. London: Continuum, 2007.
Dunkel, Mario, Emily Petermann, and Burkhard Sauerwald, eds. *Time and Space in Words and Music: Proceedings of the 1st Conference of the Word and Music Association Forum, Dortmund, November 4–6, 2010*. Frankfurt: Peter Lang, 2012.
Dunn, Peter N. *Spanish Picaresque Fiction: A New Literary History*. Ithaca: Cornell University Press, 1993.
Eckstein, Lars. "A Love Supreme: Jazzthetic Strategies in Toni Morrison's *Beloved*." *African American Review* 40, no. 2 (2006): 271–83.
Eco, Umberto. *A Theory of Semiotics*. Bloomington: Indiana University Press, 1976.
Ehland, Christoph. *Picaresque Perspectives—Exiled Identities: A Structural and Methodological Analysis of the Picaresque as a Literary Archetype in the Works of James Leslie Mitchell*. Heidelberg: Winter, 2003.
Eicher, Thomas. "Was heißt (hier) Intermedialität?" In *Intermedialität: Vom Bild zum Text*, edited by Thomas Eicher and Ulf Bleckmann, 11–28. Bielefeld: Aisthesis, 1994.
Ellison, Mary. *Extensions of the Blues*. London: Calder; New York: Riverrun, 1989.
Ellison, Ralph. "Blues People." In *Shadow and Act*, 247–58. New York: Random House, 1964.
———. *Invisible Man*. 1952. New York: Modern Library, 1994.
Encyclopedia of Poetry and Poetics. Edited by Alex Preminger. Princeton: Princeton University Press, 1965.
Enquist, Anna. *Contrapunt*. Utrecht: De Arbeiderspers, 2008.
Fahy, Thomas. *Night Visions*. New York: Harper, 2004.
Finnegan, Ruth. *Literacy and Orality: Studies in the Technology of Communication*. Oxford: Blackwell, 1988.
Fischer-Lichte, Erika. *The Transformative Power of Performance: A New Aesthetics*. Translated by Saskya Iris Jain. London: Routledge, 2008.
Fleischman, Suzanne. *Tense and Narrativity: From Medieval Performance to Modern Fiction*. Austin: University of Texas Press, 1990.
Fowler, Roger, ed. *A Dictionary of Modern Critical Terms*. London: Routledge & Kegan Paul, 1987.
Franklin, Don O. "Viewing the *Goldberg Variations* as a Musico-Mathematical Matrix." In *Bachs Musik für Tasteninstrumente: Bericht über das 4.*

Dortmunder Bach-Symposion 2002, edited by Martin Geck, 231–50. Dortmund: Klangfarben, 2003.

Freedman, William. *Laurence Sterne and the Origins of the Musical Novel*. Athens: U of Georgia P, 1978.

Fritsch, Esther. *Reading Gossip: Funktionen von Klatsch in Romanen ethnischer amerikanischer Autorinnen*. Trier: Wissenschaftlicher Verlag Trier, 2004.

Fubini, Enrico. *The History of Music Aesthetics*. Translated by Michael Hatwell. London: Macmillan, 1991.

Fuller, Jack. *The Best of Jackson Payne*. New York: Knopf, 2000.

Gailly, Christian. *Be-bop*. Paris: Les Éditions de Minuit, 1995.

———. *Bebop* [German translation]. Translated by Astrid Wintersberger. Munich: Luchterhand, 1995.

———. *Un soir au club*. Paris: Les Éditions de Minuit, 2001.

Gates, Henry Louis, Jr. *The Signifying Monkey: A Theory of Afro-American Literary Criticism*. New York: Oxford University Press, 1988.

Genette, Gérard. *Narrative Discourse: An Essay in Method*. Translated by Jane E. Lewin. Ithaca: Cornell University Press, 1983.

———. *Palimpsests: Literature in the Second Degree*. Translated by Channa Newman. Lincoln: University of Nebraska Press, 1997.

Gier, Albert. "Musik in der Literatur: Einflüsse und Analogien." In *Literatur intermedial: Musik—Malerei—Photographie—Film*, edited by Peter Zima, 61–92. Darmstadt: Wissenschaftliche Buchgesellschaft, 1995.

Göbel, Walter. "African American Picaresque: Some Examples." In *Das Paradigma des Pikaresken—The Paradigm of the Picaresque*, edited by Christoph Ehland and Robert Fajen, 273–87. Heidelberg: Winter, 2007.

Goetsch, Paul. "Fingierte Mündlichkeit in der Erzählkunst entwickelter Schriftkulturen." *Poetica* 17 (1985): 202–18.

———. "Der Übergang von Mündlichkeit zu Schriftlichkeit: Die kulturkritischen und ideologischen Implikationen der Theorien von McLuhan, Goody und Ong." In *Symbolische Formen, Medien, Identität*, edited by Wolfgang Raible, 113–29. Tübingen: Narr, 1991.

Gould, Glenn. *Goldberg Variations*, BWV 988, *Partita No. 5*, BWV 829. By Johann Sebastian Bach. Rec. October 1954 and June 1955. Naxos, 2007.

———. "The 'Goldberg' Variations." In *The Glenn Gould Reader*, edited by Tim Page, 22–28. New York: Knopf, 1984.

———. *A State of Wonder: The Complete "Goldberg Variations" 1955 and 1981*. 3 discs. Rec. 1955, 1981, 1982. Sony, 2002.

Grove's Dictionary of Music and Musicians. Edited by Eric Blom. 5th ed. London: Macmillan, 1954.

Gudas, Fabian. "Theme." In Brogan, *New Princeton Handbook of Poetic Terms*, 311–12.

Gutmann, Katharina. *Celebrating the Senses: An Analysis of the Sensual in Toni Morrison's Fiction*. Tübingen: Francke, 2000.

Haimberger, Nora. *Vom Musiker zum Dichter: E. T. A. Hoffmanns Akkordvorstellung.* Bonn: Bouvier, 1976.
Hansen-Löve, Aage A. "Intermedialität und Intertextualität: Probleme der Korrelation von Wort- und Bildkunst—am Beispiel der russischen Moderne." In *Dialog der Texte: Hamburger Kolloquium zur Intertextualität,* edited by Wolf Schmid and Wolf-Dieter Stempel, 291–360. Vienna: Gesellschaft zur Förderung Slawistischer Studien, 1983.
Harding, D. W. *Words into Rhythm: English Speech Rhythm in Verse and Prose.* Cambridge: Cambridge University Press, 1976.
Hartman, Charles O. *Free Verse: An Essay on Prosody.* Princeton: Princeton University Press, 1980.
Hawkins, Alfonso W., Jr. *The Jazz Trope: A Theory of African American Literary and Vernacular Culture.* Lanham, MD: Scarecrow, 2008.
Hawthorn, Jeremy. *A Glossary of Contemporary Literary Theory.* London: Edward Arnold, 1992.
Heffernan, James A. *Museum of Words: The Poetics of Ekphrasis from Homer to Ashbery.* Chicago: University of Chicago Press, 1993.
Hens, Gregor. *Thomas Bernhards Triologie der Künste: Der Untergeher, Holzfällen, Alte Meister.* Rochester, NY: Camden House, 1999.
Higgins, Dick. *Horizons: The Poetics and Theory of the Intermedia.* Carbondale: Southern Illinois University Press, 1984.
Hoene, Christin. "Sounding through Time and Space: Music in Postcolonial South-Asian Literature." In Dunkel, Petermann, and Sauerwald, *Time and Space in Words and Music,* 87–98.
Hoesterey, Ingeborg, and Ulrich Weisstein, eds. *Intertextuality: German Literature and Visual Art from the Renaissance to the Twentieth Century.* Columbia, SC: Camden House, 1993.
Hoffmann, Ernst Theodor Amadeus. *Kreisleriana.* 1814/1815. Ditzingen: Reclam, 1983.
Holmes, Lauren, Emily Petermann, and Carolyn Sinsky. "Towards a New Typology of Intermediality." Unpublished paper presented at the Graduate Student Conference of the Twentieth-Century Colloquium, Yale University, May 1, 2008.
Horace. "Ars Poetica." In *Horace for Students of Literature: The "Ars Poetica" and Its Tradition,* translated by Leon Golden. Emory University Department of English, 1995. http://www.english.emory.edu/DRAMA/ArsPoetica.html.
Huke, Thomas. *Jazz und Blues im afro-amerikanischen Roman von der Jahrhundertwende bis zur Gegenwart.* Würzburg: Königshausen & Neumann, 1990.
Huston, Nancy. *The Goldberg Variations.* [*Les Variations Goldberg,* 1981]. Montréal: Nuage, 1996.
Hutcheon, Linda. "Historiographic Metafiction." In *Theory of the Novel: A Historical Approach,* edited by Michael McKeon, 830–50. Baltimore: Johns Hopkins University Press, 2000.
———. *A Theory of Adaptation.* London: Routledge, 2006.

Huxley, Aldous. *Point Counter Point*. 1928. Normal, IL: Dalkey Archive, 2001.

Iser, Wolfgang. *The Act of Reading: A Theory of Aesthetic Response*. London: Routledge & Kegan Paul, 1976.

———. "The Reading Process: A Phenomenological Approach." In *The Implied Reader: Patterns of Communication in Prose Fiction from Bunyan to Beckett*, 274–94. Baltimore: Johns Hopkins University Press, 1974.

Jakobson, Roman. "A Few Remarks on Peirce, Pathfinder in the Science of Language." In *Selected Writings*, vol. 7, 248–53.

———. "A Glance at the Development of Semiotics." In *Selected Writings*, vol. 7, 199–218.

———. "Linguistics and Poetics." In *Selected Writings*, vol. 3, 18–51.

———. "Musicology and Linguistics." 1932. In *Language in Literature*, edited by K. Pomorska and S. Rudy, 455–57. Cambridge: Harvard University Press, 1987.

———. "Quest for the Essence of Language." In *Selected Writings*, vol. 2, 345–59.

———. *Selected Writings*. 8 vols. Berlin: Mouton de Gruyter, 1966–88.

———. *Semiotik: Ausgewählte Texte 1919–1982*. Edited by Elmar Holenstein. Frankfurt: Suhrkamp, 1992.

———. "Visual and Auditory Signs." 1964. In *Selected Writings*, vol. 2, 334–37.

Jarrett, Michael. *Drifting on a Read: Jazz as a Model for Writing*. Albany: State University of New York Press, 1999.

Jazz-Lexikon. Edited by Martin Kunzler. Reinbek bei Hamburg: Rowohlt, 1988.

Jenkins, Henry. *Convergence Culture: When Old and New Media Collide*. New York: New York University Press, 2006.

———. "Transmedia Storytelling 101." In *Confessions of an Aca-Fan: The Official Blog of Henry Jenkins*, March 22, 2007. http://henryjenkins.org/2007/03/transmedia_storytelling_101.html.

Jones, Gayl. *Liberating Voices: Oral Tradition in African American Literature*. Cambridge: Harvard University Press, 1991.

Jones, LeRoi (Amiri Baraka). *Blues People: The Negro Experience in White America and the Music That Developed from It*. New York: Morrow Quill, 1963.

Jonke, Gert. *Chorphantasie*. Vienna: Droschl, 2003.

———. *Schule der Geläufigkeit*. 1977. Frankfurt: Suhrkamp, 2006. Translated by Jean M. Snook as *Homage to Czerny: Studies in Virtuoso Technique*. Champaign, IL: Dalkey Archive, 2008.

Josipovici, Gabriel. *Goldberg: Variations*. 2002. New York: Harper Perennial, 2007.

Joyce, James. *Ulysses*. 1922. New York: Vintage, 1986.

Kacandes, Irene. *Talk Fiction: Literature and the Talk Explosion*. Lincoln: University of Nebraska Press, 2001.

Kaufman, Moisés. *33 Variations*. 2007. Directed by Moisés Kaufman, Eugene O'Neill Theater, New York, March 25, 2009.
Keiler, Allan R. "Two Views of Musical Semiotics." In *The Sign in Music and Literature*, edited by Wendy Steiner, 138–68. Austin: University of Texas Press, 1981.
Kernfeld, Barry. *What to Listen for in Jazz*. New Haven, CT: Yale University Press, 1995.
Kouwenhoven, John A. "What's 'American' about America." In O'Meally, *Jazz Cadence of American Culture*, 123–36.
Kristeva, Julia. *La revolution du langage poétique: L'avant-garde à la fin du XIXe siècle, Lautréamont et Mallarmé*. Paris: Seuil, 1974.
———. "Le Texte clos." *Langages* 12 (1968): 103–25.
Krüger, Anja. "Literary Photo-Fictions." PhD diss., University of Konstanz. In progress.
Kruse, Bernhard Arnold. "Interview mit Robert Schneider." *Der Deutschunterricht* 2 (1996): 93–101.
Kühn, Dieter. *Goldberg-Variationen: Hörspieltexte mit Materialien*. Frankfurt: Suhrkamp, 1976.
———. "Nachwort." In *Goldberg-Variationen: Hörspieltexte mit Materialien*, 111–58. Frankfurt am Main: Suhrkamp, 1976.
Labinger, Jay A. "Encoding an Infinite Message: Richard Powers's *Gold Bug Variations*." *Configurations* 3, no. 1 (1995): 79–93.
Leech, Geoffrey N. "Variation." In Fowler, *A Dictionary of Modern Critical Terms*, 256–57.
Lessing, Gotthold Ephraim. *Laokoon, oder Über die Grenzen der Malerei und Poesie*. 1766. Ditzingen: Reclam, 1986.
Leubner, Martin. "Adaption." In *Metzler Lexikon Literatur*, 3rd ed., edited by Dieter Burdorf, Christoph Fasbender, and Burkhard Moennighoff, 5. Stuttgart: Metzler, 2007.
Levine, Lawrence W. "Jazz and American Culture." In O'Meally, *Jazz Cadence of American Culture*, 431–47.
Link, Jürgen. *Literaturwissenschaftliche Grundbegriffe*. Munich: Fink, 1974.
Lock, Graham, and David Murray, eds. *Thriving on a Riff: Jazz and Blues Influences in African American Literature and Film*. Oxford: Oxford University Press, 2009.
Lotspeich, C. M. "Poetry, Prose, and Rhythm." *Publications of the Modern Language Association (PMLA)* 37, no. 2 (1922): 293–310.
Ludigkeit, Dirk. "Collective Improvisation and Narrative Structure in Toni Morrison's *Jazz*." *LIT* 12 (2001): 165–87.
Malone, Jacqui. "Jazz Music in Motion: Dancers and Big Bands." In O'Meally, *Jazz Cadence of American Culture*, 278–97.
Marquis, Donald M. *In Search of Buddy Bolden: First Man of Jazz*. 1978. Rev. ed. Baton Rouge: Louisiana State University Press, 2007.
Marsalis, Wynton, and Robert G. O'Meally. "Duke Ellington: 'Music Like a Big Hot Pot of Good Gumbo.'" In O'Meally, *Jazz Cadence of American Culture*, 143–53.

Marshall, Paule. *The Fisher King*. New York: Simon & Schuster, 2000.
Mayer, Sylvia. *"The Name of the Sound": Das Motiv des Klanges in den Romanen Toni Morrisons*. Heidelberg: Mattes, 1996.
McEwan, Ian. *Saturday*. New York: Doubleday, 2005.
McInerney, Jay. *Bright Lights, Big City*. New York: Vintage, 1984.
McLuhan, Marshall. *Understanding Media: The Extensions of Man*. New York: McGraw-Hill, 1964.
McPherson, James A. "Some Observations on the Railroad and American Culture." In *Railroad: Trains and Train People in American Culture*, edited by James A. McPherson and Miller Williams, 3–17. New York: Random House, 1976.
Melnick, Daniel C. *Fullness of Dissonance: Modern Fiction and the Aesthetics of Music*. Rutherford, NJ: Fairleigh Dickinson University Press, 1994.
Meyer, Michael, ed. *Literature and Music*. Amsterdam: Rodopi, 2002.
Michaels, Anne. *Fugitive Pieces*. 1996. New York: Vintage, 1998.
Miller, Stuart. *The Picaresque Novel*. Cleveland: Press of Case Western Reserve University, 1967.
Moeller, Hans-Bernhard. "Review of *Intertextuality: German Literature and Visual Art from the Renaissance to the Twentieth Century*, ed. Ingeborg Hoesterey and Ulrich Weisstein." *South Central Review* 13, no. 4 (1996): 69–71.
Monson, Ingrid. *Saying Something: Jazz Improvisation and Interaction*. Chicago: University of Chicago Press, 1996.
Morrison, Toni. "Foreword." In *Jazz*, xv–xix. New York: Vintage Press, 2004.
———. *Jazz*. 1992. New York: Penguin, 1993.
———. "Unspeakable Things Unspoken: The Afro-American Presence in American Literature." 1989. In *Within the Circle: An Anthology of African American Literary Criticism from the Harlem Renaissance to the Present*, edited by Angelyn Mitchell, 368–98. Durham: Duke University Press, 1994.
Müller, Jürgen E. "Intermedialität und Medienwissenschaft: Thesen zum State of the Art." *montage a/v*. 3, no. 2 (1994): 119–38.
Munton, Alan. "Misreading Morrison, Mishearing Jazz: A Response to Toni Morrison's Jazz Critics." *Journal of American Studies* 31, no. 2 (1997): 235–51.
Murray, Albert. *The Blue Devils of Nada*. New York: Pantheon, 1996.
———. "The Function of the Heroic Image." In O'Meally, *Jazz Cadence of American Culture*, 569–79.
———. *The Hero and the Blues*. Columbia: University of Missouri Press, 1973.
———. "Improvisation and the Creative Process." In O'Meally, *Jazz Cadence of American Culture*, 111–13.
———. *The Magic Keys*. New York: Pantheon, 2005.
———. *The Seven League Boots*. New York: Pantheon, 1995.
———. *The Spyglass Tree*. New York: Pantheon, 1991.

———. *Stomping the Blues*. New York: Da Capo, 1976.
———. *Train Whistle Guitar*. 1975. New York: Vintage, 1999.
Nattiez, Jean-Jacques. *Music and Discourse: Toward a Semiology of Music*. [*Musicologie générale et sémiologie*, 1987] Translated by Carolyn Abbate. Princeton: Princeton University Press, 1990.
The New Grove Dictionary of Jazz. 2nd ed. Edited by Barry Kernfeld. 3 vols. London: Macmillan, 2002.
The New Princeton Handbook of Poetic Terms. Edited by T. V. F. Brogan. Princeton: Princeton University Press, 1994.
Niemöller, Heinz Hermann. "Polonaise und Quodlibet: Der innere Kosmos der *Goldberg-Variationen*." In *Johann Sebastian Bach Goldberg-Variationen*, special issue of *Musik-Konzepte* 42 (1985): 3–28.
Nischik, Reingard M. "Literaturadaption." In *Metzler Lexikon Literatur- und Kulturtheorie*, 2nd ed., edited by Ansgar Nünning, 377–78. Stuttgart: Metzler, 2001.
O'Meally, Robert G., ed. *The Jazz Cadence of American Culture*. New York: Columbia University Press, 1998.
Ondaatje, Michael. *Coming Through Slaughter*. 1976. New York: Vintage, 1996.
Ong, Walter. *Orality and Literacy: The Technologizing of the Word*. London: Routledge, 1982.
Osteen, Mark, ed. *Blue Notes: Toward a New Jazz Discourse*. Special issue of *Genre* 37, nos. 1–2 (2004).
———. "Blue Notes: Towards a New Jazz Discourse." In *Blue Notes: Toward a New Jazz Discourse*, special issue of *Genre* 37, nos. 1–2 (2004): 1–46.
The Oxford Concise Companion to English Literature. Edited by Margaret Drabble and Jenny Stringer. Oxford: Oxford University Press, 1996.
Paech, Joachim. "Intermedialität: Mediales Differnzial und transformative Figurationen." In *Intermedialität: Theorie und Praxis eines interdisziplinären Forschungsgebiets*, edited by Jörg Helbig, 14–30. Berlin: Schmidt, 1998.
Pater, Walter. "The School of Giorgione." 1877. In *Three Major Texts: (The Renaissance, Appreciations, and Imaginary Portraits)*, edited by William E. Buckler, 153–68. New York: New York University Press, 1986.
Pautrot, Jean-Louis. *The André Hodeir Jazz Reader*. Ann Arbor: University of Michigan Press, 2006.
Perahia, Murray. *Bach: Goldberg Variationen*. Sony, 2000.
Petermann, Emily. "The Concept of Time Implied by the Theme-and-Variations Form: Novels Based on Bach's *Goldberg Variations*." In Dunkel, Petermann, and Sauerwald, *Time and Space in Words and Music*, 61–71.
———. "Jazz Novels and the Textualization of Musical Performance." In *Word and Music Studies: Essays on Performativity and on Surveying the Field*, edited by Walter Bernhart and Michael Halliwell, 211–27. Word and Music Studies 9. Amsterdam: Rodopi, 2011.
———. "Unheard Jazz: Music and History in Michael Ondaatje's *Coming Through Slaughter*." In *Apropos Canada / À propos du Canada: Fünf*

Jahre Graduiertentagungen der Kanada-Studien, edited by Eugen Banauch, Elisabeth Damböck, Anca-Raluca Radu, Nora Tunkel, and Daniel Winkler, 223–33. Canadiana 8. Vienna: Peter Lang, 2010.

Peters, Erskine A. "Dozens." In Brogan, *New Princeton Handbook of Poetic Terms*, 56–57.

Petri, Horst. *Literatur und Musik: Form- und Strukturparallelen*. Göttingen: Saches & Pohl, 1964.

Pfister, Manfred. "Bezugsfelder der Intertextualität: Zur Systemreferenz." In *Intertextualität: Formen, Funktionen, anglistische Fallstudien*, edited by Ulrich Broich and Manfred Pfister, 52–58. Tübingen: Niemeyer, 1985.

Phillips, Arthur. *The Song Is You*. New York: Random House, 2009.

Powell, David. "Dimensions narratives et temporelles du jeu musical dans trois romans de Nancy Huston." *Francophonies d'Amerique* 11 (2001): 49–64.

Powers, Richard. *The Gold Bug Variations*. 1991. New York: HarperCollins, 1992.

Prieto, Eric. "Ethnography, Improvisation, and the Archimedean Fulcrum: Michel Leiris and Jazz." *International Journal of Francophone Studies* 6, no. 1 (2003): 5–16.

Propp, Vladimir. "The Structural and Historical Study of the Wondertale." In *Theory and History of Folklore*, edited by Anatoly Liberman, 67–81. Manchester: Manchester University Press, 1984.

Proust, Marcel. *Swann's Way*. [*Du côté de chez Swann*, 1913]. Translated by C. K. Scott-Moncrieff and Terence Kilmartin. Revised by D. J. Enright. London: Chatto and Windus; New York: The Modern Library, 1992.

Rae, Ian. *From Cohen to Carson: The Poet's Novel in Canada*. Montreal: McGill-Queen's University Press, 2008.

Rajewsky, Irina O. "Intermedialität 'light'?: Intermediale Bezüge und die 'bloße Thematisierung' des Altermedialen." In *Intermedium Literatur: Beträge zu einer Medientheorie der Literaturwissenschaft*, edited by Roger Lüdeke and Erika Greber, 27–77. Göttingen: Wallstein, 2004.

———. *Intermedialität*. Tübingen: Francke, 2002.

———. "Intermediality, Intertextuality, and Remediation: A Literary Perspective on Intermediality." *Intermedialités* = *Intermedialities* 6 (2005): 43–64.

Rampe, Siegbert, ed. *Bachs Klavier- und Orgelwerke: Das Handbuch*, vol. 2. Laaber: Laaber, 2008.

Raussert, Wilfried. *Negotiating Temporal Differences: Blues, Jazz, and Narrativity in African American Culture*. Heidelberg: Winter, 2000.

Rice, Alan J. "Finger-Snapping to Train-Dancing and Back Again: The Development of a Jazz Style in African-American Prose." *The Yearbook of English Studies* 24 (1994): 105–16.

———. "'It Don't Mean a Thing If It Ain't Got That Swing': Jazz's Many Uses for Toni Morrison." In Simawe, *Black Orpheus*, 153–80.

———. "Jazzing It Up a Storm: The Execution and Meaning of Toni Morrison's Jazzy Prose Style." *Journal of American Studies* 28 (1994): 425–32.

Richardson, Brian. *Unnatural Voices: Extreme Narration in Modern and Contemporary Fiction.* Columbus: Ohio State University Press, 2006.
Rowell, Charles, and Albert Murray. "'An All-Purpose, All-American Literary Intellectual': An Interview with Albert Murray." *Callaloo* 20, no. 2 (1997): 399–414.
Rubenstein, Roberta. "Singing the Blues / Reclaiming Jazz: Toni Morrison and Cultural Mourning." *Mosaic* 31, no. 2 (1998): 147–63.
Sanders, Julie. *Adaptation and Appropriation.* New York: Routledge, 2006.
Saussure, Ferdinand de. *Course in General Linguistics.* [*Cours de linguistique générale*, 1916.] Edited by Charles Bally and Albert Sechehaye. Translated by Roy Harris. Chicago: Open Court, 2005.
Schanze, Helmut. *Medienkunde für Literaturwissenschaftler.* Munich: Fink, 1974.
Scher, Steven P. "Notes Towards a Theory of Verbal Music." *Comparative Literature* 22 (1970): 147–56.
———. *Verbal Music in German Literature.* New Haven: Yale University Press, 1968.
Scherman, Tony. "The Omni-American." *American Heritage* 47, no. 5 (1996): 68–77, http://web.ebscohost.com/ehost/detail?sid=717ed526-1a74-4716-9600770a046a0195%40sessionmgr114&vid=1&hid=122&bdata=JnNpdGU9ZWhvc3QtbGl2ZQ%3d%3d#db=aph&AN=9608133795.
Schneider, Robert. *Schlafes Bruder.* 1992. Munich: DTV, 1999.
Schröter, Jens. "Intermedialität: Facetten und Probleme eines aktuellen medienwissenschaftlichen Begriffs." *montage a/v* 7, no. 2 (1998): 129–54.
Schulenberg, David. *The Keyboard Music of J. S. Bach.* London: Victor Gollancz, 1993.
Schuller, Gunther. *Early Jazz: Its Roots and Musical Development.* 1968. New York: Oxford University Press, 1986.
Shockley, Alan. *Music in the Words: Musical Form and Counterpoint in the Twentieth-Century Novel.* Farnham: Ashgate, 2009.
Simawe, Saadi A., ed. *Black Orpheus: Music in African American Fiction from the Harlem Renaissance to Toni Morrison.* New York: Garland, 2000.
Smyth, Gerry. *Music in Contemporary British Fiction: Listening to the Novel.* Basingstoke: Palgrave Macmillan, 2008.
Snead, James A. "Repetition as a Figure of Black Culture." In O'Meally, *Jazz Cadence of American Culture,* 62–81.
Spielmann, Yvonne. *Intermedialität: Das System Peter Greenaway.* Munich: Fink, 1998.
Tally, Justine. *The Story of Jazz: Toni Morrison's Dialogic Imagination.* London: LIT, 2001.
Tillmann, Markus. *Populäre Musik und Pop-Literatur: Zur Intermedialität literarischer und musikalischer Produktionsästhetik in der deutschsprachigen Gegenwartsliteratur.* Bielefeld: transcript, 2012.
Todorov, Tzvetan. "Les categories du récit littéraire." *Communications* 8 (1966): 121–51.

Tolstoy, Leo. "The Kreutzer Sonata." 1889. In *The Kreutzer Sonata and Other Stories*. Edited and translated by David McDuff, 25–118. London: Penguin, 1986.

Viol, Claus-Ulrich. *Jukebooks: Contemporary British Fiction, Popular Music, and Cultural Value*. Heidelberg: Winter, 2006.

Voerknecht, Liesbeth M. "Thomas Bernhard und die Musik: *Der Untergeher*." In *Thomas Bernhard: Traditionen und Trabanten*, edited by Joachim Hoell and Kai Luehrs-Kaiser, 195–206. Würzburg: Königshausen & Neumann, 1999.

Wagner, Peter. "Introduction: Ekphrasis, Iconotexts, and Intermediality—the State(s) of the Art(s)." In *Icons—Texts—Iconotexts: Essays on Ekphrasis and Intermediality*, edited by Peter Wagner, 1–40. Berlin: de Gruyter, 1996.

Walker, Ronald G. "'I Have to Have My 12': Chapter Division and Rhythm in *Under the Volcano*." *Malcolm Lowry Review* 45–46 (1999–2000): 114–27.

Wicks, Ulrich. *Picaresque Narrative, Picaresque Fictions: A Theory and Research Guide*. New York: Greenwood, 1989.

Wild, Peter, ed. *Noise*. New York: HarperCollins, 2009.

———, ed. *Paint a Vulgar Picture: Fiction Inspired by The Smiths*. London: Serpent's Tail, 2009.

———, ed. *Perverted by Language: Fiction Inspired by The Fall*. London: Serpent's Tail, 2007.

Williams, Martin. *Jazz Masters of New Orleans*. New York: Macmillan, 1967.

Williams, Peter. *Bach: The Goldberg Variations*. Cambridge: Cambridge University Press, 2001.

Wilson, Olly. "Black Music as an Art Form." In O'Meally, *Jazz Cadence of American Culture*, 82–101.

Wolf, Werner. "Intermedial Iconicity in Fiction: Tema con variazioni." In *From Sign to Signing: Iconicity in Language and Literature 3*, edited by Wolfgang G. Müller and Olga Fischer, 339–60. Philadelphia: John Benjamins, 2003.

———. *The Musicalization of Fiction: A Study in the Theory and History of Intermediality*. Amsterdam: Rodopi, 1999.

———. "The Role of Music in Gabriel Josipovici's Goldberg: Variations." *Style* 37, no. 3 (2003): 294–317.

Wright, Terence. "Rhythm in the Novel." *Modern Language Review* 80, no. 1 (1985): 1–15.

Yaffe, David. *Fascinating Rhythm: Reading Jazz in American Writing*. Princeton: Princeton University Press, 2006.

———. "White Negroes and Native Songs: Jazz and Writing in America." *Chronicle of Higher Education*, May 14, 2004, B7–10.

Ziolkowski, Theodore. "Literary Variations on Bach's Goldberg." *Modern Language Review* 105, no. 3 (2010): 625–40.

Zyroff, Ellen. "The Author's Apostrophe in Epic from Homer through Lucan." PhD diss., Johns Hopkins University, 1971.

Index

adaptation, 2, 14n15, 17, 19, 22, 25, 36n10, 37n18, 48n3. *See also* transmediality
Adorno, Theodor W., 32–33
African American musics, 13n8, 44–46, 76, 78, 89, 90. *See also* blues music; jazz
African American studies, 41–43
African music, 50, 67n5, 71, 90, 121, 137n4. *See also* rhythm: African polyrhythms
Albright, Daniel, 21, 68n12
alla breve. *See* time notation
antiphony, 45, 70, 71, 89–94, 97, 99, 100, 101, 108. *See also* call and response; dialogism
Armstrong, Louis, 51, 68n17, 77, 79, 106, 107, 118, 129, 142n48
Arroyas, Frédérique, 146, 147n4, 154, 155, 173, 181n12, 207, 208n6
attacca. *See* time notation
audience interaction, 3, 9, 10, 11, 25, 90, 91, 100–101, 107, 114, 124, 126, 127, 155, 159, 188, 191, 201–2, 206, 207, 211, 212
augmentation. *See* time notation
aura of a work of art, 15n19, 205, 207, 201n19

Bach, Johann Sebastian, 13, 108, 146, 151, 152, 159, 163, 182n22, 191, 206
Bach, Johann Sebastian, works by, 13n6m, 180n4, 181n5; *Aria mit verschiedenen Veränderungen* (*The Goldberg Variations*, BWV 988), 4, 8, 11, 27, 107, 108, 143, 144, 145, 149, 150, 151–53, 155, 156, 161–62, 164, 165–66, 167–68, 169, 172, 174, 175, 182n22, 183, 187, 188–89, 190, 202; *Musikalisches Opfer* (Musical Offering, BWV 1079), 162–63, 191
Baker, Houston A., Jr., 42, 63. *See also* blues matrix
Bakhtin, Mikhail, 104n28, 112
Baraka, Amiri. *See* Jones, LeRoi
Barthes, Roland, 191, 207
beat (in rhythm), 50, 53, 57, 63, 66n1, 70, 71, 77, 78, 101n5, 124, 182n24, 184n44
Beethoven, Ludwig van, 4, 6, 13n7, 13n9, 14n17, 79–80, 143, 146n1, 147n1, 149, 175, 180n4, 197
Benjamin, Walter, 15n19, 204–5, 207, 210n19
Bernhard, Thomas, works by: *Der Untergeher*, 8, 145, 146, 147n4, 208n5, 213, 215, 216; musical structures in, 14n14, 183n33, 208n7; role of performer in, 7, 11, 188, 193–97, 198, 206, 209n9, 209n17
blues matrix, 42, 45, 64
blues music, 9, 41–42, 43, 44–45, 51, 62, 63–65, 69n21, 78, 129; blues form, 71, 79, 84, 102n10, 133; in fiction, 75, 76, 94–95, 105n39; quotation of song lyrics, 60, 62, 66, 132, 133
Bolden, Charles "Buddy," 8, 123, 126, 141n37
Borshuk, Michael, 47n3, 105nn36–38, 141n40
break, 10, 76, 85; definition of, 79, 129; improvisation on the, 76, 86, 102n10, 108, 127–33. *See also* improvisation
Brown, Calvin S., 5, 37n16, 145, 154–55, 155, 174, 181n8, 182n27

Burgess, Anthony, works by, 6: "K. 550 (1788)," 14n17, 147n1; *Napoleon Symphony*, 2, 4, 14n17, 143, 146n1

call and response, 3, 4, 7, 9, 26, 47, 69n25, 70, 71, 72, 89–101, 104–5, 108, 141n40, 212; and Bakthinian dialogism, 104n28; and church sermons, 69n25, 90, 91–97, 99, 104n31; definition of, 89–90; and reader involvement, 91, 100, 105n36, 141n40. *See also* antiphony

canon. *See* variation: types of

carnival, 112

Cartiér, Xam Wilson, works by, 43: *Be-bop, Re-bop*, 8, 46, 138n6 *Muse-Echo Blues*, 8, 12n5, 46, 138n6; breaks in, 85; improvisation in, 9–10, 110, 115; multiple narrators in, 118–19; rhythm and timbre in, 55–62, 212; tense-switching in, 9–10

chase, 97, 100, 104n33. *See also* cutting contest; trading fours

chorus structure in jazz, 4, 7, 9, 26, 47, 70, 76, 78–87, 97, 127, 128, 140n32, 185n48, 212, 217; definition of, 78–79

Clüver, Claus, 39n33, 103n25

collective improvisation. *See under* improvisation

Coltrane, John, 66n2, 78, 128, 134, 135–37

communication: Jakobson's aspects of, 30, 34; Molino's three levels of, 30, 31, 34, 45, 46, 47, 72, 199, 205, 213

composition. *See* performance: in relation to composition

context (as imitated by another medium), 3, 4, 9, 15n18, 25, 26, 27, 33, 35, 39n27, 40n41, 47, 68n15, 90, 92, 94, 97, 101, 106–42, 154–56, 173, 181n12, 188, 193, 199, 201, 202, 204, 208n1, 212, 214

Cooper, G. Burns, 50–51, 53–54, 56

counterpoint, 2, 27, 145, 183n33, 208–9n7

Crouch, Stanley, works by: *Don't the Moon Look Lonesome*, 8, 46, 98, 115, 138n7, 214; call and response in, 9, 92–95, 212; chorus structures in, 84–85, 104n30; riffs in, 73–74, 101n6, 102nn7–8

Culler, Jonathan, 34

Cusk, Rachel, works by: *The Bradshaw Variations*, 8, 11, 14n16, 145, 146, 180n4, 211, 214, 215; cyclical patterns in, 173–74, 176; musical structures in, 151, 164, 165, 166, 167, 172; role of performer in, 11, 188, 197–98, 206; theme of, 158–61

cut time. *See* time notation

cutting contest, 97, 100, 104n34, 108, 118, 140n32, 142n43. *See also* chase; trading fours

cycle/cyclical time, 10, 83, 102n18, 154, 173–80, 185n52, 186n53

death of the author, 191, 206–8

dialogism, 70, 90, 97, 100, 104n28, 105n36, 112, 165. *See also* antiphony; call and response

dialogue, 66n2, 85, 91, 92, 94, 97, 98–101, 118, 121, 156, 157, 158, 164, 166, 171, 206, 208n1

Dillon, Sarah, 12n1, 201n20

Eco, Umberto, 7, 32

effect (as imitated by another medium), 25, 26, 79, 102n7, 104n28, 124, 185n48, 216

ekphrasis, 103n25, 167, 182n16

Ellington, Duke, 50, 63, 64, 107, 108, 128

Ellison, Ralph, 41–42; *Invisible Man*, 104n31, 138n6, 142n45, 142n48

Enquist, Anna, works by: *Contrapunt*, 143, 144

esthesis. *See* communication: Molino's three levels of

Fischer-Lichte, Erika, 107–8, 209n10

Fleischman, Suzanne, 110, 116, 140nn27–29
focalization, 19, 74, 109, 119, 134, 135, 138n7, 159, 164, 165, 166, 183n34
Forkel, Johann Nikolaus, 187, 188–89, 190
formalism, in literary analysis, 103n19, 139n20; in music analysis, 2; structuralism, 7, 19, 36n11
free indirect discourse, 74, 84, 109, 119, 133
free verse. *See under* poetry
Fritsch, Esther, 110, 111, 112, 139n14
Fubini, Enrico, 1–2, 12n2
fugue (*fughetta*). *See* variation: types of
Fuller, Jack, works by: *The Best of Jackson Payne*, 8, 46, 103–4n26, 141n35, 147n3, 209n8, 214, 215, 216; call and response in, 9, 89, 91–92, 95–97, 100, 212; as greatest-hits album, 87–89; multiple voices in, 97, 98, 104n27, 109, 121–22, 217; rhythm in, 67n3; riffs in, 101n5

Gailly, Christian, works by: *Be-bop*, 8, 46, 214; focalization in, 109, 119, 134, 135, 137–38n5; improvisation in, 10, 108, 115, 129, 130, 133–37; multiple voices in, 119
Un soir au club, 138n7
Gates, Henry Louis, Jr., 43, 99, 105n38, 128, 139n20
Genette, Gérard, 12n1, 138n5, 210n20
gigue/giga. *See* variation: types of
Goldberg, Johann Gottlieb, 188, 189, 208n1
Goldberg Variations (BWV 988). *See* Bach, Johann Sebastian, works by: *Aria mit verschiedenen Veränderungen* (*The Goldberg Variations*, BWV 988).
Gould, Glenn, 173, 185n50, 187, 188, 193, 194, 197, 202–3, 209n9

Gould, Glenn, works by: *Goldberg Variations* (1955), 137n2, 162, 172, 173, 177, 184nn42–43, 185n47, 187, 188, 193, 202, 203, 204, 213; *Goldberg Variations* (1981) 137n2, 174, 177, 184n43, 193, 203
Gutmann, Katharina, 104n35, 112

Hanslick, Eduard, 2
Hens, Gregor, 146, 183n33, 196, 208n7
Hughes, Langston, 41, 47n3, 68n18
Huke, Thomas, 43–44
Huston, Nancy, works by: *Les Variations Goldberg / The Goldberg Variations*, 5, 8, 27, 145, 146, 186n54, 193, 198, 207–8, 208nn3–4, 209nn13–14, 216, 217; cyclical patterns in, 177–80, 217; musical structures in, 151, 164, 165, 167, 169, 171–72, 173, 184nn39–42; relationship between composition and performance in, 11, 181n14, 187, 189–90, 191–93, 201, 206, 208, 208n6, 213, 216; role of reception in, 11, 188, 199–202, 206, 208, 209n12, 214; theme of, 154–56, 181n12
Hutcheon, Linda, 1, 19, 22, 36n10, 141n42
hybridity, 13n8, 44, 57, 67n9, 78, 84, 105n39, 112, 121–22

imitation, 3, 19, 22, 25, 26, 27, 36n10, 47, 48n3, 49, 68n20, 110, 11, 129, 137, 146n1, 147n1, 166, 167–68, 173, 195, 208, 217; functions of, 12, 35, 137, 144, 215; and thematization, 7, 17, 22–23, 24, 61, 91–92, 167, 171, 185n46
improvisation, 44, 49, 91, 127–30, 191, 208n1, 213; as characteristic of jazz, 9, 47, 70, 106, 127; collective improvisation, 9, 90, 101, 108, 118, 123, 127, 140n31; formulaic improvisation, 72, 128; as imitated by fiction, 4, 9, 57, 58, 68n14, 89,

improvisation—*(cont'd)*
  110, 126, 130–37, 138n5; motivic improvisation, 71, 77, 78, 128, 133–37; paraphrase improvisation, 128; solo improvisation, 10, 57, 79, 86, 108, 109, 127, 129. *See also* break
interarts studies. *See* word and music studies
intermediality, 1, 3, 11, 12, 16–27, 207, 211, 215; categories vs. features of, 7, 23, 36nn4–6, 37–38n19; in contrast to intramediality, 19–20; in contrast to multimediality and transmediality, 17–19, 37n18; definitions of, 17, 28, 35n3; existing models of, 7, 21–23, 61; musico-literary intermediality, 6, 27; new model of, 7, 9, 23–27, 104n28, 217
intertextuality, 1, 16, 19–20, 38n26, 83–84, 124
intramediality. *See* intertextuality
Iser, Wolfgang, 100, 113, 139n22, 140n26, 152

Jakobson, Roman, 7, 29, 30, 32, 34, 39n29, 39nn35–36, 40n37. *See also* communication: Jakobson's aspects of
Jarrett, Michael, 44, 45–46, 52, 67n6
jazz. *See individual features, i.e.*, call and response; improvisation; performance; rhythm; timbre
jazz novels. *See individual authors and titles*
Jenkins, Henry, 36n9
Jones, Gayl, 43, 98, 111, 138n11
Jones, LeRoi (Amiri Baraka), 41–42
Jonke, Gert, works by: *Chorphantasie*, 4, 13n9, 14n17, 147n1, 217; *Schule der Geläufigkeit*, 14n17, 147n1
Josipovici, Gabriel, works by: "Fuga," 5
  Goldberg: Variations, 5, 8, 12n5, 27, 145, 146, 182n17, 211; cyclical patterns in, 175; musical structures in, 151, 162–63, 164, 165, 171, 173, 183–84n34; relationship between composition and performance in, 11, 187, 190–91, 206, 216; role of reception in, 206; theme of, 152, 156–58

Kacandes, Irene, 111, 138n12
Kaufman, Moisés, works by: *33 Variations*, 147n1, 217
Keyserlingk, Hermann Carl, Reichsgraf von, 188–89, 200, 208n1, 209n11, 209n12
Kouwenhoven, John, 50, 79–81, 87, 129, 217
Kristeva, Julia, 19–20
Kühn, Dieter, works by: *Goldberg-Variationen*, 143, 145, 208n1

Labinger, Jay, 146, 165, 170, 176, 181n10, 183n29, 183n31
Lasswell, Harold D., 20
Lessing, Gotthold Ephraim, works by: *Laokoon*, 20, 21
Lotspeich, C. M., 54, 55

Marsalis, Wynton, 46, 50, 63, 64, 80, 104n29, 107
Marshall, Paule, works by: *The Fisher King*, 85, 138n7
McLuhan, Marshall, 20, 111
McPherson, James, 63–64, 69n26
meaning: musical, 1, 13n7, 32–35, 39n36, 42, 45, 46, 144, 187, 191, 192–93, 204, 205, 206–7, 213–14; role of reader/listener in construction of, 11, 34, 100, 109, 161, 169, 181n12, 204, 205, 206–7, 211, 214, 217; semiotic, 28–29, 30–31, 73, 104n32
media combination. *See* multimediality
media transposition. *See* adaptation; transmediality
medium, 3, 5, 7, 12n5, 17, 18, 19, 22, 23, 24, 25, 26, 27, 28, 33, 36n9, 37n18, 38, 39, 45, 61, 111, 188, 190, 192, 202, 207, 211, 213,

215, 216; definitions of, 20; media groups, 22, 37n12
Mercier, Pascal, works by: *Nachtzug nach Lissabon*, 143–44
metafiction. *See* metareferentiality
metamediality. *See* metareferentiality
metareferentiality, 3, 11, 12, 24, 38n26, 40n38, 89, 99, 109, 127, 133, 137, 141n42, 144, 196, 215, 216
Michaels, Anne, works by: *Fugitive Pieces*, 2, 3, 13n7, 13n8
mimesis, 22, 30, 60
modernism, 2, 5–6, 12n3, 21, 42, 53
Molino, Jean, 30. *See also* communication: Molino's three levels of
Morrison, Toni, 41, 72, 101, 101n1, 102n14, 111, 139n14
Morrison, Toni, works by: *Jazz*, 8, 46, 103n22, 138n6, 139nn13–15, 139nn17–18, 214, 216, 217; call and response in, 9, 72, 100–101, 104–5n35; improvisation in, 9, 10, 57, 72, 110, 132–33, 142n44, 213; multiple voices in, 86, 119–21; orality in, 110–14; rhythm in, 65; riffs in, 71–72; tense-switching in, 117–18
multimediality, 12n5, 16, 17–18, 21–22, 23, 24, 36n6, 37n18, 38n20, 39n28, 208n1, 217
multiple voices. *See under* voice
Munton, Alan, 41, 72, 85, 101n3
Murray, Albert, 43, 45, 46, 47nn2–3, 52, 81, 82, 90–91, 102nn9–10, 105n39, 129, 142n45, 142n47, 213
Murray, Albert, works by, 57, 67n9, 213, 217:
   The Magic Keys, 8, 46, 102–3n18, 131, 138n6, 216
   The Seven-League Boots, 8, 138n6
   The Spyglass Tree, 8, 102n17, 138n6
   Train Whistle Guitar, 2, 7, 8, 46, 102n11, 103n18, 138n6; call and response in, 69n25; chorus structures in, 81–84; improvisation in, 10, 68n14, 108, 110, 114–15, 130–32, 213; rhythm in, 62, 66; riffs in, 74–76, 102n10; second person address in, 123–24; trains in, 65–66, 69n21, 69n24
musical meaning. *See under* meaning
musical novel, 1, 8, 12n4, 14n15, 14n17, 16, 27, 31, 34, 36n10, 67n10, 147n1, 211, 213–17; definition of, 2–5, 7

Nattiez, Jean-Jacques, 7, 30, 34, 205

Ondaatje, Michael, works by: *Coming through Slaughter*, 8, 46, 57, 70, 102n7, 141n34, 141n42, 142n43, 147n3, 214, 215, 216; multiple voices and text fragments in, 85–86, 121, 122–23; as a parade, 124–27; rhythm in, 65, 77, 102n7; riffs in, 69n23, 76–78, 102n7
orality, 43–44, 68n19, 106, 108–17, 129, 138n9, 138n11, 139n16, 139n20; gossip, 9, 103n22, 108, 110, 111, 112–13, 129, 139n14; oral storytelling, 9, 66, 68n19, 108, 110–12, 115, 116, 138n11, 139n16. *See also* performance: in storytelling; Signifyin(g)

palimpsest, 1, 12n1, 36n10, 207–8, 210n20
Parker, Charlie, 8, 51, 129, 106–7, 134, 135–36, 137, 137n1
Pater, Walter, 1, 21, 33
Peirce, Charles S., 7, 28–29, 39n29
Perahia, Murray, works by: *Bach: Goldberg Variationen*, 184n43, 185n47
performance: amateur, 11, 135, 188, 197–98, 206; imitated by fiction, 43, 68n15, 68n19, 108–42, 154–55, 178, 187–88, 190–205, 207–8, 212–13, 216; live performance situation, 3, 4, 9–10, 15n18, 27, 35, 47, 49, 90–91, 106–8, 124, 133, 154–55, 169, 178, 199, 207,

performance—*(cont'd)*
212 (*see also* context); recorded (*see* recording) ; in relation to composition, 10–11, 15n18, 26, 47, 106–7, 108, 109, 110, 114–15, 126, 137n3, 139n18, 163, 181n14, 187, 188, 190–93, 194, 201, 204, 206, 207, 208n1, 208n6, 211, 213, 216; in relation to reception, 34, 35, 100–101, 107–8, 124, 127, 188, 199–202, 206–7, 209n10, 211 (*see also* audience interaction; reception); in relation to the idea of the original work, 11, 15n18, 40n41, 106–7, 187, 188, 191, 192–93, 207; in storytelling, 115–16, 117, 140n28
Petri, Horst, 145, 173
Phillips, Arthur, works by: *The Song Is You*, 2, 4
poetry: as a bridge between prose and music, 49, 52–55, 216–17; free verse, 53, 54, 55, 57, 59, 61, 68n11; poetic meters in musical novels, 61–63; prose poetry, 68n11; rhythm in musical novels, 55–61
poet's novel, 53, 54, 57, 67n10
poiesis. *See* communication: Molino's levels of
polyphony, 2, 6, 26, 150; Bakhtinian, 104n28
postmodernism, 5, 11, 12n3, 15n18, 78, 110, 114, 122, 125, 144, 188, 191, 193, 207, 208n6, 214
Powers, Richard, works by: *The Gold Bug Variations*, 2, 8, 27, 38n21, 145, 180, 181n10, 190, 193, 199, 207, 211, 216; cyclical patterns in, 176–77, 217; musical structures in, 10, 13n8, 144, 146, 151, 164–65, 166–67, 168, 170, 171, 172–73, 173–74, 176–77, 182n25, 183n31, 183n33, 184n42, 185n51; relationship between reception, composition, and performance in, 188, 205, 209–10n17; role of reception in, 11, 188, 202–5, 206–7, 213, 214; theme of, 153–54, 156, 181n11
The Time of Our Singing, 3, 13n8

quodlibet. *See* variations, types of

Rae, Ian, 57, 67n10, 68n12
railroad, 9, 49, 63–66, 68n20, 69n21, 69n24, 69n25, 69n26, 71, 76–77, 80, 98–99
Rajewsky, Irina, 7, 18, 21, 22–23, 24, 35n3, 36n6, 36n9, 37n18, 37n19, 38n26, 39n33
reader-response criticism, 34, 100, 113
reception: of music by fiction, 34–35, 45, 46–47, 187, 188, 190; in musical novels, 3, 10, 35, 199–205, 212. *See also* audience interaction; performance: in relation to reception
reception theory. *See* reader-response criticism
recording, 27, 193, 199, 202–5, 207, 209n9, 209n10, 213; as innovative practice, 209n9 (*see also* Gould, Glenn). *See also under* performance
repetition: and call and response, 94; and chorus structures, 87, 102n18; musical, 32, 35, 84, 104n31, 128, 139n16, 151, 162, 164, 169, 179, 191, 203, 213; and rhythm, 50–51, 52, 56, 65; and riffs, 9, 71, 72–73, 75, 77, 78, 102n7, 212; textual, 49, 68n13, 83, 84, 104n32, 112, 116, 131, 133, 134, 137, 139n16, 169, 193; and variation, 32, 173, 175, 212
rhythm, 45, 49–51, 57, 68n20, 71, 79, 101n2, 102n7, 128, 129, 180n3, 200; African polyrhythms, 50, 67n4; in literature, 49, 51, 52–55, 55–57, 58, 59, 61–63, 65–66, 67n3, 67n7, 67n8, 68n11, 76, 77, 101n5, 102n7, 111, 133, 208–9n7, 212, 216–17 (*see also* poetry); swing, 50; syncopation,

50, 67n4; of trains, 63–66, 68n20, 71, 77, 80 (*see also* railroad)
Richardson, Brian, 114, 124, 139n21, 141n38, 141n39
riff: imitation in fiction, 3, 4, 7, 9, 65, 69n23, 70–78, 101n5, 101n6, 102n7, 102n10, 212; in jazz, 70–71, 90, 128
romanticism: romantic concept of the artist as genius, 2, 11, 13n6, 188, 193, 197; romantic conceptions of music, 1, 2, 96, 189, 200

Saussure, Ferdinand de, 7, 19, 20, 28–29, 30, 32, 39n29, 39n30, 207
scat singing, 26, 59, 68n17
Scher, Steven Paul, 5, 13n10, 37n16
Schneider, Robert, works by: *Schlafes Bruder*, 3, 13n6
Schubert, Franz, 150, 175, 180n4
Schulenberg, David, 164, 182n19, 182n23, 183n28, 186n53
Schuller, Gunther, 50, 51, 67n4, 67n5, 68n17, 70–71, 106, 127, 137n3
self-reflexivity. *See* metareferentiality
semiology. *See* semiotics
semiotics: communication, 10, 16, 18, 19, 20, 29, 30–31, 34, 39n32, 110, 111;, 112, 188, 194, 199, 201, 205, 206, 207; development of, 28–30, 39n29; intrinsic vs. extrinsic reference, 31, 32–33; as language-biased, 19, 28; of music, 31–35; semiotic systems, 4, 7, 18, 19, 20, 22, 30–31, 32, 39n33. *See also* signs
Shockley, Alan, 4, 6, 147n1
signifyin(g), 42, 43, 48n3, 66, 69n21, 99, 104n34, 105n38, 128
signs: definition of, 30–31; as dual, 20, 28–29, 30, 39n30, 67n9; musical vs. verbal, 3, 4, 7, 9, 12n5, 16, 20, 21, 31–33; Peircean trichotomy of the (icons, indices, symbols), 29–30, 39n31, 64; referentiality, 22, 28, 30–34, 39n27, 40n37, 73, 76, 77, 87, 88, 94, 96, 99, 133, 140n33, 151, 184n38 (*see also* metareferentiality); sign systems (*see* semiotics: semiotic systems)
Snead, James A., 51, 71, 73, 85, 94, 103n21, 104n31
sound, as imitated by text, 9, 10, 24, 25, 47, 49–69. *See also* rhythm; timbre
storytelling. *See under* orality. *See also under* performance
stress patterns in English, 31, 49, 52, 53, 54, 56–57, 61, 62, 77
structure, musical, 31, 32; in the *Goldberg Variations*, 4, 10, 35, 143, 144, 149–51, 161–62, 164, 165–66, 166–69, 171, 174, 175, 181n9, 182n19, 183n32; as imitated by text, 2, 3, 13n9, 14n14, 25–26, 27, 35, 38n24, 43, 47, 49, 70–105, 131, 133, 143, 144, 147n1, 149–86; in jazz, 4, 9, 45, 70–71, 78–81, 87, 89–91, 129, 130, 132
surface elements (as imitated by another medium), 25, 26, 38n24. *See also* sound
swing. *See under* rhythm

Tabori, George, works by: *Goldberg-Variationen*, 144
Tally, Justine, 111, 112, 138n10
tempo. *See under* time notation
temporality, 5, 10, 13n8, 25, 31, 52, 81, 84–85, 111, 165, 176–80, 185n50, 186n55
thematization, 3, 12, 17, 24, 25–27, 38, 39n28, 59, 76, 138n10, 144, 168, 187, 190; functions of, 91–92, 100, 104n28, 185n46; and imitation, 7, 17, 22–23, 24, 25, 61, 91–92, 167, 171, 185n46, 195, 203, 207, 208, 212
theme-and-variations form, 3, 4, 5, 7, 10, 25, 27, 75–76, 143, 149–50, 151, 153, 161, 173, 185n48, 212; as cyclical, 175–80, 185n52, 186n53. *See also* variation

timbre, in music, 3, 9, 31, 45, 47, 49, 51–52, 66n1, 89, 106; as imitated by fiction, 9, 10, 25, 59, 66n2, 212, 216

time notation, 10, 168, 169–71, 212; *alla breve*, 166, 168, 170, 171, 182n25, 184n44, 185n46; *attacca*, 167, 169, 177, 203; augmentation, 170, 182n24; cut time, 162, 170, 171, 182n25, 185n46; tempo, 57, 60, 101n5, 107, 124, 155, 166, 168, 172–73, 184n43, 185n50, 198

Tolstoy, Leo, works by: "The Kreutzer Sonata," 14n17

trading fours, 86, 96, 97, 100, 104n33, 212. *See also* chase; cutting contest

trains. *See* railroad

transmediality, 16, 17, 18–19, 22, 25, 36n5, 36n9, 37n18, 38n25. *See also* adaptation

variation, 4, 5, 10, 13n9, 32, 79, 86, 129, 143, 144, 149–61, 164, 189; as connected to repetition, 128, 173, 175, 212; as principle shared by music and literature, 27, 145, 149, 151, 173, 180n1; principles for variation, 10, 153, 155–56, 164, 185n49, 206; strategies for ending, 174–75, 178; types of: canon, 10, 144, 155, 163–66, 167, 174, 177, 181n13, 183–84, 204; fugue/fughetta, 13, 24, 150, 162, 163, 167, 168, 170; gigue/giga, 168; overture, 162, 168; quodlibet, 164, 168, 185n51, 204. *See also* theme-and-variations form

voice: double- or multivoicedness, 3, 85–87, 104n28, 105n38, 108, 118–23, 128, 217 (*see also* call and response); instrumentation, 31, 89, 118, 167, 183n30, 184n35, 212; in literature, 5, 9, 49, 57, 66n2, 97, 98–100, 108–10, 114–15, 138, 166, 196, 208–9n7, 213; in music, 51, 59, 89, 90, 155, 165–67, 170 (*see also* timbre)

Wilson, Olly, 45

Wolf, Werner, 5, 7, 13n10, 20, 21–22, 23, 24, 35n2, 37n16, 38n23, 38n26, 38n27, 39n28, 61, 146, 152, 154, 155, 158, 168, 171–72, 182n15, 184n38

word and music studies, 4, 5, 6, 14n13, 22, 44, 145

work of art, concept of, 11, 15n18, 15n19, 17, 30, 34, 40n38, 100, 114, 137, 187, 188, 204–5, 206, 207–8, 210n19, 211

Ziolkowski, Theodore, 14n16, 145, 147n2, 181n12, 182n17, 183–84n34

www.ingramcontent.com/pod-product-compliance
Lightning Source LLC
Chambersburg PA
CBHW030539230426
43665CB00010B/953